The Exploitation Theory

of

Socialism-Communism

The Idea That All Unearned Income (Rent, Interest and Profit) Involves Economic Injustice

An Extract

Eugen von Böhm-Bawerk

Third (Revised) Edition

Libertarian Press

Post Office Box 218
South Holland, Illinois 60473, U.S.A.

Publisher's Outline to This Third (Revised) Edition

This "book" consists of Böhm-Bawerk's Chapter XII entitled, "The Exploitation Theory," an Extract from *History and Critique of Interest Theories,* which is the first volume of the famous three-volume work of Böhm-Bawerk, with the general title, CAPITAL AND INTEREST.

The publisher has a "sentiment" against having much preliminary material in front of a book which has the standing of a classic; he holds that the real book should come first, or at least early. Therefore, the unorthodox method is here being followed of placing some of what are ordinarily introductory remarks *after* the book itself. The sequence of contents is as follows:

PREFACE TO THE FIRST EDITION of The Exploitation Theory by Dr. Hans F. Sennholz
This Preface professionally evaluates the specific material in Böhm-Bawerk's chapter on "The Exploitation Theory."

TABLE OF CONTENTS of The Exploitation Theory
(as edited here)

THE EXPLOITATION THEORY OF SOCIALISM-COMMUN-ISM, the idea that all Unearned Income (Rent, Interest and Profit) Involves Economic Injustice (the book itself)
The analysis is famous; it is a classic on one of the most important subjects in economics.

EVALUATION OF CAPITAL AND INTEREST by Ludwig von Mises
This is an enlightening perspective of Böhm-Bawerk's *whole* three-volume work. It was first printed in *The Freeman,* August, 1959, published by The Foundation for Economic Education, Inc., Irvington-on-Hudson, New York 10533.

PUBLISHER'S POSTSCRIPT   This is intended as a reader's help, and pertains to the difficult problems a reader will have in understanding Böhm-Bawerk because the reader begins, not at the *beginning* of a book as is the systematic method of good readers, but with Chapter XII out of a massive, technical, three-volume book on economics having altogether 66 chapters.

THE MARXIAN THEORY OF WAGE RATES
by Ludwig von Mises
This is a reprint of an article which appeared in May 30, 1961 issue of *Christian Economics,* published by Christian Freedom Foundation, Inc., 7960 Crescent Avenue, Buena Park, California 90620. This is a comprehensive appraisal of the general character of Marx's publications.

PORTRAIT OF AN EVIL MAN,   a reprint of an article in *The Freeman,* written by Erik von Kuehnelt-Leddihn. This is an unfavorable appraisal of Karl Marx; if overly so, it is an offset to many overly favorable appraisals.

For the present "book," it was not possible to retain its original pagination; footnotes, to simplify matters for readers, were moved forward from the rear to the pages where they belonged, thereby assisting the readers but disarranging the original pagination. It was not feasible to change the original page references; therefore, the original pagination is shown (for easy reference) in the outer margins. Footnote cross references match the original pagination of CAPITAL AND INTEREST.

As English-language publishers of works of Böhm-Bawerk, our appraisal of Marx in the late twentieth century differs from Böhm-Bawerk's appraisal in the late nineteenth century. Böhm-Bawerk's appraisal was *before* the portentous *political* rise of socialism-communism. We appreciate Böhm-Bawerk's objectivity and courtesy when he does not reprobate with vehemence the intellectual structure that Karl Marx developed in his book, *Das Kapital;* and also when he does not expatiate on how unadmirable a person Marx truly was. Böhm-Bawerk did not adequately anticipate the bane—the curse—that socialism-communism has proved itself in fact to be.

What was *one* chapter in the original book has been divided into six sections in this paperback Extract (see Table of Contents). This is a device to emphasize Böhm-Bawerk's main subdivisions of thought.

Sideheadings in this book are new and were not in the original text of Böhm-Bawerk; they are the responsibility of the publisher only.

For the publication of an independent "book," it is natural to elaborate a short title of a chapter by the addition of words to provide a more descriptive identification, to wit: **The Exploitation Theory of Socialism-Communism, the idea that All Unearned Income (Rent, Interest and Profit) Involves Economic Injustice.**

Socialism and communism are *linked* in this title, but that is done justifiably; the *economics* of Marx and Rodbertus are the economics of *both* socialists and communists.

The Publisher

June 5, 1975
South Holland, Illinois 60473 U.S.A.

Acknowledgments

To reprint material previously published, we are indebted to:

The Annals (January, 1891 issue)
    American Academy of Political and Social Science
    3937 Chestnut Street
    Philadelphia, Pennsylvania 19104

Christian Economics (May, 1961 issue)
    Christian Freedom Foundation, Inc.
    7960 Crescent Avenue
    Buena Park, California 90620

The Freeman (August, 1959 and September, 1973 issues)
    The Foundation for Economic Education, Inc.
    Irvington-on-Hudson, New York 10533

Harry W. Laidler, *Social Economic Movements*
    Thomas Y. Crowell Company
    666 Fifth Avenue
    New York, New York 10022

Walter Lippmann, *The Good Society*
    Little Brown and Company
    34 Beacon Street
    Boston, Massachusetts 02106

Preface to the First Edition

Exploitation Theory Has Conquered the World *

AS THE DEVELOPMENT of the exploitation theory was one of the most portentous events of the nineteenth century, its general acceptance and triumphant spread constitutes the most ominous event of the twentieth century. There cannot be any doubt that the exploitation theory has conquered the world. Today more than one-third of mankind lives under communism whose leaders make their arrogant and militant pronouncements from the platform of socialist dogma. Another third of mankind in what is sometimes called the "free world" lives under economic systems that are unmistakably socialistic. Practically all the rest have organized systems of social and economic organizations in which the exploitation theory is the guidepost for governmental intervention.

In United States, Exploitation Theory Sways Public Opinion

Even in the United States, this bulwark of the free world, the exploitation theory has swayed public opinion. It makes its appearance in the popular notion that the unhampered capitalistic economy delivers the wage earners to the discretion and power of wealthy industrialists. The individual worker is said to be helpless and in need of legal protection in his bargaining with management whose primary concerns are power and profit. The unbridled market system with its profit motive and unhampered competition as it prevailed in this country before World War I is condemned for having inflicted hardship and deprivation on many generations of workers. Such notions, which are popular versions of the exploitation theory, have invaded our colleges and universities, indeed all channels of education and communication. They have radically changed our political parties and our churches. They have given rise to a gigantic labor union movement and to the "New Deal" in social and economic matters. In fact, the exploitation theory determines our basic economic policies on all levels of government.

* Sideheadings by Publisher

Popular Labor Legislation Is
Based on Ideas in Exploitation Theory

The ever-growing mass of labor legislation is one of the fruits of the exploitation theory. Its advocates credit modern social policy for having reduced the work week to 48, 44 and 40 hours a week, or even less. They applaud labor legislation for having eliminated women's and children's labor. And they ascribe the present rate of wages to the minimum wage rates set by authoritative intervention. Indeed, practically all labor improvements are credited to social legislation and labor union intervention.

Compulsory social insurance, including unemployment assistance, stem from the same intellectual roots. Capitalism is said to be incapable of giving sustenance to the unemployed, sick, or aged laborers. Therefore, social policy must assure decent living conditions to an ever-larger part of the population.

Modern Taxation Reflects Exploitation Theory

Also modern taxation reflects our adoption of the exploitation theory. Most taxes aim not only at raising revenue but also at correcting or alleviating the alleged evils of our economic system. Some taxes aim at a "redistribution" of wealth and income. Confiscatory rates are imposed on entrepreneurs and capitalists whose income and capital are thus transformed into goods for consumption by the "underprivileged." Other taxes aim at changing business customs and conduct or at regulating production and trade.

Labor Unions Derive Justification
For Existence From Exploitation Theory

Our labor unions derive their very justification for existence from the exploitation theory. Few Americans would disclaim the boast of union leaders that their unions have raised, and still are raising, wages for all workers through association and collective bargaining. American public opinion believes that recent history has proved the beneficial nature of trade unionism without which workers would be subjugated to the greed and arbitrariness of their employers. Because of the common fear of labor exploitation, the people suffer strikes or threats of strikes, union coercion and violence, and endless agitation of hate and envy by labor leaders against the wicked selfishness of exploiters. To many millions of Americans membership in a labor union is an important social duty and strike an essential task.

Many Intellectuals Accept Exploitation Theory

But it is not only the millions of working men who stand united against the alleged evils elaborated by the exploitation theory. Without their enthusiastic encouragement by most economists, sociologists, historians, and political scientists, society would hardly tolerate union extortion and violence. On the campuses of our colleges and universities our intellectuals work diligently to debunk the individual enterprise system for its "basic contradictions" and "fundamental flaws." According to them, society is composed of classes that are consciously banded together to protect their group interests. A "new order" is rising out of the ashes of the "old" capitalist system throughout the world. And their chorus, finally, was completed by the artists who introduced the capitalist exploiter in modern literature and entertainment. It was a combination of all these forces that swayed American public opinion and led this nation to the brink of socialism.

Böhm-Bawerk Could Not Have
The Grim, Practical Perspective on Exploitation Theory
That People in the Late Twentieth Century Have

When Professor von Böhm-Bawerk first directed his pen against the exploitation theory, the unhampered market system still prevailed in all civilized countries. It is true, as a result of the agitation by Marx and his academic disciples, powerful socialist parties had emerged especially in Europe. But their influence on the economic policies of governments was yet negligible. It was a period of unprecedented progress for the world economy. Free trade united mankind in peaceful co-operation and prosperous division of labor. Men and capital moved freely from country to country unrestrained by political boundaries. Capital accumulation proceeded rapidly and labor productivity increased year by year. Wage rates and working conditions improved continuously, and industry aided by rapid technological progress provided a growing population with new and better products.

Böhm-Bawerk's Analysis of Exploitation Theory
Was the Earliest, and Still Stands in the Forefront

The rise of the exploitation theory and other socialist dogma cannot be explained by reference to historical experience. The battle between the two systems is decided by interpretation and explanation of the facts, by ideas and theories. This is why Böhm-Bawerk's analysis stands in the forefront of the battle.

His "Exploitation Theory," which constitutes an extract from his great treatise *Capital and Interest,* is a landmark in the critique of socialist thought. Until the appearance of *Socialism* by Ludwig von Mises some 38 years later, it was practically the only systematic critique of the economics of Karl Marx. With devastating logic and painstaking detail Böhm-Bawerk's thesis explodes the socialist contentions. Its rigorous reasoning and mastery of detail are cogent and convincing. Its conclusions are free from personal feelings and prejudice. And its presentation is elegantly simple. In short, there are few analyses in the history of economic thought that can be called its equal.

Böhm-Bawerk's inquiry explodes the very foundation of socialism on which the exploitation theory is built. According to the socialists, all economic goods are solely the product of labor and their value is determined by the amount of labor which their production costs. Böhm-Bawerk demonstrates that it contradicts both itself and the realities of our world. "Considered from the point of view of theoretical soundness," Böhm-Bawerk concludes, "it occupies one of the lowest places among all theories of interest. Grievous as may be the errors in logic made by the representatives of other theories, I hardly think that anywhere else are the worst errors concentrated in such abundance—frivolous, premature assumptions, specious dialecticism, inner contradictions and blindness to the facts of reality."

Disastrous Economic and Social Consequences

Considered from the point of view of its economic and social consequences, it engenders disaster. The labor legislation which its adoption entailed not only reduces labor productivity and wage rates but also sows discontent and social conflict. The minimum-wage legislation, and other attempts at raising wages above those determined by the market, are creating unemployment and depression, which in turn breed radical collectivism. The compulsory social insurance makes its recipients wards of the state by destroying self-reliance, individual responsibility and independence. The confiscatory taxes on the capital and income of our entrepreneurs and capitalists, imposed for the benefit of those who earn less, hamper economic growth and cause stagnation. They encourage waste and inefficiency, depress wages, cause economic rigidity, and create social classes. The labor unions, finally, not only reduce labor efficiency through a multiplicity of measures, cause maladjustments and unemployment, but also act as most efficient propagators of the socialist ideology. All these policies and measures together are ushering in all-round economic regulation and government omnipotence.

This booklet deals with a great deal more than the academic question of which theory is conclusive or fallacious—the exploitation theories of Rodbertus and Marx or the criticism of Böhm-Bawerk. Its crucial thesis is the defense of the individual enterprise system from the onslaught of socialism which breeds totalitarianism and communism.

Hans F. Sennholz

Grove City College
Grove City, Pa.
January 1960

Contents

The Exploitation Theory
of
Socialism-Communism

The Idea That All Unearned
Income (Rent, Interest and Profit)
Involves Economic Injustice

An Extract

I
Historical Survey of Exploitation Theory

A. General Characteristics of Exploitation Theory

1. Mortal Struggle Between Socialism and Capitalism

I NOW come to that notable theory the formulation of which may not be one of the pleasantest scientific events of the nineteenth century, but is certainly among its most portentous. It stood at the cradle of modern socialism and grew up with it. And it constitutes today (1884) the focal point about which attack and defense rally in the war in which the issue is the system under which human society shall be organized.[1]

2. Socialist Theory of Origin of Interest Is That It Is EXPLOITATION

The theory has as yet no short and distinctive name. If I wanted to give it the name of a characteristic displayed by its principle followers, I could call it the *socialist* theory of interest. But if I am to be guided by a principle which I consider more appropriate, and make use of the theoretical content of the doctrine itself as the source of its name, I could find no appellation more suitable, I think, than the *exploitation theory*. Compressed into a few sentences, the essential nature of the doctrine might, for the time being, be described as follows.

All goods that have value are the product of human labor, and

Cross references by Böhm-Bawerk himself are based on original pagination of CAPITAL AND INTEREST, which are shown by these figures in the margin.

1. This was written in 1884, and was retained in the editions of 1900, 1914 and 1921.

indeed, from the economist's point of view, the product of human labor *exclusively*. The workers however do not receive the entire product which they alone have produced. The capitalist exercises the control over the indispensable means of production which the institution of private property guarantees him, and he uses such control to secure for himself a part of the workers' product. His means of doing so is the wage contract which permits him to purchase the labor of the true producers, who are forced by hunger to accept the contract. The price the capitalist pays them is a fraction of what is produced by them, and the rest of the product falls into the lap of the capitalist at the cost of no exertion to himself. *Interest therefore consists in a portion of the product of the labor of others, acquired by exploiting the situation which places the worker under coercion.*

B. Pre-Socialist Economists
Influenced by Exploitation Theory

3. Adam Smith and David Ricardo As Ambiguous Sources

242   THE genesis of that doctrine had been foreshadowed long before and had in fact become inevitable because of the peculiar turn taken by the economic doctrine of value after Smith and even more after Ricardo. It was generally taught and believed that the value of all goods, or at least of the very great majority of economic goods, is measured by the amount of labor they embody, and that this labor is the origin and the source of the value of goods. Such being the case, it was inevitable that sooner or later the question should arise, why the worker did not receive the entire value to which his work had given rise. And as soon as that question had been raised, it was impossible to find any answer except one which could conform to the spirit of that same theory of value. That answer was that, after the fashion of the drones, one group of society, namely the capitalists, appropriates unto itself part of the value of the product produced solely by the other party in society, namely the workers.

To be sure, the originators of the labor theory of value did not as yet give this answer, as we have seen. Several of their earliest followers likewise avoided giving that answer. They did make the point quite emphatically that labor has the power to create value, but in their general conception of economic life they followed faithfully in the path of their masters. Two such were the German economists, Soden and Lotz. But the answer was nevertheless inherent in their doctrine and followed as its necessary logical consequence. It needed but a suitable motivating incident and a disciple addicted to the lure of the syllogism, to guarantee that it rise to the surface sooner or later. So Smith and Ricardo may be considered the unwilling godfathers of the exploitation theory. And they are regarded as such, even by the followers of the theory. They, and they almost alone, are spoken of by even the most dogmatic of socialists with the sort of respect that is due the discoverers of the "true" law of value. The only fault that is laid at their door is the lack of logical persistence which would have enabled them to crown their theory of value themselves with the exploitation theory.

4. Others as Forerunners of Exploitation Theory

Anyone fond of conducting research into the genealogies, not only of families but of theories as well, can probably find many a pronouncement of bygone centuries which fits in well with the school of thought behind the exploitation theory. Entirely aside from the canonists, whose conclusions agree with those of the "exploitationists" more by accident than by design, there is Locke, for one. On one occasion[2] he points out with great emphasis that labor is the source of all goods, and on another[3] he calls interest a fruit of the labor of others. Another is James Steuart who reveals a similar line of thought but couches it in terms that do not align him so unmistakably with this school.[4] Sonnenfels belongs to this group too. He occasionally describes capitalists as that class of persons "who do not toil and who feed on the sweat of the working classes."[5] Then there is Büsch who also calls interest (by which, to be sure, he means only loan interest) an "income from property derived by means of the industry of others."[6] These examples could probably be multiplied, if one made an industrious search of the older literature.

5. Sources of More-Explicit and More-Aggressive Exploitation Theories

Nevertheless, the birth of the exploitation theory as a conscious and integrated doctrine can be ascribed only to a later period. It was preceded by two preparatory developments. The first of these, as I have

2. *Civil Government*, Book II, Chap. v, Sec. 40. I should like to quote from his essay "On the History of England's Political Economy" a connected passage which reads as follows. "Nor is it so strange, as perhaps before consideration it may appear, that the property of labour should be able to overbalance the community of land. For it is labour indeed that puts the difference of value on everything; and let any one consider what the difference is between an acre of land planted with tobacco or sugar, sown with wheat or barley, and an acre of the same land lying in common without any husbandry upon it, and he will find that the improvement of labour makes the far greater part of the value. I think it will be but a very modest computation to say that of the products of the earth useful to the life of man 9/10 are the effects of labour; nay, if we will rightly estimate things as they come to our use, and cast up the several expenses about them—what in them is purely owing to nature, and what to labour—we shall find that in most of them 99/100 are wholly to be put on the account of labour."

3. *Consideration of the Consequences of the Lowering of Interest*, 1691, p. 24; cf. foregoing p. 28 f.

4. See foregoing p. 29 f.

5. *Handlungswissenschaft*, 2nd ed., p. 430.

6. *Geldumlauf*, Chap. III, Sec. 26.

already mentioned, was the development and the popularization of Ricardo's theory of value, which furnished the theoretical soil in which the exploitation theory found a bed naturally adapted for its thriving growth. The other was the victorious spreading of capitalist mass production which, by creating and exposing a yawning gulf between capital and labor, at the same time moved the question of interest derived without labor into the forefront of the great social problems.

Under the influence of such forces as these our own era seems to have been ready ever since the third decade of the nineteenth century for the systematic development of the exploitation theory. I choose to ignore the "practical communists" whose aspirations naturally stemmed from similar concepts, but who may be disregarded in a history of economic *theory*. Aside from these the earliest theorists to develop the exploitation theory in any considerable detail were William Thompson in England and Sismondi in France.

6. William Thompson on Exploitation of Laborers

The cardinal principles of the exploitation theory were developed briefly but with notable clarity and acuity by Thompson.[7] He starts with the theoretical premise that labor is the source of all value and arrives at the practical conclusion that the producer is entitled to the entire proceeds of what he has produced. He makes the statement that the worker, despite this claim to the full produce of his labor, actually is limited to a wage that is barely sufficient for subsistence, while the additional value that can be derived from an equal amount of labor by the use of machines and other capital is taken by the capitalists who have amassed it and advanced it to the workers. Land rent and interest therefore represent deductions from the full produce of labor, to which the worker is entitled.[8]

There is a division of opinion as to how far Thompson influenced subsequent writings. At any rate he has left few discernible traces. In the economic literature of England there has been little tendency to continue the Thompson trend,[9] and the most illustrious socialists in

---

7. *An Inquiry into the Principles of the Distribution of Wealth most Conducive to Human Happiness,* 1824. For a treatment of Thompson and his immediate predecessors Godwin and Hall, see Anton Menger, *Das Recht auf den vollen Arbeitsertrag,* Stuttgart, 1886, Secs. 3-5; also Held, *Zwei Bücher zur sozialen Geschichte Englands,* Leipzig, 1881, p. 89 ff. and p. 378 ff.

8. See Anton Menger, *op. cit.,* Sec. 5.

9. Two works of Hodgskin belong to this period and to this trend; one is his little known *Popular Political Economy* and the other is his anonymously published treatise under the significant title *Labour Defended against the Claims of Capital.* I was not able to see the books themselves, and was made aware of them only through quotations from them in the writings of some of his English contemporaries. Particularly Read and Scrope often quote from them, voicing sharp opposition to their content. The complete title of the anonymous work is, *Labour Defended against the Claims of Capital; or the Unproductiveness of Capital Proved,* by a labourer, London 1825. I deduce that Hodgskin is its author from a remark by Scrope on p. 150 of his *Principles of Political Economy,* London 1833. I submit a few characteristic passages, as quoted by Read. "All the benefits attributed to capital arise from co-existing and skilled labor" (from the introduction). Later the admission is made that more and better products can result from working with instruments and machines than without, but to that is added

French and German economic literature do not reveal any external resemblance to him. Anton Menger[10] recently defended with great vigor the opinion that Marx and Rodbertus borrowed their most important socialist theories from older English and French models, and especially from Thompson. But it is difficult to determine whether that is so. I for my part consider his argument not at all convincing. When a doctrine is floating in the atmosphere, as it were, the fact that it is taken up by a writer need not necessarily be evidence that he has borrowed it. Nor does it constitute proof or disproof of his originality in such event, to say that he expressed a few years earlier or later a fundamental idea that was in the air. On the contrary, the true test of his creativeness is his ability to make original additions to the idea and so advance the erection of a sound and vital theoretical structure. In the world of science, in any case, the intuitive, groping expression of an idea is often a much easier and less meritorious achievement (I say this despite examples of the opposite) than is the sound proof, corroboration and development of that same idea. Let me remind the reader of the position occupied by Darwin with respect to the vaguely prophetic thoughts of Goethe on the subject of evolution. The same is true of Adam Smith, who seized upon the germ of an idea expressed much earlier by Locke, and successfully developed it into his famous "industrial system." In our present case I feel that the development of the labor theory of value virtually put the word "exploitation" into people's mouths. But it seems to me, furthermore, that Rodbertus and Marx seized upon and developed the idea in such original fashion, that I, for one, should not be willing to characterize them as "borrowers," in their relationship either to each other, or to their predecessors.[11]

244

7. Sismondi on Exploitation of Laborers

On the other hand, it should be pointed out that the influence of Sismondi was indubitably strong and far reaching. If I cite him as a representative of the exploitation theory, it is done with a bit of reservation. For Sismondi outlined a doctrine which has all the essential features of the theory of exploitation with one exception. He refrains from pronouncing an adverse judgment on interest! It is simply a case of his belonging, as a writer, to the period of transition. While he is essentially converted to the cause of the new theory, yet he has not broken with

the following remark. "But the question then occurs what produces instruments and machines, and in what degree do they aid production independent of the labourer, so that the owners of them are entitled to by far the greater part of the whole produce of the country? *Are they or are they not the produce of labour?* Do they or do they not constitute an efficient means of production separate from labour? *Are they or are they not so much inert, decaying, and dead*

matter, of no utility whatever, possessing no productive power whatever, but as they are guided, directed and applied by skillful hands?" (p. 14).

10. See Anton Menger, *op. cit.,* preface, p. v, then pp. 53, 79 ff., 97 and many others.

11. A. Wagner said somewhat the same thing in *Grundlegung,* 3rd ed., Part I, p. 37, footnote 1, and Part II, p. 281.

the old one so completely that he can avoid shying away from its novel viewpoint.

The great work of Sismondi which exercised so much influence, insofar as our subject is concerned, bears the title, *Nouveaux principes d'économie politique*.[12] In this work Sismondi's thesis sets out from premises which he shares with Adam Smith. He accepts the latter's principle that work is the sole source of all wealth,[13] and agrees with it warmly (*p. 51*). He is displeased because the three types of income, namely rents, profits and wages are frequently attributed to three different sources, namely land, capital and labor. In actual fact, says Sismondi, all income arises only from labor, and those three categories are merely so many different ways of participating in the fruits of human labor (*p. 85*). For the worker, by whose activity all goods are produced, has "in our stage of civilization" not been able to retain control of the necessary means of production. In the first place, arable land is usually the private property of another, and the owner demands a part of the fruits of the worker's labor, in return for supplying the cooperation of the "productive force" termed land. Such part constitutes land rent. In the second place, the productive worker ordinarily does not possess a sufficient supply of provisions on which to live during the time he is performing his labor. Nor does he own the raw materials and the frequently costly instruments and machines necessary for production. The rich, who own all these things, thus acquire a certain control of the
245 labor of the poor. Without doing any of the work themselves, they take in advance the best part of the fruits of that labor, to compensate themselves for the advantages which they put at the disposal of the poor (*la part la plus importante des fruits de son travail*). This "best part" is interest (*pp. 86 and 87*). Thus, by reason of the organization of society, wealth has achieved the ability to reproduce itself through the labor of others (*p. 82*).

And although the laborer's daily efforts produce far more than his daily needs, there is little left over for him, after he has shared with the landowner and the capitalist, beyond his bare subsistence, which he receives in the form of wages. The worker needs his subsistence much more than the entrepreneur needs the worker's labor. He needs his subsistence to be able to live, whereas the entrepreneur needs his labor only to make a profit. And so the bargain almost always turns out to

---

12. First ed., 1819; 2nd ed., Paris, 1827. I quote from the latter. In an earlier work by Sismondi, (1803), entitled *De la richesse commerciale*, which occupied ground much closer to the classical viewpoint, there is included an interesting remark. It is to the effect that the employing of every productive worker involves an exchange of present for future goods. The present goods are the wages of the worker, the future goods are the product of his labor that will be received in the future (*op. cit.*, p. 53). A quotation found in Salz's *Beiträge*

zur Geschichte und Kritik der Lohnfondstheorie, 1905, p. 65, was responsible for drawing my attention to the foregoing early mention of a thought which I used extensively many decades later in my theory of interest (cf., for instance, my *Positive Theory*, Chap. II, p. 297 ff. and p. 310).

13. A principle which Smith, incidentally, by no means adhered to with unfailing consistency. In addition to "labor" he not infrequently cites "land" and "capital" as the sources of goods.

the disadvantage of the worker, and he must almost always content himself with the most meager subsistence, while the lion's share of the advantages that accrue from the increased productivity that comes about through division of labor falls to the entrepreneur (*p. 91 f.*).

Anyone who has followed Sismondi's exposition thus far, and has also read the sentence which states the "rich devour the product of the labor of the others" (*p. 81*) will necessarily expect Sismondi to conclude by declaring interest an unjust and extortionate gain that is to be condemned. But that is not the conclusion Sismondi draws. Suddenly shifting ground, he manages to conjure up a few obscure and ambiguous clichés in favor of interest, which finally stands before us robed in righteousness. First he says of the landowner that he earned a *right* to land rent by the original labor of making the land arable, or even by settlement of virgin territory (*p. 110*). Similarly he endows the owner of capital with a right to interest based on the "original labor" to which the capital owes its existence (*p. 111*). These two types of income have one characteristic in common, in that they constitute income derived by virtue of ownership, and they may therefore be contrasted with income which is derived by virtue of the performance of labor. And yet Sismondi manages to establish their good repute by demonstrating that they, too, owe their origin to labor, being different only in that their honorable origin dates back to an earlier era. For the worker, through new labors, acquires every year a new claim to income, while property owners in an earlier period of time and through original labors acquired a permanent claim which makes each year's work more advantageous[14] (*p. 112*). "Everyone," he concludes, "receives his share of the national income only in proportion to what he or his representatives contribute or have contributed to the creation of that income." Of course, Sismondi does not offer any answer to the questions whether and how this last statement can be reconciled with his earlier ones, according to which interest is something taken in advance out of the fruits of other persons' labor.

However, others very soon and very decidedly drew the conclusions which Sismondi himself did not dare to draw from his own theory. He is the connecting link between Smith and Ricardo on the one side, and the subsequent doctrines of socialism and communism on the other. Those two economists, with their theory of value, had supplied the originating impulse of which the exploitation theory was born, but had not themselves formulated any such theory. Sismondi virtually worked out what was in essence a theory of exploitation, without as yet giving it any application to the social and political field. He was followed by that massive force which, under the names "socialism" and "communism," pursued the logical sequence of the old doctrine of value to the very ultimate limit of its theoretical and practical implications, arriving finally at the dictum, "Interest is exploitation, and so it must go." 246

14. Those who wish to, may regard these words as a highly compressed statement of James Mill's remuneration theory. See foregoing p. 195 f.

C. Socialists

IT WOULD not be of any theoretical interest for me to cull the voluminous socialist writings of the nineteenth century for quotations from all the statements which proclaimed the theory of exploitation. I should be forced to weary the reader with a multitude of parallel passages which hardly vary in wording, and which reveal an extremely uninteresting monotony in content. Moreover, the very large majority of them do not go beyond merely asserting the cardinal principles of the exploitation theory without offering any better proofs than an appeal to the authority of Ricardo and adding a few commonplaces. The simple fact is that the majority of the "scientific" socialists exercised their intellectual power less in proving the fundamental correctness of their own theories than in launching corrosive attacks on those of their opponents. I shall therefore restrict myself to mentioning a few out of the mass of socialistically tinged writers who became especially important for the development or dissemination of our theory.

8. Proudhon on Exploitation of Laborers

The author of the *Contradictions économiques,* P. J. Proudhon, is outstanding among such writers for the clarity of his views and the brilliance of his argumentation, and these qualities made him the most effective apostle of the exploitation theory in France. Since we are more concerned with content than with form, I shall forego quoting detailed samples of his style, and restrict myself to summarizing the kernel of Proudhon's doctrine in a few sentences. It will be at once apparent that, except for a few peculiarities of language, Proudhon's doctrine does not differ much from the general outline of the exploitation theory, as we have already given it.

To begin with, Proudhon accepts as established the principle that labor creates all value. Hence the worker has a natural claim to ownership of his entire product. By his wage contract he foregoes that claim in favor of the owner of the capital and in return for a wage which is *smaller* than the product which he foregoes. Herein he is cheated. For he is not aware of his natural right, nor of the magnitude of his concession, nor yet of the significance of the contract which the property owner makes with him. In this transaction the owner takes advantage of error and surprise, not to say deceit and sharp practice (*erreur et surprise, si même on ne doit dire dol et fraude*).

This is the explanation of the fact that the modern worker is not able to buy his own product. His product costs more in the open market than he has received in wages. It costs more by the amount of all sorts of gains which are caused by the existence of the right of property and which, known under most varied terms such as profit, interest, yield, rent, tithes, etc., constitute just so many "tolls" (*aubaines*) which are imposed on labor. For instance, what 20 million workers have produced for a year's wages of 20 billion francs, costs 25 billions because of and inclusive of those gains. But that means "that the workers who, to be able to live, must buy back the same products, are compelled to buy back for five, the things they produced for four, or in other words that they must fast one day out of every five." And so, interest is an additional tax on labor, a pre-emptive reduction (*retenue*) of wages.[15]

9. Rodbertus on Exploitation of Laborers

The German Rodbertus is fully the peer of Proudhon in the purity of his presentation, by far his superior in the profundity of his thinking and his prudent insight, but admittedly far inferior to the passionate Frenchman in the vividness of his language. For the historian of economic theories he is the most important of the personalities that deserve mention at this point. For a long time his scientific significance went unrecognized and, strangely enough, because of the very fact that his work is so predominantly scientific. Because he did not make his appeal as others did directly to the populace, because he restricted himself primarily to scientific investigation of the social question, because he was moderate and restrained in his practical proposals as they affected the most immediate interests of the great masses, his reputation lagged for a long time behind that of other far lesser men who took over his intellectual wares second hand, and in their own fashion made them palatable for the interested multitude. Only in modern times has full justice been done to Rodbertus, that most charming socialist, and recognition paid to him for what he is, the father of modern scientific socialism. Instead of the passionate attacks and oratorical antithesis in which the great throng of socialists loves to indulge, Rodbertus has bequeathed to us a profoundly and honestly reasoned theory of the distribution of goods. Mistaken as it may be in many respects, it nevertheless contains enough that is valuable to assure its originator lasting pre-eminence among economic theorists.

I wish to reserve the privilege of returning later, and in some detail, to his formulation of the theory of exploitation. In the meantime I should like to go on to a consideration of two theorists who succeeded him in time, and who differed as completely from one another as they did from Rodbertus.

---

15. See various passages in Proudhon's numerous writings. Particularly *Qu'est ce que la propriété*, 1840; in the Paris ed. of 1849, p. 162; *Philosophie der Not*, a German translation by William Jordan, 2nd ed., p. 62, p. 287 f.; *Verteidigungsrede vor den Assisen von Besançon*, delivered February 3, 1842 (Edition of Complete Works, 1868, Vol. II). Particular attention is directed to Diehl's comprehensive work *P. J. Proudhon, seine Lehre und sein Leben,* in three sections, Jena 1888-1896.

10. Ferdinand Lassalle on Exploitation of Laborers

One of these is Ferdinand Lassalle, the most eloquent, but as to content the least original of the socialist leaders. I mention him here only because his brilliant eloquence enabled him to exercise great influence on the spreading of the theory of exploitation. But his contribution to its theoretical development is just about nil. I can therefore dispense with quotations or excerpts from his doctrine, which does not differ in content from that of his predecessors, and restrict myself to commenting in a footnote on one or two of the most striking passages.[16]

While Lassalle is an agitator exclusively, Karl Marx is pre-eminently a theorist, and indeed, after Rodbertus, the most distinguished theorist of socialism. Although his doctrine coincides in many respects with the pioneering research of Rodbertus, he displayed undeniable originality and a high degree of keen logic in developing his doctrine into a distinctive whole with which it will likewise be our duty shortly to become thoroughly acquainted.

D. Acceptance of Exploitation Theory Not Restricted to Socialists

11. Ideas of Guth on Exploitation of Laborers

ALTHOUGH the exploitation theory was developed chiefly by theorists of the socialist "persuasion," the ideas peculiar to it were adopted by writers in other literary circles as well. And these writers were many, and of many kinds.

Some of them declare themselves for the exploitation theory, lock, stock and barrel, or decline to subscribe only to the most extreme practical applications of it. One of that sort is, for example, Guth.[17] He accepts all the essential principles of the socialists and their content in their entirety. For him labor is to be regarded as the sole source of value.

---

16. The one work of Lassalle's which contains the fullest exposition of his opinions on the interest problem, and which at the same time represents the most brilliant display of his genius for agitation, is his *Herr Bastiat-Schulze von Delitzsch, der ökonomische Julian, oder Kapital und Arbeit* (Berlin, 1864). Chief passages to be noted are the following. Labor is "the source and creator of all values" (pp. 83, 122, 147). But the worker does not receive the entire value, but only the market value of labor, considered as merchandise, which is the equivalent of its cost of production, that is to say, bare subsistence (p. 186 ff.). All surplus falls to the share of capital (p. 194). Interest is therefore a deduction from the product of the labor belonging to the laborer (p. 125, and in very drastic form on p. 97). Opposition to the doctrine of the productivity of capital is found on p. 21 ff. The abstinence theory is opposed on p. 82 ff. and especially on p. 110 ff. Compare also the other works of Lassalle.

17. *Die Lehre vom Einkommen in dessen Gesamtzweigen*, 1869. I quote from the 2nd ed. of 1878.

Interest comes into being because the unfavorable conditions under which labor competes force its wages to lag behind the value of its product. In fact, Guth does not scruple to introduce the harsh term "exploitation" as the technical term which describes that process. But in the end he recoils from the practical consequences of this principle and takes refuge behind a few hedging provisos. "Far be it from us to imply that the exploitation of the worker, as the source of the original margin of gain, is an act which violates the tenets of justice. Rather, it is based on a voluntary agreement between employer and employee which, to be sure, is entered into under conditions which are usually unfavorable to the latter." The sacrifice which the "exploited" worker makes is rather to be thought of as only an "advance against something to be returned." For the accumulation of capital brings about a progressively greater productivity on the part of labor. As a result, the products of labor become cheaper, the worker can buy more, and hence his real wage rises. At the same time "increased demand brings about a wider sphere of possible employment, whereupon his money wage also rises." Hence "exploitation" resembles an investment of capital which indirectly and in increasing measure brings in returns to the worker.[18]

12. Ideas of Dühring on Exploitation of Laborers

Dühring is another whose theory of interest stands entirely on socialist ground. *"Interest is in its nature an appropriation of the principal portion of the product of labor. . . . The* increase in productivity and the saving in labor are effects of improved and more extensive means of production. But the fact that the obstacles and difficulties encountered by production become less, and the further fact that *unskilled labor, by the acquisition of technical skill, makes itself more productive, do not justify any claim that an inanimate instrument should absorb even the least bit of a surplus over and above what is required for its replacement.* Therefore interest is not a concept that could be developed on the basis of considerations that apply solely to production, or that would fit into the pattern of a system of economics. It is a form of appropriation and the result of distributional circumstances."[19]

Another group of writers accepts the ideas of the exploitation theory in eclectic fashion, incorporating some of them with their other views on the interest problem. Examples of this group are John Stuart Mill and Schäffle.[20]

Still others were sufficiently impressed by socialist writings to adopt individual features of the doctrine, even though they were unwilling to

249

---

18. *Op. cit.,* 109 ff., 122 ff. Cf. also p. 202 ff., foregoing.

19. *Kursus der National- und Sozialökonomie,* Berlin, 1873, p. 183. A bit later (p. 185), in a statement patently reminiscent of Proudhon's *droit d'aubaine* (toll right)

he declares *interest* to be a "toll" that is levied for the relinquishment of economic power. The rate of interest represents the toll or tax rate.

20. See Chap. XIII.

accept the structure in its entirety. It seems to me that the most important event of this nature was that a renowned group of German university professors, the "socialists of the chair" revived the old principle
that *labor is the only source of all value,* that is to say, the only power
which can "create value."

E. Essential Principle of the Theory, Namely, That Labor Is the Only Source of All Value

IT IS a strange fate that has befallen this principle, the acceptance
or rejection of which is of tremendous import in passing judgment on
the most important economic phenomena. It had originated with the
English economists, and in the first decades following the publication
of Smith's system had shared the widespread acceptance which the
latter had enjoyed. Later, under the influence of the teachings of Say,
who developed the theory of the three factors of production, nature, labor
and capital, and then under the further influence of Hermann and Senior,
the principle was discredited among the great majority of economists,
even in England. For a time the socialist authors were almost the only
group who kept it alive at all. Then, when the German "socialists of
the chair" adopted the principle as they took it out of the pages of a
Proudhon, a Rodbertus and a Marx, the principle once more acquired
strong support among scholarly economists. And now it almost seems
as if the reputation enjoyed by the distinguished leaders of that school
might enable it, from this point, to embark upon a second triumphal
course through the economic writings of all nations.[21]

Whether or not this is a desirable development will be shown by a
critical appraisal of the exploitation theory, to which the ensuing pages
will be devoted.

21. Written in 1884. Since that time there has, I think, been a reversal of this tendency. For a few years the labor value theory, in conjunction with the dissemination of socialist ideas, rather gained currency than otherwise. But in most recent times, among theorists in all countries, the principle has lost ground, chiefly to the theory of marginal utility, which has been gaining more and more headway.

II
General Structure of This Description and Critique of Exploitation Theory

1. How Rodbertus and Marx Came To Be Selected

THERE were several avenues open to me by which to approach 250 the task of a critique of the exploitation theory. One of those would be to appraise all the representatives of the theory individually. And while that would have been the most accurate way, the high degree to which the individual expositions coincide would have resulted in unnecessary and wearisome repetition. Another way would have been to base my critique on the general system which is common to all the individual expositions of it, without taking up a detailed consideration of any one of them individually. That procedure however would have exposed me to two complementary evils. On the one hand I should have been in danger of really failing to do justice to certain individual shades of difference. On the other hand, even if I had escaped the first danger, I should most certainly have been charged with making my task too easy, and with having made an appraisal, not of the actual theory, but of a version of it which I had wilfully distorted. And so I decided to approach the problem by a third avenue, and that was to select from the great multiplicity of individual statements of the theory a very few which I consider the best and the most complete, and to subject these individually to criticism.

For that purpose I selected the exegeses by Rodbertus and Marx. They are the only ones which offer a reasonably profound and coherent foundation. Rodbertus's is, in my opinion, the best presentation of the theory. Marx's however is the most widely recognized, the one that is, so to speak, the official pronouncement of modern socialism. By subjecting both of them to a detailed examination, I am looking at the exploitation theory, I think, "with its best foot forward." I am trying to adhere to a policy which Knies put so well when he said, "He who would be victorious on the field of scientific research, must allow his adversary to advance in all the panoply of his armor and in the fullness of his strength."[22]

2. What Is and What Is Not Here Being Considered

One preliminary remark will perhaps prevent misunderstandings. The sole purpose of the pages which immediately follow is to make a critical estimate of the exploitation theory *as a theory,* in other words, to attempt to determine whether the origin of the economic phenomenon called interest really lies in those circumstances to which the exploitation theory ascribes that origin. Conversely, it is not my intention to render any verdict at this point with respect to the *practical* side of the problem of interest or its implications from the point of view of *social legislation.* Nor do I plan to judge its goodness or badness, nor to advocate the retention or abolition of interest itself. To be sure, I do not by any means propose to write a book on interest and take refuge in silence concerning the most important question which is connected with it. But I cannot profitably discuss the "practical" side of the subject until there is complete clarity with respect to the theoretical side, and I must therefore reserve such discussion for my second volume. But at this point—I repeat —it is my intention only to seek to establish whether interest, be it good or bad, exists for the reasons which the exploitation theory alleges.

251

22. *Der Credit,* Part II, Berlin, 1879, p. VII.

III
Rodbertus's Theory of Interest [23]

A. Detailed Presentation of Rodbertus's Theory

1. Rodbertus Considers His Theory To Be Based on Smith and Ricardo

THE point of origin for Rodbertus's theory of interest is the principle "introduced into the science of economics by Smith and more firmly corroborated by the Ricardo school" to the effect that "all goods, economically considered, are only the product of labor and cost nothing except labor." Rodbertus elucidates this principle, which is habitually expressed in the form "only labor is productive" by stating it as follows. *Firstly,* only those goods belong to the class that may be termed economic goods, which have cost labor, while all other goods, no matter how necessary and useful they may be to man, are *natural* goods which have nothing to do with economics. *Secondly,* all economic goods are *solely* a product

23. A rather complete list of the numerous works of Dr. Karl Rodbertus-Jagetzow is available in Kozak's *Rodbertus' sozial-ökonomische Ansichten,* Jena, 1882, p. 7 ff. By preference I used the second and third letters to von Kirchmann in the somewhat revised reprint which Rodbertus published in 1875 under the title *Zur Beleuchtung der sozialen Frage.* I have also used his *Zur Erklärung und Abhilfe der heutigen Kreditnot des Grundbesitzes,* 2nd ed., Jena 1876, as well as Rodbertus's work, posthumously published by Adolf Wagner and Kozak under the title *Das Kapital,* which was originally his fourth *Social Letter* to von Kirchmann (Berlin, 1884). Rodbertus's theory of interest was at one time made the subject of an exceedingly searching and conscientious investigation by Knies in his *Der Credit,* Part II, Berlin, 1879, p. 47 ff. In the main I agree with Knies's estimate. Nevertheless I cannot forego instituting a new and independent critical examination, since my theoretical views diverge sufficiently widely from Knies's, for me to have essentially different opinions on several points. On the subject of Rodbertus see A. Wagner's *Grundlegung,* 3rd ed., Part I, Sec. 13 and Part II, Sec. 132; likewise, H. Dietzel's *C. Rodbertus,* Jena 1886-1888.

of labor, and from the economist's point of view are not to be conceived of as produced by nature or any other power, but only by labor. Any other view belongs in the field of the physical sciences rather than economics. *Thirdly,* all goods are, economically considered, the product of only that labor which performed the material operations which were necessary to their production. But such labor includes not only that labor which produces the good directly, but also such labor as creates the instrument which serves in the production of the good concerned. Grain, for instance, is the product not only of the labor that drove the plow, but also of that which built that plow, etc., etc.[24]

2. How Rodbertus Formulates His Claims for Laborer

The manual workers who create the entire good have a natural and just claim, at least "according to the idea of pure justice," to acquire title to their entire product.[25] But there are two important reservations. In the first place, the system of division of labor under which a great many cooperate to produce a single product, makes it a technical impossibility that each worker receive his product in kind. Therefore in place of the claim to the whole *product* must be substituted the claim to the entire *value* of the product.[26] Furthermore there must be some provision made out of the sum of all products, for a share for all those who render useful service to their fellow men without participating directly in the making of the product, as for instance, clergymen, physicians, judges, naturalists and also, in Rodbertus's opinion, the entrepreneurs who "know how to employ a large number of workers productively by means of a capital."[27] But such labor, which is only "indirectly economic," will have to urge its claim to be compensated, not out of the "original distribution of goods," in which only producers share, but out of a "secondary derivative distribution of goods." Hence the claim which, under the idea of pure justice, can be advanced by the manual workers, is to be construed as a claim to *the whole value of the product of their labor in the original distribution,* undiminished by reason of the secondary claims to compensation by other useful members of society.

252

Rodbertus finds that under the present organization of society this natural claim is not realized. For workers today receive only part of the value of their product at the original distribution in the form of wages, while the rest falls to the share of the owners of land and of capital in the form of surplus proceeds (*Rente*). Rodbertus defines surplus proceeds as "all income that is received without work, purely on the basis

---

24. *Zur Beleuchtung der sozialen Frage,* pp. 68, 69.
25. *Soziale Frage,* p. 56; *Erklärung und Abhilfe,* p. 112.

26. *Soziale Frage,* pp. 87 and 90; *Erklärung und Abhilfe,* p. 111; *Kapital,* p. 116.
27. *Soziale Frage,* p. 146; *Erklärung und Abhilfe,* Part II, p. 109 ff.

of ownership of property."[28] It includes two kinds of income, *interest on land* and *interest on capital goods.**

3. Rodbertus's Statement of the General Problem of Interest

Rodbertus now asks, "Since all income is the product of labor, why do some members of society draw income, and in fact original income, though they have not stirred a finger to produce it?" With those words Rodbertus has framed the general theoretical problem of interest.[29] His answer to the problem is as follows:

Surplus proceeds owe their existence to the combined effect of two facts, the one economic and the other legalistic. *The economic reason* lies in the fact that since the introduction of the division of labor, the workers' labor produces more than they need for their subsistence and for the continued performance of such labor. As a result, others, too, *can* live off that labor. *The legal reason* lies in the existence of private ownership of land and of capital goods. Since the workers are excluded by this institution of private property from control of the conditions indispensable to production, they cannot produce at all except as employees of the proprietors and under the terms of a previously concluded agreement. And the latter, in return for making the conditions of production available, impose upon the workers the obligation to cede a portion of the product of their labor as surplus proceeds. Indeed, the cession takes place under the still more onerous guise of a surrender by the workers of title to the entire product of their labor in favor of the proprietors, who then return to them only a part of its value as wages, limiting such wages to the indispensable minimum required for subsistence and for the continued performance of their labor. The power which compels the workers to accept this contract is hunger. But let us read it in Rodbertus's own words.

"Since there can be no income, except as it is the result of labor, an excess of proceeds over labor costs depends on two indispensable pre- 253 requisites. First, there can be no surplus proceeds unless the labor at

---

28. *Soziale Frage*, p. 32.   29. *Soziale Frage*, p. 74 f.

* Translators' note: Rodbertus's concept of *Rente* corresponds to what economists today would call "surplus of gross proceeds over labor costs." They conceive of this magnitude as a complex which includes four elements: (a) the price of the entrepreneur's own labor employed in the production process; (b) the entrepreneur's profit proper; (c) interest on the entrepreneur's capital; and (d) interest on borrowed capital. In the hope that these connotations will remain more vividly present, the translators will generally render Rodbertus's *Rente* by the more precise modern term "surplus of proceeds over labor costs," or more briefly and simply, "surplus proceeds." Rodbertus's distinctive terms *Kapitalgewinn* and *Grundrente* might be conveyed in modern terminology by rendering them as "interest derived from the utilization of capital goods" and "interest derived from the use of land." We are dealing with but a single economic phenomenon, namely *interest*, but in two manifestations with respect to factors of production. One is interest on capital goods, the other is interest on land.

least produces more than is required for the continuation of the labor. For it is impossible for anyone to draw an income regularly without himself doing any work unless there is such a margin. Second, there can be no surplus proceeds, unless conditions exist which deprive the workers of this margin in whole or in part, and divert it to others who do not work themselves. For the workers are, in the nature of things, in possession of their product at the outset. That labor does create such a margin is the result of economic factors, in particular such as increase the productivity of labor. That this margin is wrested in whole or in part from the workers and is diverted to others, is the result of legalistic factors. Just as law has from the beginning been in coalition with power, so in this instance this diversion takes place only by the continued exercise of compulsion.

"Originally this compulsion was exercised by the institution of slavery, which came into existence at the same time as tillage of the soil and private ownership of land. The workers who created a margin in the product of their labor were slaves, and the master to whom the slaves and hence their product itself belonged, gave the slaves only just so much as was required for the continuation of their labor, and kept the rest, the margin, for himself. When all the land in a country is privately owned, and when at the same time title to all capital has passed into private hands, then this ownership of land and capital exerts the same compulsion on liberated or free workers. This brings about a twofold effect. The first effect is the same as that produced by slavery, in that the product itself does not belong to the workers, but to the owners of land and of capital. The second effect is that the workers, who own nothing, are glad enough to receive from the masters who own land and capital even a part of their own product to support themselves, that is to say, to allow them to continue their labor. Only now the commands of the slave owner have been replaced by the contract between worker and employer, a contract which is free only in form but not really in substance. Hunger makes almost a perfect substitute for the whip, and what formerly was called fodder is now called wages."[30]

According to this argument all surplus proceeds are the fruit of *exploitation*,[31] or as *Rodbertus* occasionally puts it still more caustically,[32] a *theft* of the product of other men's labor. This description is appropriate to all classes of surplus proceeds in equal degree, whether it be interest on capital or on land, or even the derivatives of these two, namely hire and loan interest. The two latter are as fully justified a charge against the entrepreneurs who pay them, as they are unjustified charges against the workers, at whose expense they are ultimately collected.[33]

30. *Soziale Frage*, p. 33. Similarly and in greater detail on pp. 77 to 94.

31. *Soziale Frage*, p. 115 and frequent other instances.

32. *Op. cit.*, p. 150; *Kapital*, p. 202.

33. *Soziale Frage*, pp. 115, 148 f.; cf. also his *Herr Bastiat-Schulze von Delitzsch, ibid.*, pp. 115-119.

4. Rodbertus, on the Greater Labor's Productivity, the Greater the Exploitation

The amount of excess proceeds increases with the productivity of labor. For under the system of free competition the worker receives generally, and in the long run, just the amount necessary for subsistence, that is to say, a definite concrete quantity of the product. Now the greater the productivity of labor, the smaller is the percentage of the total value of the product which that concrete quantity of the product represents. 254 And the greater is the percentage of the product and of the value, which is left over as the portion of the owners, that is to say, their interest.[34]

Although the foregoing statements indicate that all interest is basically a unified mass of completely homogenous origin, in practical economic life it is commonly recognized that it takes two different forms, namely interest on capital goods and on land. Now Rodbertus explains the reasons and the laws of this duality in exceedingly individual fashion. Throughout his investigation he proceeds, it must be noted by way of introduction, from the theoretical assumption that the exchange value* of all products is equal to their labor cost.[35] He assumes, in other words, that all products are exchangeable, one for another, on the basis of their relative cost in terms of labor. The remarkable thing about this assumption is that Rodbertus knows that it is not in accordance with fact. But he thinks that the deviation from actuality is only a matter of the "real exchange value sometimes being greater and sometimes being smaller." He feels furthermore that there is always a gravitational tendency in evidence toward the point which is "the natural, and hence also the equitable exchange value."[36] He rejects entirely the idea that it should be a *normal course of events* for goods to be exchanged on the basis of some standard other than the labor that has been expended on them. He excludes the possibility that deviations from that basis might be the result, not of fortuitous and momentary market fluctuations, but of the operation of a definite law which influences value in a different direction.[37] I call attention to this circumstance at this point, for it will be important later.

5. Rodbertus Divides Production Into Raw Production and Manufacture

The production of goods viewed as a whole is divisible, according to Rodbertus, into two parts; *raw production* avails itself of the help of the land to produce raw materials, and *manufacture* works up the raw ma-

---

34. *Soziale Frage*, p. 123 ff.
35. *Op. cit.*, p. 106.
36. *Soziale Frage*, p. 107; similarly pp. 113, 147; also *Erklärung und Abhilfe*, p. 123.
37. *Soziale Frage*, p. 148.

* Translators' note: *Exchange value* is the capacity of a good to obtain in exchange a quantity of other goods. *Price* is the exchange ratio between money and that quantity of other goods.

terials into further products. Before the introduction of the division of labor, the obtaining of raw materials, and the further processing of them were performed in immediate succession and by the same entrepreneurs, who then also received the entire resulting surplus proceeds without differentiation. At that stage of economic development there was as yet no division of interest into that derived from the utilization of capital goods and that derived from the use of land. But once the division of labor had been introduced, the entrepreneurs of raw production and of the subsequent manufacture became different persons. The preliminary question is the determination of the proportion in which to divide surplus of proceeds over labor costs resulting from the entire productive process. What shall be the respective shares of the producers of the raw materials and of the entrepreneurs who do the manufacturing?

The answer to the question lies in the nature of interest. Interest, being a deduction from the value of the product, is a percentage thereof. The amount of interest that can be gained from a given productive pro-
255 cess is determined by the exchange value of the product. But since the exchange value of the product, again, is determined by the quantity of the labor expended, raw production and manufacture will share the total surplus proceeds in the proportion born to each other by the *respective labor costs* of these two branches of production. Let us consider a concrete example. This example is not in Rodbertus's book, but I insert it to guard against confusion in this difficult line of reasoning.

6. No Relationship Between Amount of Capital Employed and Interest Received on Capital

If 1,000 working days are required to produce a given quantity of raw materials, and the processing of it requires another 2,000 working days, and if the overall surplus proceeds means a deduction of 40% from the exchange value of the product for the benefit of the proprietors, then the proprietors of the raw production will receive the product of 400 days, and the manufacturing entrepreneurs that of 800 days, as interest. The amount of *capital* employed in each of the productive processes is immaterial for purposes of this division. It is true that the rate of interest is computed on the basis of the capital employed, but it is not determined by the amount of that capital but by the quantities of labor that were applied.

The very fact that the magnitude of the capital employed has *no* determining influence on the amount of interest that may be realized from one branch of production, becomes a causative factor in the origination of interest on land. Rodbertus elucidates as follows. Interest, although it is the product of labor, is regarded as the yield of wealth, because it is conditioned by the possession of wealth. Since in manufacture only capital goods, and not land are employed, the entire amount of interest which is derived specifically from manufacturing is regarded as the yield of capital, or as interest on capital. By following the custom of computing the ratio of the amount of yield to the amount of capital which returns that yield, people arrive at a position in which they speak of the definite percentage of return that can be earned by capital employed in manufacture. That rate of yield, which will be approximately uniform in all activities because of the recognized influence of competition, will also become a criterion for the computation of the yield on capital engaged in raw production. That will be true, if for no other reason, because a far greater part of the "national capital" is employed in manufacture than in agriculture. For, as is readily comprehensible, the yield of the vastly predominant portion of capital can dictate the rate of yield which is to be deemed acceptable in the case of the smaller portion. For that reason those engaged in raw production will consider that portion of their total surplus proceeds which represents the customary rate of earnings calculated on their capital employed, to be their interest on capital. The rest of the surplus proceeds over labor costs however will be thought of as the yield of the land, and constitutes the additional residuum of interest on land.

According to Rodbertus the latter *must* always necessarily be left over in the production of raw materials by the terms of that one presupposition that products are exchanged on the basis of the labor incorporated in each. And this is Rodbertus's argument to prove it. The amount of interest that can be derived from *manufacture* depends, as   256
was pointed out earlier, not on the quantity of capital expended, but on the amount of work performed in the process of manufacture. This labor consists of two components, direct manufacturing labor, and that indirect labor "which because of the exhaustion of instruments and tools must be taken into account." Of the various elements of which capital expenditure is composed, only a few have any influence on the amount of surplus proceeds, namely those that consist in wages and in expenditures for machines and tools. Capital expenditure for raw materials, however, does not exert such an influence because this expenditure offers no counterpart corresponding to any labor cost expended in the manufacturing stage of the production process. And yet this part of the expenditure *does* add to the amount of capital which serves as the basis for computing the yield which the surplus proceeds represent. The result is that part of the capital outlay—the expenditure for raw materials—increases the capital devoted to manufacture but does not increase the yield. And the further result ensues that the presence of such a part of the capital obviously and necessarily reduces the ratio which interest, represented by the yield, bears to the increased capital employed in manufacture. In other words, it depresses the rate of interest on manufacturing capital.

7. Rodbertus's Distinction of Difference
Between Interest on Land and Interest on Capital

Now interest in the field of raw production will also be calculated at this lower rate. But in the case of raw production the situation is more favorable. For since agriculture begins its production *ab ovo*—"from scratch" as it were—and does not process any material which comes to it from a preceding production, its capital outlay does not include the component "raw material." The only thing it might offer as occupying an analogous position would be the land itself. That however is assumed in all theories to cost nothing. Consequently participation in the distribution of surplus proceeds is limited to those parts of capital only which have had some influence on the amount of those proceeds. And as a further consequence it follows that the ratio of the surplus proceeds earned to the capital employed must be more favorable in agriculture than it is in manufacturing. But since the rate of earnings in agriculture must be computed at the lower rate prevailing in and borrowed from the field of manufacturing, there must always be an additional residuum for the landowner, which he receives as interest on land. This, according to Rodbertus, is the origin of interest on land and of its distinction from that on capital.[38]

8. Rodbertus Surprisingly Asks No Abolition of Private Property or Unearned Income

In order to make my presentation complete, I should like to state briefly that in spite of the severe theoretical condemnation which represents Rodbertus's verdict in judging the predatory character of interest, he does not desire the abolition of either private ownership of capital nor of the income from it. Rather does he ascribe to private ownership, both of land and of capital "an educative power" which we cannot forego, "a sort of domestic power which we should be able to replace only if we had for that purpose a completely different national system of education. But for that we do not as yet have even the necessary conditions."[39] In the meantime he thinks of private title to land and to capital goods as a "species of public office which entails national economic functions—functions which consist in guiding the economic labor and the economic resources of the nation as best befits the national needs." From this favoring point of view interest can be looked upon as a sort of salary which those "public officials" receive for the exercise of their functions.[40]

257

I have already remarked that this observation of Rodbertus, recorded rather casually and as a mere footnote, constitutes the earliest mention of a thought which some subsequent writers, particularly Schäffle developed into a peculiar variant of the remuneration theory.

---

38. *Soziale Frage*, p. 94 ff., especially pp. 109-111; *Erklärung und Abhilfe*, Part I, p. 123.
39. *Erklärung und Abhilfe*, p. 303.
40. *Erklärung und Abhilfe*, p. 273 f. In Rodbertus's posthumously published *Kapital* his verdict against private ownership of capital is more severe. And though he does not advocate its abolition, he wishes to see it replaced (p. 116 ff.).

B. Deficiencies of Rodbertus's System

THAT brings me to my critique of Rodbertus's doctrinal system. Let me say at once and without mincing matters that I consider the interest theory which is a part of it to be completely erroneous. I am convinced that it suffers from a series of grave theoretical defects. In the following pages I shall attempt to set forth those defects as clearly and as impartially as I can.

9. Böhm-Bawerk: It Is Downright Wrong To Maintain That All Goods, ECONOMICALLY CONSIDERED, Are Solely a Product of Labor

The first stumbling block which my critical appraisal encounters is the cornerstone on which he erects his structure. He lays down the principle that all goods, economically considered, are only the products of labor.

First of all, what does he mean by "economically considered"? Rodbertus clears that up by an antithesis and contrasts the point of view of economic science to the point of view of the physical sciences. He expressly concedes that goods are physically the product, not only of labor but also of the forces of nature. If nevertheless goods are supposed from the economist's point of view to be only the product of labor, he can mean only one thing. He must mean that the cooperation of natural forces in the process of production is a factor to which we may be completely indifferent when we study human economy. On one occasion Rodbertus expresses this point very strongly when he says, "All other goods (other than those which have cost labor), no matter how necessary or useful they may be to man, are natural goods, with which *economics has no concern.*" "Whatever preliminary results nature has achieved may be a cause for human gratitude, for man has been spared just that much work. *But economics takes them into account only insofar* as labor has complemented the work of nature."[41]

That is just downright wrong. Even purely natural goods, whenever they are rare in comparison with the need for them, are the concern of economics. Or does a nugget of pure gold that falls as a meteorite on a landowner's property, or a silver mine which he happens to discover on his land mean nothing to the economist? Will the owner allow the gold or silver which he has received as a gift from nature to lie disregarded, or will he give it away, or squander it, merely for the reason that nature has presented it to him without any exertion on his part? Or will he not take care of it just as carefully, protect it from the greed of others, prudently dispose of it on the market, in short, husband it with the same economy as he would in the case of gold and silver which he had

41. *Soziale Frage*, p. 69.

acquired through the labor of his hands? And is it really true that economics concerns itself with those goods which have cost labor, only to the extent to which *labor* has complemented the work of nature? If that were so, the economic behavior of men would treat a barrel of the choicest Rhine wine as the absolute equivalent of one of those local country wines which, though well tended, is by nature a mediocre vintage. For approximately the same amount of human labor has been expended on each. The fact that nevertheless the Rhine wine often has an economic value 10 times as great, is an eloquent refutation which life offers of Rodbertus's theory.

Negations of that kind are so obvious that Rodbertus could really have been expected to intrench his first and most important fundamental principle behind very carefully prepared defenses against them. But such expectations are unfulfilled. Rodbertus has marshalled a few items intended to make his thesis convincing. But they consist partly of some not overly persuasive references to authorities, and some just as unconvincing argumentation which does not touch the point at issue, but evades it.

10. Smith and Ricardo Are, Despite Their Fame, Inadequate Authorities

The former category includes his oft-repeated invoking of Smith and Ricardo as authorities to support that principle "concerning which there is no more dispute among progressive economists," which has acquired full citizenship among English economists and is at least represented in France, and "what is the most important, has been indelibly impressed on the consciousness of the people, so that it is proof against the sophistries of a doctrine freighted with ulterior motives."[42] We shall have occasion a little later to establish the interesting fact that Smith and Ricardo merely allege the axiomatic truth of the principle we are discussing without furnishing any proof of it whatsoever. And furthermore, both of them have themselves failed to adhere consistently to that principle, as has been very nicely demonstrated by Knies.[43] Now it is obvious that in a scientific discussion even authorities furnish proof, not by the weight of their names, but by the cogency of the reasons that they advance. But since in this case the names are not represented by any reasons at all, nor even by a consistently maintained statement, the conclusion is inescapable that all Rodbertus's invoking of authorities effects no actual strengthening of his position; and furthermore that that position is entirely unsupported except for such arguments as he himself is able to advance for his thesis.

11. Rodbertus's Errors on "Costing"

In this connection we must give consideration to a rather long argument in the first of five theorems which Rodbertus entitled *Zur Erkenntnis unserer staatswirtschaftlichen Zustände*. And we must deal with his *Zur Erklärung und Abhilfe der heutigen Kreditnot des Grundbesitzes*.

42. *Soziale Frage*, p. 71.   43. *Credit*, Part II, p. 60 ff.

In the former Rodbertus begins by developing with entire correctness the point that we deal in our economy with goods that cost labor,
and why we must do so. He is quite right in placing in the foreground
the quantitative disparity between "the infinitude and the insatiability   259
of our capacity for desiring," that is to say, of our wants on the one
hand, and our limitations on the other hand, as to time and energy.
He mentions only secondarily and more by way of intimation, that labor
is "toilsome," and a sacrifice of "freedom" and the like.[44] Similarly, he
expounds, with reasons, the unimpeachable truth that an expenditure of
labor must be considered "costs." "One simply needs," says Rodbertus,[45]
"to grasp the concept behind the word 'to cost.' It means more than
saying that 'a' is necessary for the production of 'b.' The essential
point is not only that an outlay has been made of something which
therefore is no longer present to be laid out for something else, but
also this outlay has been made by a person who *feels* the irrevocability
of it. The latter point constitutes the reason why only man can experience
cost."

That is entirely right! Nor is it any less right, as Rodbertus goes
on to say, that both criteria of cost are applicable to labor. For the
outlay of labor which every good has caused "is no longer there to be
expended on another good," and thus the first criterion is satisfied. And
the outlay is felt by no one but man, for it is an outlay of his energy
and his time, and both of these are a finite quantity, in contrast to the
limitless series of goods—all of which satisfies the second criterion.

12. Rodbertus's Approach to Labor Costing Must
Be Extended to Costing Other Elements of Production

But now it devolves upon Rodbertus to prove that the phenomenon
of "costing" and hence the right to recognition as an economic factor
applies to labor alone, and is not applicable to any other element. He
has to concede, first of all, "that one thing (in addition to labor) is
necessary and is active in the production of a good. And that one thing
—barring ideas which are supplied by the mind—is material which is
supplied by nature, plus natural forces which "in the service of labor
assist in accomplishing a transformation or an adaptation of material."
But nature's contribution fails to meet both criteria of cost. For the
active forces of nature says Rodbertus are "infinite and indestructible.
The force that combines the substances necessary to the production of
a kernel of grain, is always at the disposition of those substances. The
material that nature supplies for *one* good is concededly not available
for the production of a different one. But one would have to personify
nature if one wished to argue that therein lay a reason for speaking of
'costing' and one would have to speak of *her*—i.e., Mother Nature's—

---

44. *Zur Erkenntnis unserer staatswirt-*   45. *Op. cit.*, p. 7.
schaftlichen Zustände, 1842. See First The-
orem, pp. 5 and 6.

costs. Material is not an outlay which *man* makes to produce a good. Only those things may be termed costs of a good which are a *cost to man*."[46]

Of the two parts which comprise the foregoing dual conclusion, the first one which denies the applicability of criterion number one is quite obviously fallacious. Yes, the forces of nature *are* perpetual and indestructible. But for purposes of expenditure for production it is not a question of whether those forces continue to exist at all, but a question of whether they continue to exist and to operate in a manner which makes them capable of a repetition of their productive useful functioning. And in this respect—which is the only respect that is pertinent to our discussion—there is of course no such thing as continued existence and indestructibility. When we have burned our coal, the chemical characteristics of carbon, it is true, continue to exist after it has combined with the oxygen in the air to provide us with the desired heat. But the effectiveness of its properties does not now go beyond remaining, as atoms of carbon, in combination with atoms of oxygen to form carbon dioxide. There is no possibility, for the present, of a repetition of the functioning of these forces of nature. The expenditure of chemical forces which we have made by burning coal as an element in the production of a good cannot be repeated toward the production of an additional good.[47] Exactly the same thing is true, of course, of materials used in production. And Rodbertus really admits it. To be sure, he does so only inadequately, when he says they are not "for the time" available for use in another good. As a matter of fact they are unavailable not only "for the time" that they are incorporated in the first good, but regularly continue to be unavailable subsequently for the production of another good. Thus when I use wood for dowel beams, that wood is unusable, not only during the 100 years of its service in the house as a dowel beam and of its gradual decomposition there, but also after it has rotted. And it cannot serve for the production of another good for the reason that its chemical elements, admittedly still in existence, are nevertheless in a condition that makes them no longer adapted for service to man. Somewhat later, while discussing an objection that he raises himself, Rodbertus abandons his first argument, and places his sole reliance on the contention that the second criterion is lacking, the requirement that costs must apply to a person.

But in this respect, too, Rodbertus is at fault. Even the expenditure of rare gifts of nature constitutes an expenditure the irrevocability of which is felt as a loss by the person concerned. It thus meets that requirement of Rodbertus's definition of the meaning of "to cost," and it does so for the same reason which he himself says applies to labor. Now

46. *Op. cit.*, p. 8.
47. It is readily understandable that if Rodbertus had been consistent he would have had to maintain that labor (the force "labor," as it were) is also eternal and indestructible since the chemical and physical forces residing in the human organism, like all others, do not disappear from the universe!

Rodbertus is making an inquiry into the reason for our being compelled to deal economically with labor and its products. The answer that he supplies does not ascribe our sense of compulsion, as one might expect, to the unpleasantness that is associated with labor. Instead he says, and repeatedly emphasizes, that the cause lies in the quantitative limitation of labor in comparison with the infinitude of our wants. And what is the meaning of this thesis? Surely, Rodbertus can mean only that, as it is, we have but an inadequate supply of labor for the complete satisfaction of our wants, and that therefore any waste of labor creates a still larger deficiency. But Rodbertus's reason would be just as valid, even if labor were entirely unconnected with any feeling of pain, annoyance, compulsion or the like. It would be so even if labor afforded the worker pure unalloyed pleasure, provided the amount of labor continued to be inadequate for the production of all desired goods. A person thus feels a loss because of a wasted expenditure of labor—or indeed any expenditure of labor—simply because he thereby loses the satisfaction of a want that would otherwise be obtainable.[48] And exactly the same thing takes place when a rare gift of nature is wastefully consumed, or consumed at all. If I dissipate a valuable deposit of coal or other mineral, either wantonly or by extravagant mining methods, then I am wasting a quantity of facilities for satisfying wants which I could have fulfilled if I had acted economically—satisfactions which I fritter away by my uneconomical behavior.[49]

261

13. Rodbertus's First Major Error:
Goods Are the Product of Manual Labor Only

Rodbertus does not lose sight of this objection, which it is almost impossible to overlook. The objection might be raised, he says, that for the owner of a stand of timber, costs include, in addition to the labor that he expends on felling trees, etc., the cost of the material itself, "since it has been used for one good and hence cannot be used for another, and since it therefore represents an expenditure which the owner feels as a deprivation."[50] But Rodbertus evades this objection with a bit of sophistry. He claims that the objection is based on a "fiction" inasmuch "as it consists in making a provision of statutory law into the basis of an economic action, which should of course be governed only by valid natural law." Only from the point of view of statutory law, says Rodbertus, can it be assumed that natural resources have any "owner" before

---

48. Who would deny, for instance, that even one who controls the labor of others —be he employer, patriarch or slaveowner —also has a rational motive for dealing economically with the labor *of others*? In such case it is of course no longer a question of the labor involving a loss of *his* time, an expenditure of *his* energy, a sacrifice of *his* personal freedom. Patently the significant factor, as I pointed out in the text, is the satisfaction of wants—his wants or his family's.

49. The provisions found in all legislation prohibiting wasteful methods of operating mines, supply a palpable refutation of Rodbertus, since they make the economical management of rare natural resources an out and out duty—and for very well-founded reasons.

50. *Op. cit.*, p. 9.

any labor has been expended on them. The situation would be entirely altered, if private ownership of land were abolished.

But of course that would not alter the case at all, with respect to its decisive feature. If standing lumber is a relatively rare natural resource at all, then it follows from the very nature of things and irrespective of any provision of law, that any wastage of rare natural resources affecting weal or woe, must proceed from persons. The legal provisions are concerned only with the question of which specific persons suffer the deprivation. Under a system of private ownership of land the proprietor is the person interested, and the one who feels the loss; under a system of socialized property in land, the entire circle of society would be the persons concerned; in the absence of any system of law and order it would be the incumbent in actual control, be he the first or the strongest. But it would be unavoidable that the loss or any diminution of rare natural resources, would affect disadvantageously a person or a group of persons in the satisfaction of human wants. One might imagine an exception if the forest had no human inhabitants at all, or if the inhabitants, from some noneconomic motive such as a religious one, refrained on principle from using wood in any way, shape or form. In such case, to be sure, there would be no economic treatment of wood. But it would be not because purely natural resources are incapable, as a matter of principle, of being the subject of a loss involving deprivation to a person. It would be because the factual circumstances applying in the given case were such as to exclude such personal relationships, which in and of themselves might very well have been involved.

In a later work Rodbertus devotes another short bit of argumentation to his thesis, advancing what is apparently the same idea, though it appears, in part, in somewhat different guise. Everything can be called a product, he says, which achieves economic relationship to us by means of labor. All such products are to be credited, economically speaking, 262 solely to human labor, because labor is the only original force and the only original expenditure with the help of which human economy is transacted.[51] This line of reasoning encounters, first of all, the counter argument that it is highly doubtful whether the premise from which he proceeds is itself correct. And certainly Knies's attacks upon its soundness were delivered with great decision, and were backed, in my opinion, with cogent arguments.[52] In the second place, even if his premise were correct, his conclusion from it would not be. Even if labor were the only original force with which man carries on his economic activity, I still

51. *Erklärung und Abhilfe*, Part II, p. 160; similarly *Soziale Frage*, p. 69.

52. *Credit*, Part II, p. 69; Rodbertus's statement that "labor is the only original force and the only original expenditure with the help of which human economy is transacted," which is the sole reason he advances in support of his own argument, is purely and simply a factual error. What an astonishing delusion, especially on the part of a landowner, to maintain that it is impossible for the generative power active in our limited parcels of land to be left "lying dead," or to be "dissipated on the growth of weeds," etc., etc.! Such absurd reasoning would in the end justify the statement that the loss of X acres to the owner of Y square miles of land "does not signify any economic loss" in an economy.

cannot see why man should not have grounds for conducting his economy through the instrumentality of additional forces besides the "original forces." Why not through certain achievements of that original force, or the achievements of other original forces? Why not through that meteorite we discussed some pages ago? Why not through that fortuitously discovered jewel? Or the natural coal deposits? The simple fact is that Rodbertus is too narrowly limited in his conception of the nature and the causative forces of human economy. Now, he is quite correct in saying that the reason why we deal economically with the original force called "labor" is "because labor is limited as to time and quantity, because labor, once put to use is used up, and finally, because it represents a sacrifice of our freedom." But those are all only intermediate reasons, not the one ultimate reason for our economic behavior. In the last analysis we carry on our economy with the help of labor, limited and onerous though it be, because if we deported ourselves uneconomically with respect to labor, we should suffer an impairment of our well-being. Exactly the same motive impels us to carry on our economy with respect to any other useful thing which we cannot forego or lose without a sacrifice of enjoyment, because the supply of it is limited. That applies whether or not it be an original force, whether or not it may have cost some original force called "labor."

The position taken by Rodbertus then becomes more untenable than ever, when he adds the further statement that goods are even to be regarded solely as products of *manual labor*. This statement, in addition to other things, excludes from consideration as economically productive activity even the indirect intellectual labor of the supervision of production labor. And it leads to a host of internal inconsistencies and faulty conclusions which exclude any possibility of doubt as to the erroneous character of the statement itself, and which were unearthed by Knies in such striking fashion that it would be superfluous repetition on my part to go into the matter again.[53]

And so Rodbertus finds himself, after the setting up of his very first fundamental principle, at loggerheads with fact. Now to be completely fair I am compelled to make an admission at this point which Knies could not make from his point of view as a representative of the use theory. My admission is that the refutation of his initial fundamental principle is not a refutation of his theory of interest. That principle is erroneous because it misrepresents, not the contribution of capital, but

---

53. See Knies's *Der Credit,* Part II, p. 64 ff.; for instance: Any one who would "produce" coal must not only dig, but must dig in the right place. He can perform the same manual labor of digging at thousands of places, without the slightest success. But the difficult and necessary service of correctly locating the place for digging has to be taken on by some special person—say a geologist. And without a further exercise of "intellectual power," it is impossible to sink a shaft. Now, if those things and others are necessary, how can the digging be the only "economic" service?—If in the making of pills, the choice of ingredients, the determination of their relative amounts and the like, are taken care of by a person other than the one who does the actual rolling of the pills, can we then say that the economic value of those objects, of this manufactured medicament, is a product of the manual labor expended?

263 the contribution of nature to the production of goods. I believe with Rodbertus that if we consider all the successive stages of production as a single process, capital goods cannot be said to occupy an independent position among the costs of production. Capital goods are not as Rodbertus contends, exclusively "labor expended in the past" but they are so in part, and as a matter of fact usually they are so in greater part. As to the rest, capital goods are valuable accumulated natural forces. Let us assume a case where there is an absence of the latter. Let us assume a production process which throughout all its stages employs only free gifts of nature and labor, or uses only such intermediary goods as themselves result from nothing but free gifts of nature and labor. Wherever that condition obtains, we may truly say with Rodbertus that such goods, economically speaking, are products of labor alone. Inasmuch, then, as Rodbertus's fundamental error does not apply to the part played by capital but to the contributions made by nature, the conclusions that he draws from them on the nature of interest need not necessarily be in error. Not until subsequent developments in his doctrine exhibit essential errors shall we be able to reject it as erroneous. Such errors will, to be sure, make their appearance.

In order not to draw undue advantage from Rodbertus's first error, I shall, for all the remaining pages of this investigation, frame all my presuppositions in such a way as to eliminate completely all the consequences of that error. I shall concede that all goods are produced only by the cooperation of labor and *free* forces of nature and with the assistance of only such capital goods as are the result of the cooperation of labor and free forces of nature, without the intervention of natural material resources having exchange value. Within the limitations of this presupposition I can admit the validity of Rodbertus's fundamental principle that all goods, economically speaking, cost only labor. Let us continue.

14. Rodbertus's Second Major Error: Neglects Significance of TIME on Value

Rodbertus's next thesis is that by the laws of nature and according to the "idea of pure justice" the entire product, having been produced by the worker alone, must belong to the worker, or in lieu of it, its full value without deduction. I am fully in accord with this thesis, too, since under the terms of the limiting presupposition which I stipulated before, there can be no question of its correctness and its fairness. But I do think that Rodbertus and all the other socialists have a false conception of the realization of this truly just principle. Misled by that misconception they desire the creation of a condition which is not in accordance with the principle, but directly opposed to it. I consider it remarkable that the numerous attempts that have been made hitherto to refute the exploitation theory have touched on this decisive point only superficially at best, but never presented it in its true light. I shall therefore take the liberty of requesting my readers to devote some measure of attention to the following development of the point. This difficult subject certainly requires it.

The error that I censure I shall first name and then elucidate. The completely just proposition that the worker is to receive the entire value of his product can reasonably be interpreted to mean either that he is to receive the full *present* value of his product *now* or that he is to get the entire *future* value in the *future*. But Rodbertus and the socialists interpret it to mean that the worker is to receive the entire *future* value of his product *now*. At the same time they act as if that were entirely self-evident and the only possible interpretation of that proposition.

Let us illustrate the matter by a concrete example. Let us imagine that the production of a good, for instance a steam engine, costs five years' labor, and that the completed machine commands a price of $5,500. Let us further ignore for the moment that in actual practice the labor is distributed among many workers, and imagine that a single workman produces the machine by five years' continuous labor. Now let us ask what wage is due him in the sense of the proposition that the worker is to receive his whole product, or the full value of his product. There cannot be a moment's doubt that the answer is the whole steam engine or $5,500. But *when*? On that score, too, there can be no slightest doubt. Obviously at the expiration of five years. For by the laws of nature he cannot receive the steam engine before it is in existence, cannot gain possession of a good valued at $5,500 and created by himself, before he has created it. In that case he will have received his compensation according to the formula, "the whole future product, or its whole future value at a future time."

But it often happens that the worker cannot or will not wait until his product has been fully completed. Our worker wishes, for instance, after the expiration of one year to receive a corresponding partial compensation. The question arises, as to how that is to be measured in accordance with the aforementioned principle. I think this, too, can be settled without a moment's hesitation. The worker will get justice if he gets all that he has labored to produce up to this point. If, for instance, he has up to this time produced a pile of unfinished ore, or of iron, or of steel material, then he will be justly treated if he receives the pile of ore, of iron, or of steel, or receives the full exchange value which this pile of material has, and of course has *now*. I do not think any socialist could find fault with that decision.

How large will that value be, in relation to the price of the finished machine? Here is the point at which a superficial thinker can easily go wrong. The worker has up to this time performed a fifth of the technical work which the production of the entire machine demands. Accordingly, a superficial consideration of the problem might tempt us to answer, the present product will possess an exchange value of one-fifth of that of the whole product, that is to say, $1,100. The worker is to receive a year's wage of $1,100.

That is wrong. One thousand one hundred dollars is one-fifth of the price of a completed, present steam engine. But what the worker has produced up to this time is not one-fifth of a machine that is already finished, but only one-fifth of a machine which will not be finished for another four years. And those are two different things. Not different by a sophistical splitting of verbal hairs, but actually different as to the thing itself. The former fifth has a value different from that of the latter fifth, just as surely as a complete present machine has a different value in terms of present valuation from that of a machine that will not be available for another four years. And it will be so, just as surely as it is true in general that present goods have a value different from that of future goods.

That present goods have a higher value, in the esteem of that present in which the economic events take place, than future goods of the same kind and quality, belongs to the most widely known and most important economic facts. The causes to which this fact owes its origin, the multifarious variations in which it is manifested, and the equally multifarious consequences to which it leads in economic life, will be the subject of detailed investigation in the second volume of this work.* That investigation will be neither so easy nor so simple as the simplicity of the basic idea might lead us to expect. But even before I have completed that investigation, I think it justifiable to rely on the fact, as a fact, that present goods do have a higher value than identical future goods. The crudest empirical tests of everyday life establish it beyond any question of a doubt. If you ask 1,000 persons to choose between a gift of $1,000 today and $1,000 50 years from today all 1,000 of them will prefer to have it today. Or ask another 1,000 persons who are in need of a car, and who would be willing to pay $2,000 for a good one, how much they would give today for an equally good car to be delivered in 10 or 15 years. All of them would offer a far smaller sum, if indeed they offered anything at all, thus demonstrating that people, when acting economically, universally regard present goods as more valuable than identical future goods.

Accordingly our worker at the end of a year's work on the steam engine that will be finished in another four years has not yet earned the entire value of one-fifth of a completed engine. He has earned some smaller amount. Smaller by how much? I cannot at this point explain that without a lot of awkward anticipation. Let the remark suffice here that the amount of that difference bears an ascertained relationship to the rate of interest prevailing in the locality as well as to the remoteness of the time at which the whole product is scheduled to be completed. If I assume a prevailing interest rate of 5% then the product of the first

* PUBLISHER'S NOTE: Böhm-Bawerk refers here to his second volume, *Positive Theory of Capital* (in the three-volume opus, *CAPITAL AND INTEREST*); see pages 259-289.

year's labor will, at the end of the first year, be worth about $1,000.[54] And so, if the principle is valid that the worker is entitled to the full produce of his labor, or to the entire value thereof, then the wage for the first year of labor will amount to $1,000.[55]

If anyone has the impression, in spite of the line of reasoning laid down above, that this is too little, I offer the following for consideration. No one will question the statement that the worker is not being under-paid if at the end of five years he receives the whole steam engine or its whole price of $5,500. Let us for the sake of comparison also compute the price of the anticipated payment of wages in terms of its price at the end of the fifth year. Since the $1,000 that he receives at the end of the first year can be deposited for another four years at interest he can thus earn interest at 5% for four years. That is to say, he can receive an additional $200 (ignoring the compounding of interest) for the pos-sibility of using his money that way is open to the worker when he has received his wage. Obviously then, $1,000 paid at the end of the first year is the equivalent of $1,200 paid at the end of the fifth year. So if the worker gets $1,000 at the end of a year for one-fifth of the technical work, he is clearly being compensated by a standard which is not less favorable than if he had received $5,500 at the expiration of five years. 266

But how do Rodbertus and the socialists envision the principle that the worker is entitled to receive the entire value of his product? They demand that the entire value which the product is going to have when completed shall be used for payment of wages, but not at the conclusion of the whole process of production, but made available in installments during the course of the work. Let us weigh carefully what that means. That means, in the case of our steam engine, that the entire $5,500 which the engine will be worth at the end of five years, is received by the worker at the end of 2½ years, which is the result attained by aver-aging the installments received over five years. I must confess I find it absolutely impossible to justify this demand by that premise. How can it be according to the laws of nature and in keeping with the idea of pure justice, for someone to receive at the end of 2½ years a whole which he will not have created until the end of five years? This is so little "in accord with the laws of nature" that it is, quite on the con-trary, just naturally impracticable. It is not feasible even if we free the worker from all the bonds of his much maligned wage contract, and put him into the most favorable conceivable position of an entrepreneur entirely "on his own." As a worker and entrepreneur he will of course get the whole $5,500, but not before they are produced, that is to say, not before the end of five years. And how is a thing to be brought to

---

54. Nothing could be further from my thoughts than to intimate that the rate of interest *causes* the lower valuation of future goods. I know perfectly well that interest and interest rate are only a result of that primary phenomenon. My intention here, anyhow, is not to explain, but to depict facts.

55. At first glance these figures may ap-pear strange, but their correctness will soon be demonstrated.

pass, in the name of the idea of pure justice, through the instrumentality of the wage contract, which the nature of things denies to the entrepreneur himself?

What the socialists want is, in plain English, for the workers to get under the wage contract, *more* than their work produces, more than they could get if they were entrepreneurs in business for themselves, and more than they bring in to the entrepreneur with whom they have made the wage contract. What they have created, and what they are justly entitled to is $5,500 at the end of five years. But the $5,500 at the end of 2½ years, which is what is being claimed for them, is more than that; in fact if the interest rate is 5%, it is equivalent to about $6,200 at the end of five years. And this state of relative valuations is not, mind you, the result of social institutions of debatable merit which have created interest and established a rate of 5%. It is a direct result of the fact that we humans live out our lives in a temporal world, that our Today with its needs and cares comes before our Tomorrow, and that our Day-After-Tomorrow may perhaps not be assured us at all. Not only the "profit grasping capitalist," but every worker as well, indeed every human being makes this difference between present value and future value. How the worker would complain of being cheated, if in place of $10 out of his week's wages which are due today he were offered $10 to be paid a year from today! And is something that is not a matter of indifference to the worker supposed to be such to the entrepreneur? Is he to pay $5,500 at the end of 2½ years for $5,500 which he is to receive, in the shape of a finished steam engine, at the end of five? That is neither just nor natural! The thing that is just and natural—I am glad to concede it again—is that the worker should receive the whole $5,500 at the end of five years. If he cannot or will not wait five years, he shall still receive the entire value of what he produces. But of course it must be the *present* value of his *present* product. This value however will necessarily be smaller than the future value of the product which his labor produces, because in the economic world the law obtains that the present value of future goods is less than that of present goods. It is a law which owes its existence to no social or governmental institution, but directly to human nature and to the nature of things.

If there is any excuse for discursiveness anywhere, it might be at this point where it is a question of the confutation of a doctrine as pregnant with possibilities as is the socialist exploitation theory. And so, at the risk of seeming tedious to my readers, I shall submit a second concrete case which will, I hope, afford me an opportunity of proving the socialists' error even more convincingly.

15. Böhm-Bawerk's Illustration of Five Socialists Building a Steam Engine, And Being Paid Unequally, But Justly

In our first example I ignored the fact that division of labor is an economic actuality. Now I shall change the conditions of the problem in this respect so as to approach the realities of economic life more closely. Let us assume that five different workers participate in the labor of producing a machine, and that each of them contributes one year's work. One worker, perhaps, is a miner who procures the necessary ore, the second prepares the iron from it, the third transforms the iron into steel, the fourth constructs the necessary steel parts, the fifth finally assembles these and, in general, does the finishing. Since each of these successive workers, by the nature of his work, cannot begin his work until the one before him has completed his preparatory stage of the work, the five years' work of our laborers cannot be carried on simultaneously, but only in succession. The completion of the machine, just as in our first example, will likewise take five years. The value of the machine we shall again assume to be $5,500. Now, in conformity with the principle that the worker is to receive the full price of what he produces, what can each of the five who share the labor claim for what he accomplishes?

Let us first solve the problem for a case in which there is no introduction of an outside entrepreneur, and in which therefore the claims to compensation, or the method of dividing the article produced need to be adjusted only among the five workmen. In such a case two things are certain.

The *first* of these is that a distribution of the product itself cannot take place *until the expiration of five years,* because before that time there is nothing there to divide. For if there were any desire, at the end of the second year let us say, to distribute to the individuals as compensation the ore and the iron that had been produced in the first two years, then the raw materials would be lacking for the succeeding stages. On the contrary, it is clear that the intermediary product that is achieved each year must be excluded from any early distribution and retained for the production process until its conclusion.

The *second* thing that is certain is that there will be a total of $5,500 to be distributed among the five workers. But in what proportions?

Certainly not, as one might easily suppose at a first—and superficial —glance, in equal fifths! For that would mean a distribution favoring the worker whose labor is performed in later stages, over those whose work was done early. The worker who puts the finishing touches on the machine would receive $1,100 for his year's work immediately after its conclusion. The one who prepared the individual parts for assembling into the complete machine would receive the same amount, but would have to wait a whole year after he had completed his work to collect his compensation for it. And then there is the extreme case of the worker who mined the ore, and who would not receive his wage until four years after he had completed his work. Since a delay of that sort could not possibly be a matter of indifference to the persons concerned, everyone would want to perform the final labor, which does not suffer any postponment of compensation, and no one would want to assume the work of the preparatory stages. In order to find anyone to assume those jobs, the workers in the late stages would be compelled

268

to consent to an arrangement by which a larger portion of the ultimate exchange value of the product would be accorded to their co-workers in the preparatory stages, to compensate them for the delay. The amount of the difference would depend partly on the length of the postponement, and partly on the degree of difference in the valuation of present and future goods which prevails within our small society, as determined by the economic and cultural conditions which exist there. If the degree of that difference is, for instance, 5% per year, then the shares of the five workers would be graduated as shown below.

The first worker, whose wage is not paid to him until four years after the completion of his year's labor, receives	$1,200
The second, who waits three years	1,150
The third, who waits two years	1,100
The fourth, who waits one year	1,050
The last, who receives his wage immediately upon completion of his labor	1,000
Total	$5,500

It would be inconceivable that each of the workers should receive an equal share of $1,100, except under the hypothesis that the difference in time is a matter of indifference to them. It would be conceivable only if they all considered themselves equally well paid at $1,100, no matter whether they received that sum three or four years later, or immediately after finishing their labors. I hardly need to observe that such a hypothesis never holds, and never can hold. But in the absence of the introduction of a third party it is in any case *completely impossible for each of them to receive $1,100 immediately after completion of his labors.*

It is probably worth while in passing to call special attention to one circumstance. I do not think that anyone could find the distribution plan that I have recorded above an unjust one. And I am especially convinced that, since the workers share their own product only with each other, there can be no contention that there has been an injustice done by a capitalist entrepreneur. And yet the worker who completed the next-to-last fifth does not receive a full fifth of the ultimate price of the product. He gets only $1,050, and the last worker caps the climax by receiving only $1,000!

Now let us make the further assumption, with which reality is ordinarily in agreement, that the workers cannot or will not wait for their wages until the process of producing the machine has been completed. That leads to their entering into an agreement with an entrepreneur whereby they will receive their wage immediately upon completion of their labor, in return for which he is to become the owner of the final product. Now let us make the still further assumption that this entrepreneur is an entirely just and unselfish man, who would be thoroughly incapable of making use of any possible distress to which the workers might be a prey, in order to depress by extortionate measures their claims to wages. Let us ask what the conditions would be of a wage contract drawn up and signed under such circumstances.

The answer is fairly easy to find. Obviously the workers are being treated with complete justice if the entrepreneur offers them as a wage the same as they would have received as their distributive shares, had they been engaged in independent production. This principle gives us a reliable standard for one worker, to begin with, namely, the last of the five. The latter would have received $1,000 immediately after performing his work. So the entrepreneur, to be completely fair, must offer him the same $1,000. But the rest of our table of shares does not give us any direct standard. For since the point of time at which compensation is made is now different from the one that would have applied in the case of their own distribution of shares, the amounts set up for the latter would no longer be directly applicable. However, we have another firm criterion. For since all five workers have contributed the same amount of service toward the genesis of the product, they are in justice entitled to equal wages. And since each one is paid immediately after he has completed his labors, the wages will be equal sums. Justice is served if each worker receives $1,000 at the end of his year's labor.

If anyone should think that that is too little, I refer him to the following easy example in arithmetic. It will prove that the workers now receive exactly the same amount as they would have received through a distribution among themselves—and that amount was shown to be indubitably just. Worker No. 5 receives $1,000 from the distribution, immediately after the end of the year's work, and in the case of the wage contract he receives the same amount at the same time. Worker No. 4 receives $1,050 through the distribution, one year after his work is completed; in the case of the wage contract he receives $1,000 immediately after his work is completed. Now if he puts that out at interest for a year, he achieves exactly the same position that he would have in the case of the distribution, for he then has $1,050 one year after completing his work. Worker No. 3 receives by the distribution $1,100 two years after his work ends, by the wage contract $1,000 immediately which, put out at interest, amounts to the same $1,100 at the same time. In the same way the $1,000 which the first and second workers receive under the wage contract, with the addition of interest are exactly equal to the $1,200 and the $1,150 which, under the distribution, would have been received after four and three years respectively. And if each of the individual wage sums is the equivalent of the corresponding distributional share, then the aggregate of the wage sums must be the equivalent of the aggregate of all the distributional shares. Hence the total of $5,000 which the entrepreneur pays immediately upon performance of the labor to the workers is the exact equivalent of the $5,500 which, in the other

270

case, could have been distributed among the workers at the end of the fifth year.[56]

Any higher wage, such as a yearly wage of $1,100, would be conceivable only under one of two alternatives. Either something to which the workers are not indifferent, namely the difference in time, would have to be a matter of complete indifference to the entrepreneur, or the entrepreneur would have to have the desire to make a gift to the workers of the difference between $1,100 in present funds and $1,100 in future funds. Neither the one alternative nor the other is to be expected of the private entrepreneur, at least not as a rule. Nor could one make it a matter of the slightest reproach, and least of all would it justify a charge of injustice, exploitation, or predacity. There is only one person of whom the workers could expect such behavior as a regular thing, and that is the *state*. For the state is, on the one hand, an entity that exists in perpetuity, and is not therefore compelled to take such strict account of the temporal difference in the giving and receiving of goods. And the state, whose ultimate purpose is the welfare of all its members, can, on the other hand, afford to give instead of to bargain. And so it would

---

56. Stolzmann in his *Soziale Kategorie*, p. 305 ff. registered a few objections to this illustrative example of mine. They are, to my mind, rather inconsequential as well as mistaken. He takes as his point of departure his own erroneous impression that I had intended to have my group of workers represent a sort of archetype (or that I ought to have done so)—a little state with its own complete self-sufficient economic system. And then he raises the objection that even the last worker "could not do anything with his completed machine, could not derive a single day's livelihood from it" (p. 307). He makes the further objection that the hypothetical $1,200 that I set up as compensation for the first worker at the end of the fifth year was an inadequate substitute for his five-year-long wait. The worker would moreover have to receive five full years' wages of $5,000, "if he is not to starve during the long period in which he is forced to fold his useless and idle hands in his lap" (p. 308). I hardly need to say in refutation that it was by no means my intention to furnish an example of a self-contained archetype, but that I merely wanted to—and did—depict a little group of five persons, active in the midst of our modern economic life, and organized for the execution of a single project of production, namely, the construction of *one* machine. I refer Stolzmann to the clear wording of the conditions of my example outlined on p. 264. In addition to other points I made the one there of an "exchange value" of the machine and stated that the only factor I was ignoring was that of the division of labor. Even then I made the stipulation only for the time being and only with respect to the construction of the one machine. Hence there can also be no question of enforced idleness on the part of the participants in the production operation during the time when they were not occupied with it. Later (p. 313) Stolzmann charges me with being guilty of flagrant innuendo, when I state the hypothetical possibility that one of the workers could put out at interest the wage he had received earlier until the expiration of the fifth year. In doing so, says he, I "brand the wage earner as a capitalist." My answer to that is, that not a single word in my example excluded the possibility that one or the other of the participants might not himself possess the means which would permit him to do the waiting. On the contrary, I expressly offered on p. 264 as well as p. 269 the alternative that the workers "cannot *or will not*" wait. Stolzmann, on his pp. 307 and 309 through obvious error misquotes me by saying "cannot *and* will not." Besides all that, I expressly indicated in my Note 54 on p. 468, which also appears in my first edition, that my example was not intended to explain the phenomenon of interest itself, but merely to illustrate a certain line of reasoning with the help of some given facts. Dr. Robert Meyer in his excellent book *Das Wesen des Einkommens*, Berlin, 1887, pp. 270 ff., raises an interesting and much more profound objection. But since it requires anticipating numerous details of my *Positive Theory of Capital* to clear up his likewise mistaken exception, the discussion of it must be reserved for the third volume of this work, *Further Essays on Capital and Interest*. See Essay VI.

concededly be thinkable for the state—but *only* the state in its capacity of giant entrepreneur in the production field—to offer the workers a wage representing the entire future product of their future production and to give it to them *now*, that is to say, immediately after the performance of their labor. Whether the state shall or shall not do so, and thereby afford a practical solution of the social problem in terms of socialist doctrine, is a question of expediency, which it cannot be my purpose to discuss here. But one thing I should like to repeat here and with all possible emphasis, and that is this. If the socialist state pays out now to the workers, as wages, the entire future exchange value of their product, then that is not a *fulfillment but a violation* of the fundamental   271 principle that the worker is entitled to receive as his wage the value of what he produces. And it is a deviation dictated by social and political considerations, rather than the restoration, as the socialists allege, of a situation which of itself is natural or which accords with the idea of pure justice, but has been upset through the avidity of the capitalists for exploitation. On the contrary, it is an artificial interference intended to render possible what in the natural course of things is an impossibility, and to make it possible by means of a veiled and perpetual gift by a generous communal entity known as the state, a gift granted to its more penurious members.

And now a short practical application. It is easily perceived that the stage of distribution which I last described in our example, is the one at which we have actually arrived in our market economy. In this system too, the full value of the product of labor is not distributed as wages, but only a lesser sum, though at an earlier point in time. But the worker suffers no unjust curtailment in his claim to the full amount of what he produces, provided one condition is fulfilled, and that condition provides as follows. The total sum of wages distributed in installments must not fall short of the ultimate price of the final product by a greater amount than is necessary to bridge the gap representing the prevailing difference in the valuation of present and future goods. In other words, the total wages must not be exceeded by the price of the final product to a greater degree than is represented by the prevailing interest rate. The workers in that case receive the full value of their product at a valuation which duly reflects the point in time at which they receive their wage. Only to the extent that the total wage lags behind the ultimate exchange value of the product by a margin in excess of the prevailing interest can that lag, under some circumstances, indicate genuine exploitation of the workers.[57]

Let us return to Rodbertus. The second decisive error with which I charged him in the immediately preceding pages was his interpretation of the statement that the worker is entitled to receive the entire value of his product. I conceded the correctness of the statement but not of his unjustified and illogical interpretation, to the effect that the worker is entitled to receive *now* the entire exchange value which his completed product *will some day have.*

16. Rodbertus's Third Error:
Exchange Value of Goods Is Determined
According to Quantity of Labor Embodied in It

If we institute a search to discover what led Rodbertus into this error, we find that the source of it was still another error, and the *third* important one which I hereby charge he made in his exploitation theory. For he proceeds on the assumption that the exchange value of goods is determined exclusively by the quantity of labor which their production has cost. If that were a correct assumption, then the intermediary product, which in our example represents one year's labor, would indeed at that stage already be invested with a full fifth of the value which the completed product, with its five years of labor behind it, will one day possess. And in that case there would be justice in the claim that the worker is already entitled to a full fifth of that value as his wage.

272

17. How Rodbertus Really Misrepresents
Ricardo's Views (Namely, By an Omission)

But in the form in which Rodbertus presents it, his assumption is unquestionably wrong. Now, if challenged to prove this, I am not even under the necessity of discrediting Ricardo's famous law of value, that labor is the source and the measure of all value. I merely need to call attention to the existence of a highly important exception to that law.

---

57. I shall defer more detailed elaboration of this topic to my second volume. But I wish to protect myself against misunderstanding, and especially against any presumption that I regard any entrepreneur's profit which exceeds the prevailing interest rate as spoliative profit. To that end I should like to insert the following brief remark. There is the possibility that the total difference between the proceeds of the product and wages paid, which difference accrues to the entrepreneur, may consist of four essentially different components. (1) Risk premium to cover the risk of production failure. Correctly estimated, this will, on the average and over the course of the years, be consumed and over the course to reimburse the entrepreneur for actual losses and of course involves no deprivation for the worker. (2) A wage for the entrepreneur's own work, which of course is also quite unobjectionable. In fact, under certain circumstances such as the utilization of a new invention by the entrepreneur it can fairly be computed at a high rate without any injustice being done the workers thereby. (3) The compensation discussed in the text for the time difference between payment of wages and realization of the final product, as measured by the prevailing interest rate. (4) Finally, it is possible for the entrepreneur to increase his income still more by exploiting the distress of the workers to effect an extortionate depression of their wage. Of these four constituent elements only the last violates the principle that the worker is to receive the full value of his product.

It is an exception which Ricardo himself conscientiously registered, and which he discussed in detail in a special chapter. But Rodbertus, strange to say, takes no note of it whatever. That exception concerns the fact that, if two goods have been produced at the cost of equal amounts of labor, then a higher exchange value will attach to the one which requires for its completion either a longer period of time, or the prior performance of a greater amount of preliminary work. Ricardo accords notice to that fact in strange fashion. In Section IV of the first chapter of his *Principles* he makes the following statement: "The principle that the quantity of labor expended on the production of goods determines their relative value, *is subject to considerable modification* by reason of the use of machines and of other fixed and durable capital." In Section V he adds, "also by reason of the unequal duration of capital and the unequal rapidity with which it is returned to its owner." Sometimes the production of goods requires the use of fixed capital of great magnitude or of long duration; sometimes production is of such a nature that a long turnover period is required for the entrepreneur to recover his liquid capital. Goods so produced have a higher exchange value than goods to which these considerations apply in lesser degree or not at all, despite the fact that the latter may have cost the same amount of labor as the former. And the degree of difference in such exchange value is the amount of interest charged by the capitalist.

Even the most partisan defenders of his labor theory of value could hardly harbor any doubt that there really is such an exception to it as is here observed by Ricardo. They may be equally certain that under certain circumstances the factor of temporal remoteness may have even greater influence on the price of goods than the factor of magnitude of labor costs. I remind my readers, as examples, of the price of a wine which has been seasoned for decades, or of a 100-year-old tree in a timber forest.

But there is another very special point in connection with this exception. For it does not require any unusual keenness of perception to notice that the exception really contains the essence of originary interest. For the margin in exchange value which is acquired by those goods that require for their production an advance expenditure of capital, is the very thing that sticks to the fingers of the entrepreneur capitalist in the guise of interest, when the time comes for the distribution of the yield of the product.[58] If that difference in value did not exist, then originary

58. My opinion is not shared by Natoli who subjoins a polemic footnote to these words of my text. See his *Il principio del valore e la misura quantitativa del valore,* 1906, p. 114, Note 2. In other passages, too, he repeatedly and emphatically insists that the "Ricardian differences" in the exchange value of goods requiring production periods of different length are an entirely different matter. They are by no means identical, says Natoli, with the differences in value between present and future goods. The latter occur in the "capitalist exchange" between capitalists and workers and are the source of interest (see his p. 224 ff.). My error, says Natoli, lies in my confusing these two different phenomena (see pp. 279, 314). Yet I think I can adhere to the view I developed in my text above. And I am the more confident because Natoli himself is compelled to admit that the two phenomena, which he accuses me of "confusing," "are

273 interest would not exist either. The former makes possible the latter, encompasses it, is identical with it. There is nothing easier than to illustrate this, if indeed any one demands proof of such a patently obvious fact. Let us assume that three consumers' goods require for their production one year's labor each, but that they differ from each other in the length of the period for which this labor must be advanced. Let the first require that the year's labor be performed only one year prior to completion, the second ten years previously, the third twenty years previously. Under these circumstances the exchange value of the first good will and must be sufficient to cover the wage for one year of labor and in addition the interest for one year on the amount of the labor "advanced." It is perfectly obvious that the same exchange value is not sufficient to meet the wage for one year's labor and in addition either the ten years' interest or the twenty years' interest on an "advance" of the same amount of labor. The payment of such interest can be met only when and because the exchange value of the second and third consumers' good is correspondingly higher than that of the first, even though all three have equal labor costs. And the difference in exchange value is clearly the source from which the ten years' and twenty years' interest can and does flow.

18. What Ricardo Presents Merely as an EXCEPTION Should Have Been His Main Explanation of Interest. Rodbertus Was Too Indiscriminating and "Poor" a Reader of Ricardo

And so that exception to the labor theory of value has no lesser significance than that it is identical with the principal instance of originary interest. Whoever wants to explain the originary interest must explain Ricardo's exception. Without an explanation of the exception, there is no explanation of the interest problem. If a treatise makes it a point to deal with originary interest, and yet ignores this exception, not to say denies its existence, then that must be characterized as a blunder so gross that its equal cannot be imagined. For Rodbertus to ignore that exception is nothing short of an utter disregard of the main topic of the subject he was supposed to explain.

Nor can it be urged as an excuse for his blunder, that Rodbertus had not intended to establish a rule that was valid for real life, but merely to set up a hypothesis of which he availed himself, in order to conduct his abstract investigation with greater ease and accuracy. He does, to be sure, on occasion advance, in the guise of a mere presupposition, his dictum that the value of every good is determined by its labor costs.[59]

---

attributable to a similar and even identical cause" (p. 221). In fact, he admits. that we are concerned with phenomena which are themselves of downright "identical nature" (p. 241). Natoli's attempt to draw a line of demarcation where, in the nature of things, no such line exists, seems to me merely the counterpart of another equally futile undertaking of his. I am referring to his endeavors to take up predominantly sound ideas, garnered from the theory of marginal utility, or from the agio theory, and to stretch them on the Procrustean bed of the labor theory of value.

59. E.g., *Soziale Frage,* pp. 44, 107.

However there is no dearth of passages in which Rodbertus reveals his conviction that his law of value also has validity in real economic life.[60] And in addition it must be urged against Rodbertus that it is not permissible to assume by way of presupposition anything one wishes! Even in the case of a merely hypothetical presupposition, it is permissible to eliminate from consideration only such factual elements as are irrelevant to the question under examination. But what can be said of a scientific inquiry into interest which begins by presupposing that one of the main instances of interest does not exist? What of an explanation in which the best part of that which is to be explained is conjured away "by hypothesis"!

Rodbertus of course is right in one thing he says. If you want to discover a principle, such as that underlying interest, you cannot, says he, "have value dancing up and down";[61] you must assume the validity of a stable rule of value. But we have recorded the following fact. If goods show a greater time interval between expenditure of labor and completion of production, they will also, other things being equal, have greater value. Is not that a stable rule of value? And does not that rule of value have fundamental significance for the phenomenon of interest? And is it to be eliminated as a factor, in the same manner in which we disregard fortuitous and coincidental market conditions?[62]

274

---

60. *Soziale Frage*, p. 113 and 147; *Erklärung und Abhilfe*, Part I, p. 123. In the last mentioned instance Rodbertus says, ". . . if the value of agricultural and of manufactured products is regulated by the labor which inheres in them, *which, by and large, always takes place in real exchange* . . ." etc.

61. *Soziale Frage*, p. 111, Note.

62. The foregoing observations had been set down before Rodbertus's posthumous work, *Kapital*, was published in 1884. In it he takes a very strange position with respect to our question, and as a result I now feel inclined to be more censorious rather than more lenient in the verdict rendered in the text. It is true that he now emphasizes vigorously that his labor law of value is not an exact one but rather a mere approximation, which gives expression to a gravitational tendency (p. 6 ff.). And he does make the express admission that, because of the insistence on an excess of proceeds on the part of the entrepreneurs, a steady deviation takes place in the actual exchange value of goods, as compared with their exchange ratio as measured by the amount of labor (p. 11 ff.). But he grants far too restricted applicability to this concession. For he assumes that this divergence occurs only in the conditions that apply to individual stages in the production of a single good, and not "in general to all production stages." In some cases the production process of a good is broken down into several stages, each of which develops into a separate industry. In such case, according to Rodbertus, the value of the "separate product" that is made at each separate stage cannot maintain a ratio corresponding to the labor expended in it. The reason for this, he maintains, is that the entrepreneurs of the later stages of production are obliged to make a greater outlay for their raw materials, and hence a greater expenditure of capital, and therefore must calculate a higher interest. And that interest can be provided only out of a relatively higher value of the particular product. Correct as this concept may be, it is equally clear that it does not go far enough. The subject is inadequately covered by saying that the variation in the actual exchange value of goods from that of the labor expended thereon, is confined to the preliminary products in the process of producing a good. Nor is the problem completely met by saying that in the course of the successive stages in production these divergences compensate for each other and cancel out, so that the ultimate consumers' goods once more conform to his law of value. For the influence of the factors represented by the amount of capital advanced, and the length of time during which it is advanced, is such that the value of *all* goods is *finally and definitively* at variance with their labor costs. But my severest condemnation is reserved for his stubborn refusal to be ruled by his own admissions. He still insists on the law that all goods are distributed either in the form of wages or of interest. He bases this insistence on the the-

The consequences of this strange kind of negative presupposition made themselves apparent in due course. I have already touched upon one. Rodbertus overlooked the influence of time on the valuation of a good, and so he easily could and inevitably did commit the blunder of confusing the claim of the worker to the entire present value of his product with his claim to its future value. We shall encounter without delay a few other consequences.

19. Rodbertus's Fourth Error: His Doctrine Contradicts Itself in Important Respects; His Law of the General Tendency Toward Equalization of All Surplus Proceeds Contradicts Most Important Contentions of His Interest Theory in General, and His Theory of Interest on Land in Particular

A *fourth* charge which I level against Rodbertus is that his doctrine contradicts itself in important respects.

Rodbertus's whole theory of interest on land is based on the often and emphatically repeated pronouncement, that the absolute quantity of "interest" to be gained in a production process depends, not on the quantity of capital employed, but entirely on the quantity of labor applied in the course of the production in question. Let us assume that in a given industrial production process, for instance a shoe manufacturing business, there are 10 men employed; that each worker produces a product in one year having an exchange value of $1,000; that the necessary sustenance which he receives as wages amounts to a deduction from that amount of $500. In that case, no matter whether the capital employed is large or small, the entrepreneur has a year's excess of proceeds amounting in *toto* to $5,000. If the capital employed amounts to $10,000 ($5,000 for wages and $5,000 for materials) then the surplus proceeds amount to 50% on a base of the capital of $10,000. Now let us suppose that another productive enterprise, say a jewelry factory, also employs 10 men. Under the assumption that the value of products is determined by the amount of labor they represent, these 10 men, too, will produce a yearly product of $1,000 each, of which half belongs to them as wages, and the other half as surplus proceeds to the entrepreneur.

---

oretical assumption that all goods possess a "normal" value, by which he means a value corresponding to their labor costs. Rodbertus justifies this attitude by claiming that his "normal" value, whether in its relationship to the deriving of interest in general, or of interest on land and on capital goods in particular, is the most *impartial*. It is the only one, he says, *which does not seize by stealth any part of the thing it is supposed to explain,* which is a fair characterization of the course of any value which, from the outset, is presumed to be so compounded as to include an element which shall be the source of interest (p. 23). Now in this contention Rodbertus is flagrantly in error. He is fully as guilty of the impropriety of "seizing by stealth," as any of his opponents can possibly be. Only Rodbertus does it in the opposite direction. While his opponents have practiced their furtiveness by presupposing the *existence* of interest, he postulates its *non-existence.* For he ignores that persistent deviation from "normal value" which constitutes the well-spring and the sustenance of originary interest. And by so doing he simply presupposes the principal manifestation of the phenomenon of interest itself right out of existence.

But since gold, the material in the second case, represents a markedly higher capital value than the shoemaker's leather, the total surplus of $5,000 in the second example will be computed percentage-wise on a far larger business capital as a base. Assuming that the latter amounts to $200,000, consisting of $5,000 for wages and $195,000 for materials, then the surplus proceeds will be computed as 2½% computed on the base of the business capital of $200,000. These two examples of mine are conceived entirely in the spirit of Rodbertus's theory.

In almost every manufacturing enterprise the ratio of the number of workers employed, directly and indirectly, to the magnitude of the business capital employed will vary from the ratio obtaining in others. If consistency were to be preserved, that would mean that in almost every enterprise the rate of earnings for the business capital employed would have to vary correspondingly and within extremely wide limits. Now 275 Rodbertus himself does not dare to maintain that such is the case in real life. Instead, we find a remarkable passage in his exposition of his theory of interest on land. The assumption is there set down that, by reason of the competition between capitals throughout the manufacturing field, a uniform rate of surplus proceeds will be established. I will submit the passage in Rodbertus's own words. He makes the observation that in the manufacturing field the only factor of production in use is *capital* goods, and that therefore all surplus proceeds earned in that field are looked upon as income on capital. Then he continues as follows.

"Furthermore, the resulting rate of return will exert an influence tending toward equalization of all incomes on capital, and so will furnish a certain rate of surplus proceeds which will be the standard for the surplus proceeds from raw materials also, and for its calculation on the basis of the capital employed in raw production. For if, as a result of the generally accepted exchange value, there arises a uniformly designated criterion to express the ratio of yield to capital, then that will serve also in the case of surplus proceeds derived from a manufacturing process. In other words, it will be possible to say that the surplus in a given industry amounts to such and such a percentage of the capital employed. That percentage of surplus proceeds will then furnish a standard by which to equalize all surplus proceeds. *Wherever an industry shows proceeds at a rate exceeding the general rate, competition will cause additional capital to be attracted, and will thus cause a general tendency toward the equalization of all proceeds.* For that reason no one will invest capital, unless he can expect an income at that rate."[63]

It will be worth while to examine this passage more closely.

Rodbertus calls competition the factor which will bring about the adoption of a uniform rate of surplus proceeds in the field of manufacturing. He hints only very vaguely how that will take place. He makes the assumption that every time the rate of proceeds in an industry ex-

63. *Soziale Frage,* p. 107 f.

ceeds the uniform rate, an influx of additional capital investment will depress the rate to the uniform level. Conversely, we are presumably entitled to add, every instance of lower-than-normal rate will cause a withdrawal of capital so that the income rate will rise to the average.

Let us carry our consideration of these events a little beyond the early point at which Rodbertus breaks it off. In what way can an increase in capital investment depress an abnormally high rate of surplus proceeds to the general level? Obviously the only means will be as follows. With the increased capital the production of the particular good will be increased, and the increased supply will depress the price to the point where, after deduction of wages, the reduced surplus yield amounts to no more than its normal rate. In the example we gave of the shoe industry, we should have to imagine the procedure by which the abnormally high return of 50% would be reduced to the normal rate of 5% to be apparently as follows. Attracted by the high yield rate of 50% a great many persons will take up shoe manufacture as a new business, and in addition, those already in the shoe industry will increase their production. That increases the supply of shoes, and the price and the exchange value of shoes goes down. This process goes on until the point is reached where 10 workers in the shoe industry produce a year's product which has an exchange value, not of $10,000 but of $5,500. Now after deduction of the necessary wages of $5,000 the entrepreneur has only $500 left as his surplus proceeds. Computed on the basis of the same $10,000 capital investment as before, this represents the prevailing rate of 5%. The exchange value of shoes must remain permanently at the point which has now been reached, if the earnings in the shoe business are not to become abnormal again, in which case there would be a repetition of the entire levelling process we have just described.

In similar fashion the lower-than-normal rate of surplus proceeds in the jewelry manufacturing business of 2½% is raised to 5%. Because of the inadequate rate of earnings, participation in the jewelry business is restricted; as a result the supply of jewelry is reduced; then its exchange value rises to the point where the amount of jewelry turned out in a year by 10 workers in the industry attains an exchange ratio of $15,000. Now after deducting the same wages of $5,000, the entrepreneur has surplus proceeds of $10,000. This amount, computed on the same base of $200,000 as before, represents an interest rate of 5%. Thus the point of stabilization is reached at which the exchange value of jewelry like that of shoes in the first example, can be regarded as permanently established.

Now the equalization of abnormal rates of surplus proceeds cannot be effected without permanent changes in the exchange value of the goods concerned. That is an important point, and before I proceed any further I should like to discuss it from another aspect and remove all possible doubt. For if the exchange value of the products remained unchanged, the only way to raise an inadequate rate of earnings to the normal rate would be to supply the deficiency at the expense of the necessary wages of the workers. If, for instance, the product of 10 workers in the manufacture of jewelry retained unchanged the exchange value of $10,000 which is equal to the quantity of labor expended, then leveling of the rate of yield upwards to 5% would require an increase in the amount of yield from $5,000 to $10,000. Obviously no other method is conceivable than to eliminate entirely the wages of the 10 workers at $500 each. That would mean that the entire product is acquired by the capitalist as his return. Without even considering the point that this assumption involves a sheer impossibility, I wish merely to point out that it is equally at variance with experience and with Rodbertus's own theory. It flies in the face of experience because our experience demonstrates to us that the leveling reduction of supply in a given industry is regularly reflected in an increase in the price of the product and not in a reduction of workers' wages. Nor does experience furnish any evidence that wages are essentially lower in those industries which demand heavy investment of capital, than in the others. And yet that would have to be the case if the requirement of a greater quantitative surplus were met by a reduced wage rather than by an increased price of the product. 277 However, the assumption also violates Rodbertus's own theory. For that theory presupposes that in the long run the workers always receive the necessary cost of subsistence as a wage. And the method of leveling which I have just described would, to say the least, be a grave infraction of Rodbertus's rule.

It would be no more difficult to prove the converse proposition. To reduce returns *in excess* of the average without a change in the exchange value of the product could be effected only by *increasing* the wages of the workers above the normal. And that, too, is counter to experience and to the theory of Rodbertus itself. I believe I may claim that I have described the process of the leveling of returns in the foregoing paragraphs in entire conformity to reality and to Rodbertus's own presuppositions. In doing so I assume, be it noted, that the leveling of abnormal returns is brought about by a permanent change, be it upward or downward, in the exchange value of the products in question.

But if the year's product of 10 workers in the shoe industry has an exchange value of $5,500 and that of 10 workers in the manufacture of jewelry has an exchange value of $15,000—and they must have those exchange values, if there is to be a permanent leveling of surplus proceeds as Rodbertus presupposes—then what becomes of his other presupposition that products are exchanged on the basis of the labor they represent? And if the employment of the same quantity of labor results in surplus proceeds of $500 in one industry and of $10,000 in another, what becomes of the principle that the amount of surplus proceeds over labor costs to be gained in a production process, is not in proportion to the magnitude of the capital employed but to the labor performed? The contradiction in which Rodbertus has involved himself is as patent as it is irreconcilable. There are two possible alternatives. The first alternative is that a permanent system of exchange is really established whereby goods are exchanged at values which are in proportion to the labor that the respective goods represent, and whereby, furthermore, the magnitude of the surplus proceeds to be derived from production is really determind by the quantity of labor expended. If that alternative obtains, then any equalization of the ratio of surplus proceeds to capital is an impossibility. The second alternative is that such an equalization does take place. If that alternative obtains, then products cannot possibly continue to be exchanged at values which are in proportion to the labor they represent, nor is it possible that the quantity of labor expended shall be the only determinant of the magnitude of the surplus proceeds to be derived. Rodbertus would have been compelled to observe this manifest contradiction if he had devoted to this process of the leveling of surplus proceeds even a modicum of genuine reflection, instead of tossing off a fine phrase about the equalizing effect of competition and so contenting himself with an utter superficiality.

But actually the situation is worse than that. The whole explanation of interest derived from the use of land, which in Rodbertus's theory is so intimately bound up with the explanation of interest on capital goods, 278 is based on an inconsistency so conspicuous that it required almost incredibly gross negligence for him to overlook it.

He offers two alternatives of which only one is possible. A leveling process in the earnings on capital either is or is not brought about through competition. Let us assume it is. In that case, what justifies the assumption by Rodbertus that leveling takes place throughout the entire field of manufacture, but ceases at the borders of the field of raw production as if spellbound? If agriculture promises a temptingly higher return, why should not more capital be attracted to it? Why should not more land be placed under cultivation, more intensive methods be applied, cultivation be improved, all to the point at which the exchange value of raw products achieves harmony with the newly increased capital engaged in agriculture, so that the latter yields only the prevalent rate of return? Rodbertus's "law" says the quantity of surplus proceeds over labor costs is not in proportion to the outlay of capital, but only in proportion to the amount of labor expended. But if that law did not prevent leveling in manufacture, how will it do so in raw production? But in that case what has become of the constant excess over the prevailing rate of interest, that is to say, the additional residuum of interest on the use of land?

Or, to examine the other alternative, let us assume that leveling does not take place at all. Then there simply is no general prevalent rate of earnings; then, just as for production in general, so for agriculture in particular, there is no definite norm by which to compute what proportion of "interest" is to be counted as interest on capital goods; and finally, there is then no line of demarcation between interest on capital goods and interest on land. And so, no matter whether the leveling of surplus proceeds takes place or not, in either case Rodbertus's theory of residual interest on land dangles in mid-air. And so we find contradiction upon contradiction, and not, indeed, in the matter of trifles, but in the very fundamentals of his theory!

20. Rodbertus's Fifth Error: His GENERAL and Astounding Error, Which Makes Him Unable To Offer Any Explanation for One Important Aspect of Phenomena of Interest

Up to this point I have made detailed features the target of my criticism. I will conclude by putting the theory as a whole to the test. If the theory is sound, it must be able to supply a satisfactory explanation for the phenomenon of originary interest as we encounter it in real economic life, and in all the important manifestations of its existence. If it is not able to do that, the verdict is rendered—the theory is false.

I now maintain and shall at once prove that Rodbertus's exploitation theory might, in a pinch, serve to make intelligible the earning of interest by those portions of a capital which are invested in wages, but that it is absolutely impossible by means of his theory to explain the earning of interest by those portions which are invested in materials used in the process of manufacture. I call on the reader to judge.

A jeweler engaged principally in making pearl necklaces employs five workers who make up genuine pearls into necklaces which have a price of a million dollars yearly, and which he disposes of, on the average, in one year. He will therefore have a capital of a million dollars con-   279 stantly invested in pearls, and this capital must yield an annual income, at the prevailing interest rate, of $50,000. The question now is, how this earning of interest by the jeweler is to be explained.

Rodbertus's reply is that it is a predatory income, gained by pinching it off from the natural and just compensation of labor. But from the wages of which laborers? The five who sort the pearls and assemble them into necklaces? That can hardly be, for if one is supposed to be able to nibble off $50,000 from the just wages of five workers, that just compensation would have to be something in excess of $50,000, or of $10,000 each. That is an amount of just payment that surely can hardly be taken seriously, especially in view of the fact that the occupation of sorting and assembling pearls is not very far exalted above the level of unskilled labor.

Let us examine the problem a little more closely. Is it perhaps the workers of an earlier stage of production whose labor gave rise to the product which the jeweler is exploiting? Might it be the pearl divers? But the jeweler had no contact at all with those workers. He bought his pearls directly from the entrepreneur of the pearl fishery, or even from a middleman. And so he had no opportunity to make any deduction from the product, or from the exchange value of the product of the pearl divers. But maybe it was the entrepreneur of the pearl fishery who did so, instead of the jeweler, so that the latter's gain arises from a deduction from wages of which the former mulcted his workers? That, too, is impossible. For the jeweler would obviously still make his gain, even if the pearler had made no deduction whatsoever from his workers' wages. And even if the pearler distributes the whole million dollars which the pearls are worth, and which he received from the jeweler as the purchase price, among his pearl divers as wages, the only thing he accomplishes is that he himself receives no income. Certainly the jeweler would not sacrifice any of his earnings. For to the jeweler it is certainly a matter of complete indifference how the purchase price he pays is distributed, provided it involves no increase in that price. And so, strain your imagination as you will, you will search in vain for the workers from whose just wages the jeweler's $50,000 gain could conceivably have been withheld.

But possibly this example of mine may leave some of my readers with unresolved doubts. Some may perhaps consider it somewhat strange that the labor of the five pearlsetters should be the source from which the jeweler can derive so considerable a gain as $50,000, yet they may find it not entirely inconceivable. And so I will present a still more striking example. It is a good old example, one by which in the course of time many a theory of interest has already been tried and found wanting.

The owner of a vineyard has harvested a cask of good young wine. Immediately after the harvest this cask of wine has an exchange value of $100. He leaves the wine to lie undisturbed in the cellar, and after 12 years the wine, which has aged, now has an exchange value of $200. The difference of $100 constitutes an increment for the owner of the wine as interest on the capital represented by that wine. What laborers, pray, were predaciously mulcted of that interest on capital?

280

Since there was not a stroke of work done to the wine during the period of maturation, the only conceivable victims of exploitation are the workers who produced the new wine. The owner of the vineyard paid them too little as their wage. But then my question is, "How much should he 'in all justice' have paid them?" Even if he paid them the whole $100 that the new wine was worth at the time it was harvested, the increment, which Rodbertus brands as a gain through exploitation, would still belong to him. Yes, even if he had paid them $120 or $150 in wages, he still would be branded with the stigma of exploitation. He could not be purified short of having paid them the whole $200.

Now can it be the subject of a serious demand to ask that the "fair labor wage" for a product *worth no more than $100 shall be $200*? Does the owner know in advance whether the product will ever be worth $200 anyhow? Is it not possible that he will be forced, contrary to his original intentions, to use or to sell the wine before the expiration of 12 years? And would he not in that case have paid $200 for a product that never was worth more than $100 or $120? And how is he to recompense those other workers who produce the new wine which he sells immediately for $100? Shall he pay them $200, too? That means ruin. Or only $100? Then different workers get a different wage for completely identical work. And that certainly is an injustice, not to mention the practical difficulty that comes from not knowing before-hand whose product is going to be sold immediately, and whose is going to lie in storage for 12 years.

But there is more to come. Even a wage of $200 for a cask of new wine would not be an amount of compensation that would guarantee immunity from the charge of exploitation. For the proprietor of the vineyard can let the wine mature, not merely 12 years, but 24 years. And then the wine will be worth, not $200, but $400. Is he for that reason to be obliged "in all justice" to pay in place of $100 the sum of $400 to the workers who produced the wine for him 24 years earlier? The thought is too absurd! But if he pays $100 or even $200, he earns his interest on capital, and Rodbertus will say that by withholding a part of the exchange value of his product he has cheated the worker of some of the wage justly due him for his labor.

21. Concluding Critique of Rodbertus's Doctrine on Interest: (a) Unsound in Foundation; (b) False in Conclusions; (c) Self-Contradictory

I do not think anyone would have the temerity to maintain that the instances of the receipt of interest which have been presented here, or the numerous analogous cases that might be, have been ex-plained by Rodbertus's theory. Now a theory which fails to explain a significant proportion of the phenomena it is meant to explain, cannot be the correct one. And so this concluding investigation and summary yields just about the result which might have been expected from the critique of some of its detailed features which I submitted in my earlier comments. That result is: Rodbertus's exploitation theory is unsound in its foundations, and false in its conclusions, and it contradicts both itself 281 and the realities of our world.

In the foregoing pages it has been my aim to render a critical ap-praisal of that theory. The very nature of my task required me to forego any semblance of impartiality and to select for discussion only the errors of which Rodbertus was guilty. However, I believe I am performing an equally binding duty, when I pay tribute to the memory of this prominent figure and to his outstanding services in the development of economics. Unfortunately, the description of those services is something that lies outside the scope of my present task.

IV
Marx's Theory of Interest [64]

A. Detailed Presentation of Marx's Theory

MARX'S life work on economic theory is his large three volume work on capital. The fundamentals of his exploitation theory are laid down in the first volume, which was published in 1867 and was the only one to appear during his lifetime. The second volume, published posthumously by Engels as early as 1885, is in content closely akin to the first. It is common knowledge that there is less homogeneity between these two and the third which was published in 1894, and thus followed the preceding volume, as had the second, only after an interval of several years. Many persons, including the writer of these lines, are

64. *Zur Kritik der politischen Ökonomie,* Berlin, 1859; *Das Kapital, Kritik der politischen Ökonomie,* 3 vols., 1867-1894. Re Marx compare the article "Marx" by Engels in the *Handwörterbuch der Staatswissenschaften,* which includes a complete list of Marx's writings, continued and supplemented in the 3rd ed. of the manual by K. Diehl; then among others, Knies, *Das Geld,* 2nd ed., 1885, p. 153 ff.; A. Wagner in his *Grundlegung der politischen Ökonomie,* 3rd ed. *passim,* especially Vol. II, p. 285 ff.; Lexis in Conrad's *Jahrbücher,* 1885, new series, No. XI, pp. 452 ff.; Gross, *K. Marx,* Leipzig, 1885; Adler, *Grundlagen der Marxschen Kritik der bestehenden Volkswirtschaft,* Tübingen, 1887; Komorzynski, on the 3rd vol. of Karl Marx's *Das Kapital* in the *Zeitschrift für Volkswirtschaft, Sozialpolitik und Verwaltung,* Vol. VI, p. 242 ff.; Wenckstern, *Marx,* Leipzig, 1896; Sombart, "Zur Kritik des ökonomischen Systems von Karl Marx," *Archiv für soz. Gesetzgebung u. Statistik,* Vol. VII, No. 4, pp. 555 ff.; my own essay "Zum Abschluss des Marxschen Systems" in the *Festgaben für Karl Knies,* Berlin, 1896; published in book form in Russian at St. Petersburg, 1897, and in English at London, 1898; Diehl, "Über das Verhältnis von Wert und Preis im ökonomischen System von Karl Marx," reprint from the *Festschrift zur Feier des 25 jährigen Bestehens des staatswissenschaftlichen Seminars zu Halle a. S.,* Jena, 1898; Masaryk, *Die philosophischen und soziologischen Grundlagen des Marxismus,* Vienna, 1899; Tugan-Baranowski, *Theoretische Grundlagen des Marxismus,* Leipzig, 1905; von Bortkiewicz, "Wertrechnung und Preisrechnung im Marxschen System," in *Archiv für Sozialwissenschaft und Sozialpolitik,* Vols. 23 and 25; and many other writings of the voluminous and ever growing literature on Marx.

of the opinion that the content of the third volume is incompatible with that of the first volume, and vice versa. But Marx himself refused to admit this irreconcilability. On the contrary, he insisted in his third volume on the continued and complete validity of the doctrines he had enunciated in the first volume. Therefore a critic has both the right and the duty to regard the first volume as the true and continuing opinion of Marx, despite the existence of the third volume. And of course he commands the same right and must acknowledge the same duty to cite the third volume by way of illustration and criticism, at the proper juncture.

1. Marx's Theory on Interest More Extreme Than Rodbertus's

Marx takes as his point of departure the principle that the value of all commodities is controlled exclusively by the amount of labor which their production costs. He places greater emphasis on this principle than does Rodbertus. While the latter mentions it more or less incidentally in the casual course of his analyses and, in fact, frequently pronounces it only in the form of a theoretical presupposition, without ever wasting a word anywhere to prove it,[65] Marx places the proposition in the very forefront of his entire doctrine, and devotes to it detailed proof and elucidation.

The research area that Marx undertakes to examine in order to "get on the trail of value" (*Vol.* I, *p. 23*)[66] is originally limited by him to *commodities,* by which we must understand that he means, not all economic goods, but only those that are produced by labor for disposition on the market.[67] He begins with an "analysis of commodities" (*Vol.* I, *p. 9*). A commodity, regarded from one point of view, is a useful thing possessing properties which make it capable of satisfying human needs of some sort and therefore possessing use value. Regarded from another point of view, it constitutes a material carrier of exchange value. Then his analysis takes up the latter aspect. "Exchange value first appears as the quantitative relation, the ratio, in which use values of one kind are exchanged for use values of another kind. This relation varies constantly

282

65. Lifschitz in his *Zur Kritik der Böhm-Bawerkschen Werttheorie,* Leipzig, 1908, on p. 16, claims to have caught me contradicting myself. He cites this remark and also an early passage in this book, p. 257 ff. where I spoke of Rodbertus's "serious attempt to prove his case." But Lifschitz has either read so superficially, or thought so superficially, that he confuses two quite distinct theses. In actual fact Rodbertus did defend the thesis that all goods, economically speaking, can cost only labor. I am speaking here of the totally different thesis that the *value* of all goods is regulated solely by the *quantity* of labor cost. Lifschitz might certainly have devoted some attention to the very essential difference between these two theses, if for no other reason, then by all means on account of the completely different positions I took with respect to them on p. 262 f. and on p. 271 ff.

66. My quotations from the 1st vol. of Marx's *Das Kapital* are always taken from the 2nd ed., published in 1872, and those from the 2nd vol. are from the 1885 ed. References to the 3rd vol. concern the ed. of 1894 and, be it further noted, the first part of that volume, unless specifically stated to be otherwise.

67. Vol. I, pp. 15, 17, 49, 87 and other passages. Compare also Adler, *Grundlagen der Karl Marxschen Kritik,* Tübingen, 1887, pp. 210 and 213.

with time and place." It seems therefore to be something fortuitous. And yet behind this variation there must be a constant, and that is the object of Marx's search. He pursues that search in his well-known dialectical fashion. "Let us take two commodities, such as wheat and iron. Whatever the exchange relation may be between them, it is always possible to express that relation in an equation, of which the members are a given quantity of wheat and some quantity of iron, that is to say one bushel wheat $= x$ hundredweight iron. What is the significance of this equation? It signifies that there is something, identical in magnitude, possessed in common by two different things, namely by one bushel of wheat and x hundredweight of iron. Both things therefore are equal to a third thing which, in and of itself, is neither the one nor the other. Each of them then, insofar as it has exchange value, must be reducible to this third something."

2. Marx's Dialectics on Value

"This common element" continues Marx "cannot be any quality— geometric, physical, chemical or otherwise natural quality of commodities. Their physical properties in any event are deserving of consideration only insofar as such properties make them useful, or in other words enable them to qualify as use values. On the other hand, however, the exchange relation of commodities is apparently characterized by a disregard of their use values. Within that relation one use value is worth just as much as any other, provided only it is present in the proper proportion. Or, as old Barbon says 'one kind of commodity is as good as another, if the exchange value of both is equally great. There is no difference and no differentiating between things having equal exchange value.' In their capacity as use values, commodities are primarily of differing quality; in their capacity as exchange values they can differ only in quantity, and as such do not possess an atom of use value.

"If we disregard the use value of objects that can be classified as commodities, then they retain only a single quality, that of being products of labor. And yet the product of labor is transformed as soon as we have it in hand. If we eliminate its use value from consideration, we likewise eliminate the physical component parts and the form which render it a use value. It is no longer table or house or yarn or any other useful thing. We obliterate all the qualities it possesses which are registered by sensory perception. It is also no longer the product of carpentering labor, of building labor, of spinning labor, or of any other specific productive labor. As the useful character of the products of labor is eliminated, so also the useful character of the labors they represent is eliminated; the differing concrete manifestations of those labors also vanish; they no longer differ from each other, but are all reduced   283 to identical human labor, human labor in the abstract.

"Let us consider this residuum of the products of labor. There is nothing left of them but that aforementioned spectral objectivity, a mere coagulation of undifferentiated human labor, of an expenditure of human energy without regard to the form in which it was expended. These things are now merely symbols of an expending of human energy, an accumulating of human labor. As the crystallization of that social substantiality which they all have in common, they are—values."

Thus the concept of value is discovered and determined. It is, in the terms in which Marx's dialecticism presents it, not identical with exchange value but it stands in most intimate and indissoluble relation to it. It is a sort of conceptual distillate of exchange value. To put it in Marx's own words, value is "that common possession which asserts itself in exchange ratio or in exchange value." Conversely too, "exchange value of necessity comprises the manner in which value expresses itself, or the form in which it manifests itself" (*Vol.* I, *p. 13*).

3. Marx's "Socially Necessary Labor Time"

Marx goes on from the determination of the concept "value" to the exposition of its measure and its magnitude. Since labor constitutes the substance of value, the magnitude of the value of all goods is, quite consistently, measured by the quantity of labor they contain, or more specifically, by the labor time. But that does not mean the individual length of time that this or that person who may have fashioned the commodity happened to need for it. It means the "socially necessary labor time." Marx explains this as meaning "the time required to produce any use value when operating under the conditions of production normally prevailing in a given society, and when utilizing the degree of skill and application normally available there" (*Vol.* I, *p. 14*). "It is only the quantity of socially necessary labor, or the labor time socially necessary for the production of a use value, which determines the magnitude of its value. Any single given commodity is considered the average example of its kind. Commodities or goods which contain equal quantities of labor, or which can be produced in the same labor time, have therefore the same amount of value. The value of one commodity bears the same relation to the value of every other commodity, as the labor time necessary for the production of the one bears to the labor time necessary for the production of the other. As values, all commodities are only definite measures of crystallized labor time."

4. Marx's "Law of Value"

From these statements we can deduce the content of the great "law of value" which is "inherent in the exchange of commodities" (*Vol.* I, *pp. 141, 150*) and which controls exchange conditions. This law provides, and in the light of the preceding remarks can provide only, that commodities are exchanged on the basis of the average amount of socially necessary labor which they embody (*e.g., Vol.* I, *p. 52*). The same law is expressed in other terms, such as the statement that commodities *are exchanged at their values* (*Vol.* I, *pp. 142, 183; Vol.* III, *p. 167*) or that *one equivalent is exchanged for another* (*Vol.* I, *pp. 150, 183*). Of course, under the influence of transient fluctuations in supply and demand, prices appear that are higher or lower than those values. But 284 these "constant oscillations of market prices are self-compensatory, they cancel each other out, and finally resolve themselves into the average price which is their essential rule" (*Vol.* I, *p. 151, Note 37*). "In the fortuitous and constantly fluctuating conditions of exchange," however, it will in the long run always be true that "the socially necessary labor time will find enforcement as the controlling natural law" (*Vol.* I, *p. 52*). Marx terms this law the "eternal law of the exchange of commodities" (*Vol.* I, *p. 182*), the "law of ratio," the "natural law of equilibrium" (*Vol.* III, *p. 167*). Those instances in which commodities are exchanged at prices which are at variance with their values—and such cases admittedly do occur—are to be regarded as "accidental" deviations from the rule (*Vol.* I, *p. 150, Note 37*) and the deviations themselves as "violations of the law of the exchange of commodities" (*Vol.* I, *p. 142*).

5. Marx's "Surplus Value"

On this foundation of the theory of value Marx then erects the superstructure of his doctrinal edifice, his famous *principle of surplus value*. He probes into the source of the gain which the capitalists derive from their capital. The capitalists put in a certain sum of money, transform it into commodities and then, with or without an intervening productional process, they convert them, by means of a sale, back into more money. Whence does this increment come, this excess of the sum of money drawn out over the sum originally advanced, or as Marx calls it, this "surplus value?"

Using a dialectic method peculiar to himself, Marx begins by defining the conditions of his problem by exclusion. His first point is that this surplus value cannot arise out of the fact that the capitalist regularly purchases commodities for less than their value, nor can it be that he regularly sells them for more than their value. The problem therefore may be put in the following words, "Our . . . possessor of money must buy commodities at their value, and sell them at their value, and yet at the end of the transaction he must take more value out than he put in . . . Those are the conditions of our problem. Here lies Rhodes, here is the gap to be spanned!" (*Vol.* I, *p. 150 ff.*).

Marx finds the solution to this problem in the fact that there is one commodity, the use value of which possesses the peculiar faculty of being the source of exchange value. That commodity is the ability to labor, or labor power. The latter is offered for sale on the market under two conditions. The first of these is that the worker be personally free. For otherwise it would not be his power that were for sale, but his whole person, that is to say, he would be a slave. The second condition is that the worker be without "all those things that are necessary to the activation of his labor power." Otherwise he would prefer to act as an independent producer, and to offer his products for sale, rather than his labor power. By trading in this commodity the capitalist acquires his surplus value. And he does so in the following manner.

The value of the commodity "labor power" is regulated, as is that of any other commodity, by the labor time necessary to reproduce it. In this case that means the labor time required to produce as much of the materials needed for human sustenance as is necessary to preserve the existence of the worker. If a social labor time of six hours, let us say for example, is required to produce what is necessary for one day's sustenance, and if at the same time we may assume that those six hours are embodied in $9, then the labor power of one day is purchasable for $9. If the capitalist has completed such a purchase, the use value of the labor power is his, and he realizes it by having the worker work for him. If he had him work only just so many hours a day as are embodied in the labor power itself, and just so many as he had been compelled to pay for when he made the purchase, then no surplus value would arise. For six labor hours cannot, by our hypothesis, add to the product in which they become embodied any greater value than $9, and that is what the capitalist paid in wages. But that is not the way the capitalists do business. Even if they have purchased the labor power for a price that corresponds to six hours of labor power, they have the worker work the whole day for them. Now there are more work hours embodied in the product that is produced during that day than the capitalist had to pay for, and the product therefore has a greater value than the wages paid. And the difference is the "surplus value" which the capitalist receives.

Let the following serve as an example. Let us assume that a worker, spinning for 6 hours, converts 10 pounds of cotton into yarn. Assume that the cotton itself required 20 hours' labor for its own production, and accordingly has a value of $30. Let us assume further that during the 6 hours of spinning labor the cotton spinner causes wear and tear of the loom corresponding to 4 hours' labor, in other words representing a value of $6. Thus the total value of the means of production consumed in the spinning process will amount to $36, the equivalent of 24 work hours. During the spinning process the cotton "absorbs" an additional 6 work hours, and so the completed yarn is the product, *in toto,* of 30 work hours and consequently will have a value of $45. On the assumption that the capitalist has the employed worker labor no more than 6 hours a day, the production of the yarn has really cost the capitalist a full $45, namely $30 for cotton, $6 for wear and tear of equipment, $9 for wages. There is no surplus value.

It is an entirely different story if the capitalist has the worker work 12 hours a day. In 12 hours the worker converts 20 pounds of cotton, already representing 40 work hours and hence worth $60. Furthermore the wear and tear of machinery represents 8 work hours with a value of $12. But the worker has added in the course of a day a value of 12 work hours, that is to say a new or additional value of 6 hours. The statement now reads:

Exchange value of yarn spun in one day and representing a cost of 60 work hours	$90.00
Outlay by the capitalist	81.00
(Cotton $60, Wear and Tear $12, Labor $9)	
Remaining surplus value	$ 9.00

According to Marx, then, surplus value is a result of the capitalist's 286 having the worker labor for him for part of the day without paying for it. The work day of the worker thus comprises two distinguishable parts. In the first part, that of the "necessary labor time," the worker produces his own sustenance, or the value thereof, and for that part of his work he receives an equivalent in wages. During the second part, the "surplus work time," he is "exploited"; he produces the "surplus" without receiving any equivalent of any kind for it (*Vol.* I, *pp. 205 ff.*). "Capital is therefore not only, as Adam Smith says, control over labor. It is essentially control over unpaid labor. All surplus value, in no matter what specialized form it is later crystallized, whether profit, interest, rent or the like, is by its nature something which has materialized out of unpaid labor time. The secret of capital's ability to create values out of itself resolves itself into its control over a certain amount of unpaid work performed by others" (*Vol.* I, *p. 554*).

6. Marx's Innovations as Compared With Rodbertus's

THAT is the essence of Marx's exploitation theory, as it is set down in the first volume of *Das Kapital,* and, as we shall later see, contradicted in the third volume. He may possibly contradict it involuntarily, but at any rate he does not in any way repudiate it. In this exposition the attentive reader will recognize once more all the essential features of Rodbertus's doctrine. Even though some of them appear in somewhat altered garb, we find the elements from which Rodbertus assembled his theory of interest. Thus the principle that the value of goods is determined by quantities of labor; that only labor creates all value; that the worker under a wage contract receives a lesser value than he creates, and is forced by necessity to consent to this arrangement; that the capitalist appropriates the excess, and that the excess he thus gains bears the characteristics of the predacious fruit of the labor of others.

Because of the duplication in content of both theories—perhaps it would be more correct to say of both formulations of the same theory —everything that I said in refutation of Rodbertus's theory applies with entire validity in contravention of Marx as well. I can therefore restrict myself to a few supplementary arguments. I consider these necessary, partly in order to adapt my critique in a few matters to the peculiar formulation Marx employs, and partly to discuss a few genuine innovations by him.

Among these innovations the one that is by far the most important is his attempt to go beyond mere statement and to adduce proof for the proposition that all value is founded on labor. My refutation of that principle in Rodbertus's work was casual, as was Rodbertus's own statement of it. I did not go beyond raising such objection as consisted merely in the mention of a few indubitable exceptions to the principle. But I never really went to the root of the matter. But that is something I cannot and will not neglect in the case of Marx. To be sure, I am enter-

287 ing a field which has been plowed up frequently, and by excellent scholars, in the course of literary altercation, and so I can scarcely hope to unearth much that is new for presentation here. But I believe it would ill become me, in writing a book on the critical presentation of theories of interest, to evade the detailed examination of a principle which has been regarded as fundamental to one of the most important of those theories and placed in the vanguard of its forces. It is also unfortunate as well as true, that economic science is at a stage today where renewed efforts at critical examination can by no means be regarded as superfluous exertion. For in our time, more than ever, it is true that that proposition threatens to achieve adoption in ever widening circles, like a profession of faith. In sober truth it is nothing but a fable, once told by a great man and ever since repeated by a credulous multitude.

B. Weakness of Marx's Proof By Authority, Based on Smith and Ricardo

THE two proud names of Adam Smith and Ricardo are generally regarded as indicating the originators of the principle that the value of all goods is founded on labor. And they are just as generally regarded as the august authorities to whom all witnesses take recourse. This general practice is not without justification, but neither is it completely correct. The proposition is indeed found in the writings of both men. But Smith contradicts it every once in a while.[68] And Ricardo places such restric-

---

68. One instance is found in Chap. v of his Book II, where he says: "Not only the tenant farmer's serving-men and serving-maids are productive workers, so are his beasts of burden, too." Another is his statement: "In agriculture nature works with man; and although its work costs nothing, its products have their value, just as truly as do the products of the most highly paid workmen." Compare Knies, *Der Credit*, 2nd half, p. 62.

tions on the field in which it has validity, and so interlards his comments with exceptions to the principle that one is hardly justified in maintaining that he held forth labor as the general and exclusive factor on which the value of goods is based.[69] He begins his *Principles* with the express statement that the exchange value of goods rises from *two* sources— their *rarity* and the *quantity of work* that it cost to obtain them. Certain goods, he points out, such as rare statues and paintings, derive their value exclusively from the first source. The value of only such goods as can be reproduced, by means of labor, in any desired quantity, is determined by the quantity of labor costs. Ricardo admits that the very great majority of all goods belong to this class. But even with respect to these Ricardo feels constrained to make a further reservation. For he is forced to admit that the exchange value of even these goods is not determined by labor exclusively. On the contrary, considerable influence is exerted by the *time* which elapses between the outlay in work advanced, and the realization of the ultimate product.[70]

And so neither Smith nor Ricardo accepted the principle we are discussing as unreservedly as is popularly believed. And yet they did establish it within certain limitations. Let us examine a little further to determine to what extent this is so.

7. Neither Smith Nor Ricardo Substantiated Their Own Work

And here we make a strange discovery! Smith and Ricardo *did not furnish any proof of the principle at all,* but merely stated its validity as something quite self-evident. The famous words in which Smith expressed himself on this topic, and which Ricardo adopted word for word as part of his own doctrine, read as follows: "The real price of every article, what every article really costs him who wishes to acquire it, is the effort and difficulty of acquisition. What every article is really worth to the man who acquired it and wishes to sell it or to exchange it for something else, is *the effort and difficulty which it enables him to avoid and to unload on others.*"[71]   288

Let us pause here a moment. Smith speaks these words in a "tone of voice" as if their truth were immediately and convincingly obvious. But is it really obvious? Are *value* and *effort* concepts so indissolubly connected that the conviction is immediately forced upon us that effort is the reason for value? I do not believe that any unprejudiced person can so maintain. That I have slaved to acquire a thing is *one* fact; that the thing is worth slaving for is a second and different fact. And that both facts do not always go hand in hand is far too well corroborated by experience to admit of any possible doubt. Every one of the countless

69. On this point compare C. A. Verryn Stuart's fine study, *Ricardo and Marx,* and my discussion of it in Conrad's *Jahrbücher* Series III, Vol. I (1891) p. 877 ff.

70. See p. 272 and Knies, *Der Credit,* p. 66 f.

71. *Wealth of Nations,* Book I, Chap. V (p. 13 of the McCulloch ed.); Ricardo, *Principles,* Chap. I.

unsuccessful efforts which are wasted every day on valueless results bears witness to this, quite regardless of whether the cause be technical ineptitude, misguided speculation, or merely bad luck. No less convincing is each of the many instances in which slight effort is rewarded with high value. Examples are the settlement of a tract of land, the finding of a jewel, the discovery of a gold mine. But even if we disregard cases like these, on the ground that they are exceptions to the normal course of events, we know it to be a fact, indubitable as it is completely normal, that the same amount of effort expended by different persons has a widely differing value. The results of one month's effort by an outstanding artist is quite regularly worth 100 times as much as the results of a similar month's effort on the part of an ordinary house painter. How could that be, if effort were really the basis of value? How could it be possible if some direct psychological connection compelled our judgment of value to rely on effort and difficulty, and on nothing else? Surely no one will maintain that nature is so aristocratic as to compel our psyche, by her psychological laws, to prize the efforts of an artist as 100 times more precious than the more modest efforts of a house painter![72] I think that a little cogitation, in place of blind acceptance, will lead to the conviction that there really can be no such thing as the direct and compelling appreciation of an inner connection between effort and value, such as Smith seems to take for granted in that passage.

But does the passage really apply only to exchange value, as has been silently and fondly taken for granted? I do not believe that this can be maintained either, by anyone reading the passage with unbiased eye. It does not apply to either the exchange value, or the use value or any "value" in the strictly scientific sense. As his very use of the word "worth" rather than "value" indicates, Smith has been dealing with value in that very wide and vague sense that the word has in the mouth of the general populace. That is a very significant feature! Smith has the involuntary feeling that he could not gain approval for his principle before the forum of strictly scientific consideration, so he employs the medium of everyday language and turns his attention to the less accu-

---

72. Smith seems to reconcile himself to the phenomenon I describe here as follows: "If the one species of labour requires an uncommon degree of dexterity and ingenuity, *the esteem which men have for such talents* will naturally give a value to their produce, superior to what would be due to time employed about it. Such talents can seldom be acquired but in consequence of long application and the superior value of their produce may *frequently* be no more than a reasonable compensation for the time and labour which must be spent in acquiring them" (Book I, Chap. VI). The inadequacy of this explanation is obvious. In the first place it is clear that the higher value of things produced by especially skillful persons is not based on the "esteem which men have for such talents." How many poets and scholars have been allowed to starve, despite the high esteem which the public accorded their talents? How many unscrupulous speculators has the public rewarded with hundreds of thousands, although it did not esteem their "talents" at all? But even if we admitted that esteem were the basis of value, then we should not be citing an instance of the applicability of the law that value is based on *effort*, but on the contrary, we should be citing a violation of the law.—And when Smith attempts in the second case to attribute the higher value to the effort expended in acquiring skill, he himself admits, through the insertion of the word "frequently," that it is not possible in all cases. The contradiction therefore is still there.

rately formulated concepts of everyday life. Experience shows that he did so with some success, which in the interest of economic science is 289 much to be deplored.

The whole passage can in any event lay little claim to scientific accuracy. This is evident from the fact that its words, few though they be, contain even one more contradiction. For Smith, in one and the same breath, attributes with equal confidence to two different entities the quality of being the basis of "real" value. They are the effort which one can save oneself through ownership of a good, and the effort which one can impose upon another. But those are two quantities which, as everyone knows, are by no means identical. At the present stage of the division of labor, the effort that I should have had to expend, personally, to acquire ownership of a desired article is ordinarily very much greater than the effort it costs a technically trained worker to produce it. Which effort is it, the one which I have been "spared," or the one which I have "imposed" on someone else, that is immediately recognizable as the effort that determines the real value?

In short, the famous passage in which Adam Smith, the Old Master, introduces the labor principle into the doctrine of value, is as far removed as it well can be from what it is ordinarily claimed to be. For the claim is usually made that it must be recognized as a great and well-supported scientific fundamental proposition. But it is not compellingly self-evident; it is not supported by a single word of substantiating argument; it is clothed in the careless language, has the neglectful character of untutored speech; finally it contradicts itself. That it should have nevertheless enjoyed general credence is due, in my estimation, to the combination of two circumstances. In the first place, it was spoken by an Adam Smith; in the second place it was spoken with no vestige of substantiation. Had Adam Smith addressed himself with a single word to the intellect, instead of directly to the emotions, the intellect would not have permitted any invasion of its right to examine the evidence behind the statement in the cold light of reason. In that case its threadbare character could not have failed to be revealed. Doctrines like that can score a victory only when people are taken by surprise.

But let us listen to what Smith continues to say, and after him Ricardo. "Labor was the first price, the original purchase money that was paid for all commodities." That sentence is rather unobjectionable, but at the same time proves nothing with regard to the principle of value.

"In that early and rude state of society which precedes both the accumulation of stock and the appropriation of land, the proportion between the quantities of labour necessary for acquiring different objects *seems* to be the only circumstance which can afford any rule for exchanging them for one another. If among a nation of hunters, for example, it usually costs twice the labour to kill a beaver which it does to kill a deer, one beaver *should naturally* exchange for or be worth two deer. *It is natural* that what is usually the produce of two days' or two hours' labour, should be worth double what is usually the produce of one day's or one hour's labour."

290   We search in vain for any assignment of reason, any motivation in this statement. Smith simply says *"seems* to be the only circumstance," *"should naturally,"* *"it is natural,"* and so on. But he leaves it to the reader entirely, to convince himself of the "naturalness" of these dicta. Incidentally, that is a task which the critical reader will not find it easy to accomplish. For if it were really "natural" that products should be exchangeable solely on the basis of the relative labor time that their acquisition costs, then it would perforce be natural for a rare, gaily colored butterfly or a rare edible frog to be worth 10 times as much among the savages as is a stag. For ordinarily it takes a 10 days' search to find such a butterfly, whereas it is usually possible to get a stag with a single day's labor. That is a matter of relative values that would hardly seem so "natural" as to appear self-evident to anyone.

The upshot of the immediately preceding remarks is, I believe, this: Smith and Ricardo stated the proposition that labor is the principle of the value of goods, without any supporting argument, and as if it were completely axiomatic. But it is not an axiom. Consequently, if the proposition is to be maintained at all, Smith and Ricardo must be ignored entirely as authorities, and corroboration sought elsewhere, and independently.

Now it is a very curious fact that almost no one among their successors has done so. The same men who otherwise probed thoroughly into traditionally accepted doctrines with the scalpel of their devastating criticism, the same men who seemed to consider no time-honored doctrine so firmly entrenched as to be secure against being questioned anew, and against being required to prove itself sound, these same men have failed to show even a trace of incredulity with respect to this very principle of fundamental import, borrowed from the old doctrine. From Ricardo to Rodbertus, from Sismondi to Lassalle, no one has deemed it necessary to bolster the principle with any further support than the name of Adam Smith alone. Anything original contributed by any of them consisted of nothing but repeated assurances that the proposition is true, irrefutable, indubitable. But no one made any attempt really to prove the truth of it, really to refute objections, really to resolve any doubts. Those who look with scorn upon proof by authority are themselves content to invoke authority; the foes of statements that are mere presumptions without benefit of proof, are themselves content to make statements without proof. Only very few of the advocates of the labor theory of value are an exception to that charge, and one of those few is Marx.

C. Examination and Refutation of Marx's Basic Proposition

8. Marx Selected a Defective METHOD of Analysis

TO ANYONE seeking a genuine proof of that thesis, two methods offer obvious avenues of approach that afford a natural way to seek and find such proof. Either the empirical method or the psychological method might conceivably serve. For one might, on the one hand, simply examine the conditions under which experience tells us exchanges are made, and observe whether there is any actual harmony in evidence between the magnitude of the exchange value and the expendi- **291** ture of labor. Or one might, on the other hand, avail oneself of a mixture of inductive and deductive reasoning such as is common usage in our science, and analyze psychological motives. One might, then, ask what motives actuate people when they carry out exchange transactions, or when they determine exchange prices. Or again, we might inquire into the motives at work when they participate in production. From the nature of these motives we might draw inferences as to typical human behavior patterns. In so doing we might conceivably discover, among other things, some relation between the prices that are regularly demanded and paid for commodities, and the amount of labor necessary for their production. And yet Marx did not adopt either of these two natural courses of investigation. It is interesting to discover from his third volume that Marx himself was well aware that no result favorable to his thesis could be achieved either through an examination of the facts, or through an analysis of the motives that are operative during "competition." Instead of that he adopts a third course, one that is certainly rather strange when applied to material of that sort. It is the course of purely logical proof, of dialectic deduction based on the essential nature of exchange.

Marx found the idea ready to hand in old Aristotle, who said, "There can be no exchange without equality, there can be no equality without commensurability" (*Vol.* I, *p. 35*). He uses this idea as his point of departure. He symbolizes the exchange of two commodities by an equation, continues the logical thought process by inferring the existence of a "common element of the same magnitude" in the two things that have been exchanged and which therefore have been rendered equal. He concludes by making it his problem to discover the common element to which the equal things are "reducible" as exchange values (*Vol.* I, *p. 11; see foregoing page 281 ff.*).

9. Matters Antecedent to an Exchange Must Evidence Inequality Rather Than Equality

I should like to make one comment at this point, by way of inter-polation. Even the original presupposition that in any exchange of two things an "equality" manifests itself, seems to me open to two objections. Marx is thinking along lines that are not only out of date (which in the last analysis might not be material) but also very unrealistic. And that, in plain English, means fallacious. Wherever equality and exact equilibrium prevail, there is customarily no change in the state of quiescence previously existing. And so, since any case of an exchange brings about the result that the commodities change owners, it is rather to be taken as evidence of a previously existing inequality or lack of equilibrium, the very effect of which was to compel a change. This situation is analogous to that which results when two chemical compounds are so joined that they may interact. New compounds are created if the chemical "affinity" of an element of the first compound with an element of the second compound is of a strength which is not just equal to, but greater than its affinity with any other element or elements of the first compound. Modern economists are, as a matter of fact, unanimous in their opinion that the old views propounded by the scholasticists and theologians are 292 untenable in their espousal of an "equivalence" of the values that are exchanged. But it is not my purpose to ascribe any further importance to that point. I prefer to turn my attention to a critical examination of the logical and methodological procedures by which Marx's quest for the "common element" yields him labor as the desired distillate.

10. Marx's Erroneous Intellectual Method

Marx's procedure in his search for the "common element" that characterizes exchanges is as follows. Whatever qualities are possessed by the objects which are balanced against each other in the exchange are allowed to pass in review. Then all those which cannot meet the test are excluded under the Marxian elimination method, until at last only one quality is left. This one—the quality of being a product of labor— must then be the object of our search, the quality that is possessed in common.

This procedure is somewhat strange but not in and of itself to be condemned. But it is odd to refrain from applying positive tests to the presumptive characteristic quality. I admit that to do so would have meant to adopt one of the two methods we discussed previously, and which Marx deliberately avoided. The strangeness consists in Marx's attempt to convince himself by a purely negative procedure that that presumptive quality is just the very one he is looking for. The reason he gives is that no other qualities are what he is seeking, and there must be one such quality. Still, that method can lead to the desired result, if it is applied with the necessary care and all-inclusiveness. That is to say, if meticulous care is exercised to put into the logical sieve everything that belongs there, and to make absolutely certain that by no possible inadvertence can any single thing slip through the meshes of the sieve, which should not do so.

But how does Marx proceed?

From the outset he places in the sieve only those things possessing exchange value, which also possess the quality which in the end he means to sift out as the "common" one, and he excludes all others. His procedure is like that of one who has a strong desire to demonstrate that a white ball can be drawn out of an urn, and takes the precaution to insure that result by placing nothing but white balls in the urn. For from the outset he restricts the scope of his search for the essence of exchange value to "commodities." While in so doing he does not exactly define this concept "commodities" with meticulous care, he does nevertheless set limits that are narrower than those which define "economic goods," and he restricts the field to products of labor and excludes gifts of nature. Now it is certainly obvious that if exchange means an equivalence, which presupposes the existence of a "common element of equal magnitude," then such common element should necessarily be sought and found in all categories of goods that are made the subject of exchange. It should be present, not exclusively in products of labor, but also in such natural resources as land, timber, water power, coal deposits, stone quarries, oil wells, mineral waters, gold mines and the like.[73] Under these circumstances it is really nothing short of methodological high crime to exclude, in a search for the common element that belongs to all exchange values, all goods possessing exchange   293 value without being products of labor. It would be exactly comparable to the procedure followed by a physicist conducting a hypothetical investigation as follows. He wishes, let us say, to determine the reason for a quality possessed in common by all bodies, such as weight. His method is to sift the qualities of a single category of bodies, let us say, transparent ones. He passes in review all the qualities that are common to transparent bodies, he demonstrates with respect to all their *other* qualities that these cannot be the reason for weight. And on the basis of that proof he proclaims that transparency is the reason for weight.

It would certainly never have occurred to Aristotle, the father of the idea of equivalence in exchange, to exclude natural resources. It is all the less justifiable since some gifts of nature, such as land, belong among the most vitally important objects of wealth and commerce, and since, furthermore, it can by no means be maintained that the exchange values of natural resources are always only fortuitously and haphazardly

73. There is cogency to the objection that Knies raises to Marx's argument when he says, "It is impossible to perceive from anything contained in Marx's exposition any reason why we may not have, beside the equation: one bushel wheat = x cwt. of wood felled in the forest, the equally valid equation: one bushel wheat = x cwt. uncut timber, = y acres of virgin land, = z acres of pasture on natural meadowland." (*Das Geld,* 1st ed., p. 121, 2nd ed., p. 157.)

determined. On the one hand products of labor, too, show at times fortuitous prices. And on the other hand the prices of natural products often exhibit very distinct relationship to firmly established reasons or determining factors. It is very well known, for instance, that the purchase price of real estate is frequently determined as a multiple of the income it yields at the prevailing interest rate. It is equally certain that standing timber and coal in the mine vary in price, and not out of pure coincidence but because of differences in quality, or location, or transportation conditions.

And Marx takes every precaution to avoid being caught up in the necessity of accounting for the fact that his investigation from its inception excluded one class of goods possessing exchange value. With equal care he avoids giving any reason for doing so. In this instance, as in so many others, he exhibits the necessary skill to escape, with the slipperiness of an eel and by sheer dint of his dialectic cleverness, from the tight places into which his argument has led him. To begin with, he avoids calling to his readers' attention the fact that his concept of "commodities" is narrower than that of all goods with exchange value. With exceptional cleverness he paves the way for his subsequent restricting of the investigation to his "commodities." The very natural paving stones he uses are the words of a generalization which appears as an apparently harmless bit of verbiage at the beginning of his book. "The riches," he says, "of those societies in which capitalistic methods of production prevail, appear as a monstrously large *collection of commodities.*" This statement is completely erroneous if the expression "commodities" is accepted in the sense in which Marx uses it later of "products of labor." For nature's gifts, including land, comprise a very considerable and by no means negligible portion of personal wealth. But the insouciant reader can easily overlook this inaccuracy, because he does not know that at a later time Marx is going to assign a much narrower significance to the term "commodities."

Nor does Marx clarify this matter as he goes on. On the contrary, 294 the first few paragraphs show him wavering in his choice from among the terms "thing," "use value," "good" and "commodity" without making any sharp distinction between the last of these and the other three. On page 10 he says, "the usefulness of a thing makes it a *use value.*" And again, "an object classifiable as a commodity . . . is a *use value or good.*" On page 11 we find, "Exchange value . . . manifests itself . . . as the quantitative proportion in which *use values* of one kind are exchanged for *use values* of another kind." Be it noted that here the one Marx has cast in the rôle of the hero of the exchange value phenomenon is use value, alias good. Then Marx continues after the words, "Let us consider the matter more closely." Surely those words are not intended to announce a transition to a different and more restricted field of investigation! Yet Marx goes on to say, "A single *commodity,* a bushel of wheat, is exchanged in the most varied proportions for other *articles.*" He also says, "Let us take two further *commodities,*" etc. In the same paragraph the expression "things" even occurs again. In fact, it appears as part of a statement that is very important for our problem, to the effect that "a common element of identical magnitude exists in two different *things*" (i.e., two things which are being treated as equivalents in an exchange).

11. Marx's Fallacy Consisting in Biased Selection of Evidence

But on page 12, the page immediately following, Marx prosecutes his search for the "common element" only with respect to the "exchange value of *commodities*," without breathing the slightest word to put us upon notice that he intends to limit the field of his investigation to only a part of the things which have exchange value.[74] And on the very next page the limitation is immediately abandoned, and the conclusion that he has just established for the limited field of commodities is extended as if it had validity for the wider field of the use values of goods. "A *use value, or good,* has value only because it represents human labor in the abstract which has materialized and been rendered objective!"

If Marx had not at the crucial point restricted his investigation to products of labor, if he had looked for his common element in natural resources as well, it would have been patently manifest that labor cannot be that common element. If he had made his delimitation explicitly and avowedly, he would himself inevitably have stumbled upon his methodological blunder. And his readers too! And they would have been forced to smile at the naive artifice by which he seeks to prove his point. The end product of his process of distillation is indeed the quality of being a product of labor, as one element possessed in common by the class of things he has distilled. But Marx himself excluded beforehand from the materials he placed in his retort all things which are not products of labor, even though they deserved to be included because they are by nature things possessing exchange value. The trick was impossible to perform, except in just the way Marx performed it—surreptitiously and by employing a dialectician's device that consisted in skimming over a ticklish point with celerity and facility. I must express my sincere admiration of the cleverness with which Marx was able to make an acceptable presentation of such a fallacious procedure. But I am of course also 295 compelled to report its complete fallaciousness.

But suppose we go a bit further. After all, the end achieved by this trick of Marx's that we have just described, was no more than to admit labor into the circle of aspirants. The artificial delimitation of the field simply made it *one* quality that was possessed "in common." There was the possibility that other qualities, also held in common, might compel consideration. How was he to oust these competitors?

74. In this very paragraph he quotes a passage from Barbon which again obliterates the distinction between goods and things. "One kind of commodity is as good as another, if the exchange value of both is equally great. There is no difference and no differentiating between things having equal exchange value!"

That end he achieved by two thought processes, each of which contains only a few words, but one of the most grievous errors in logic.

The first of these is Marx's exclusion of all "geometrical, physical, chemical or other natural properties of goods." For "their physical properties in any event are deserving of consideration only insofar as such properties make them useful, or in other words enable them to qualify as use values. *On the other hand, however, the exchange relation of commodities is apparently characterized by a disregard of their use values.*" For "within that relation (the exchange relationship) *one use value is worth just as much as any other, provided only it is present in the proper proportion*" (*Vol.* I, *p. 12*).

What would Marx have said to the following argument? In an opera company there are three excellent singers, a tenor, a bass, and a baritone who receive a salary of $20,000 a year each. The question is, "What is the element possessed in common which causes them all to be paid the same salary?" My answer is, that in the matter of salaries one good voice is worth as much as any other, a good tenor voice is worth the same as a good bass voice or a good baritone, provided only it is available in the proper proportion. Consequently there is "apparently" an elimination, in the matter of salary, of the factor of good voice, and consequently the good voice cannot be the common cause of the high salaries. It is obvious that this line of reasoning is fallacious. It is equally obvious that the Marxian logical sequence, of which it is an exact copy, is no whit more correct. Both contain the same error. They confuse elimination *of a factor generally*, with elimination *of the special phases* the factor exhibits in special instances. The factor which can be disregarded in our problem is the special phase in which the factor "good voice" manifests itself. It may be immaterial whether we are paying for a tenor, a bass, or a baritone. But rest assured it is not so as to "any good voice." In the same way, consideration of the exchange relation of commodities may disregard the special phase in which their use value manifests itself, for instance whether the commodity serves to provide food or clothing or shelter, but it certainly may not disregard the use value itself. The utter impropriety of summarily dismissing use value from consideration could have been deduced by Marx from the very fact that there can be no exchange value where there is no use value. Indeed, that is a fact which Marx himself is repeatedly compelled to admit.[75]

75. He says, for instance, at the bottom of p. 15: "A thing cannot have value, if it is not a useful article. If it is not useful, then the labor it contains is also useless, does not count as labor (sic!) and hence does not create value."—Knies has already directed attention to the error I have censured above. See his *Das Geld*, Berlin, 1873, p. 123 f. (2nd ed., p. 160 ff.). Adler, in his *Grundlagen der Karl Marxschen Kritik*, Tübingen, 1887, p. 211 f. reveals that he has strangely misunderstood my argument, when he urges in refutation that good voices are not commodities in the Marxian sense. I was not concerned at all with the question whether or not "good voices" can be classed as economic goods under the Marxian law of value. I was concerned solely with drawing up a sample of a syllogism that embodies the same error that Marx makes. I could just as well have chosen an example that had no relationship whatever to the economic field. I could, for instance, just as well have proved that the one element common to variegated bodies is heaven knows what, but not the combina-

Marx is in still worse case when it comes to the next link in his chain of argumentation. "If we disregard the use value of objects that can be classified as commodities, then they retain only a single quality," Marx says, to quote him literally, "that of being products of labor." Really? Only *one* quality? Do not goods possessing exchange value have other qualities in common? For example, are they not *rare* in relation to the demand for them? Or are they not the object of supply and demand? Or are they not privately owned? Or are they not "products of nature"? For no one states more clearly than Marx himself, that they are as much products of nature as they are of labor, when he declares, "Objects classifiable as commodities are combinations of two elements, natural materials and labor," or when he quotes approvingly from Petty, "Labor is the father of it (material wealth), and the earth its mother."[76]

Now my question is, why the principle of value cannot just as well be contained in one of *these* common qualities, as in the quality of being a product of labor. For Marx has not offered a ghost of a positive reason to support the latter. His only reason is the negative one that the successfully eliminated use value is *not* the principle of exchange value. But does not this same negative reason apply with equal force to all the other qualities which commodities possess in common but which Marx overlooked?

But there is more to come. Let us look at page 12 on which Marx conjured away the influence of use value on exchange value with the argument that one use value is worth as much as any other, provided only it is present in proper proportion. There he says, with respect to products of labor, the following. "And yet the product of labor is transformed as soon as we have it in hand. If we eliminate its use value from consideration, we likewise eliminate the physical component parts and the form which render it a use value. It is no longer table or house or yarn or any other useful thing. We obliterate all the qualities it possesses which are registered by sensory perception. *It is also no longer the product of carpentering labor, of building labor, of spinning labor, or of any other specific productive labor.* As the useful character of the products of labor is eliminated, so also the useful character of the labors they represent is eliminated; the differing concrete manifestations of those labors also vanish, *they no longer differ from each other, but are all reduced to identical human labor, human labor in the abstract.*"

Is it possible to say more distinctly or more explicitly that for the exchange relation not only one use value, but also one kind of labor and labor products "is worth just as much as any other, provided only it is present in proper proportion"; in other words, that the very same

---

tion of several colors. For one combination of colors, say white, blue, yellow, black and violet, is worth just as much as a claim to classification under "variegated," as is any other combination of colors, say green, red, orange, sky-blue, etc., provided only it is present "in proper proportion." Consequently, we eliminate color and color combinations as factors!

76. *Das Kapital*, p. 17 f.

circumstances which serve as the grounds on which Marx pronounces his verdict of elimination against use value, can be made to apply to labor? Labor and use value have a qualitative and a quantitative side. As surely as the use values of table, house and yarn differ from one another qualitatively, just so surely is there such a difference in the case of the labor done in carpentering, building or spinning. And as surely as labor of different kinds is comparable on the basis of its quantity, just so surely are use values of different kinds comparable on the basis 297 of their magnitude. It is absolutely incomprehensible why the identical set of facts can lead to the elimination of the one competitor, and to the crown of olive leaves for the other! If Marx had happened to reverse the order of his inquiry, he could have eliminated labor by the very same logical succession which led him to the elimination of use value. And by the same procedure which led to the coronation of labor, he would have come to proclaim use value to be the sole surviving and thus the desired common quality, and value to be a "coagulation of use value." I think it could be maintained, not facetiously but in all seriousness, that the two paragraphs on page 12 could be interchanged. I mean that in the first paragraph in which the influence of use value is eliminated, and in the second in which labor is proved to be the desired common element, the subjects could be interchanged, without the necessity for any change in external logical correctness. That is to say, without any change in the sentence structure of the first paragraph one could in every instance replace the word "use value" with "labor and labor products," and similarly, one could replace the word "labor" throughout the second paragraph with "use value"!

12. Böhm-Bawerk's Idea That Marx Had "An Intellect of the Very First Order"

Such is the logic and the methodology of Marx's procedure in introducing into his system the fundamental proposition that labor is the sole basis of value. As I stated recently elsewhere,[77] I consider it utterly out of the question to suppose that this dialectical hocus pocus furnished the source and justification of his convictions for Marx himself. I cannot believe that this represents the procedure by which he originally attained conviction or sought to examine the facts and freely and impartially to determine their inter-relationship. I consider Marx an intellect of the very first order, and I believe it would have been impossible for a thinker of his caliber to seek the truth by paths that are in their very nature so devious and unnatural. Nor could a mind of such stature have blundered through sheer mischance or adverse fortune into all those errors of logic and of method I have just described. Had his line of research been in truth so mistaken, it could not possibly have yielded as its result, achieved without prescience or premeditation, the thesis that labor is the sole source of value.

77. "Zum Abschluss des Marxschen Systems," p. 77 ff.

I believe the true situation was quite otherwise. I do not doubt that Marx was really and sincerely convinced of his thesis. But the reasons for his conviction are not the ones he wrote into his system. He believed in his thesis, as a fanatic believes in his dogma. He doubtless embraced it because it stood under the aegis of those celebrated authorities, Adam Smith and Ricardo. And he was certainly imbued with it on the strength of the same vague and casual impressions, accepted without searching intellectual scrutiny, that had misled those illustrious intellects into the expression of similar ideas. And it is improbable that he ever reached the point where he entertained the faintest doubt of its correctness. And so for Marx himself his proposition stood firm as an axiom. But for his readers he had to furnish proof. The principle could not have been demonstrated empirically, nor along the lines of the psychology which underlies economic phenomena. And so he took recourse to rationalization of a dialectical character, a procedure, incidentally, that accorded with the bent of his mind. With an adeptness most admirable of its kind, he tinkered and puttered around, manipulating the compliant concepts and premises of his thesis, until at long last the predetermined and premeditated result was finally produced in a form that was to all outward appearances reputable and conclusive. **298**

This attempt of Marx's to play the dialectician in order to furnish his thesis with such props as would make it convincing, collapses completely, as we have just seen. But could not some support have been found for it by following either the empirical or the psychological method which Marx avoided?

13. Other Methods of Approach Than Marx Here Uses

In the second volume of this work, its positive phase, I shall show that the psychological method, for one, would not. An analysis of the psychological forces that are operative in the matter of exchange values leads to results quite at variance with Marx's thesis. And as a matter of fact, Marx's posthumously published third volume really contains an admission to that effect.[78] There still remains to be considered the attempt along empirical lines, the test of factual experience. What does that show?

14. Five Factual Exceptions Neglected by Marx

Experience shows that the exchange ratio of goods is in proportion to the quantity of labor necessary for production in the case of only some goods, and then it is only incidental. That this statement sums up the situation as it exists in hard fact ought to be well known, because the data which support it are a matter of common knowledge. And yet its truth is seldom acknowledged. It is true that the whole world, including the socialist authors, is unanimous in admitting that experience does

---

78. This topic will receive further treatment later.

not bear out the labor principle in all cases. But the opinion is very frequently encountered that the cases in which actuality coincides with the labor principle constitute a very large majority, and that the cases which are at variance with the labor principle are exceptions to the rule and relatively rare. That opinion is a very badly mistaken one. I should like to correct that opinion once and for all. To that end I will devote the succeeding pages to grouping together the "exceptions" which experience tells us exist in our economic world, in violation of the labor principle. It will become apparent that the "exceptions" preponderate so vastly, that there is hardly any room left for the "rule."

1]   In the first place, all "rare goods" are exempt from the labor principle. That means all goods which, because of some factual or legal obstacle, cannot be reproduced at all, or at least not in unlimited quantity. Ricardo lists a few examples, and these include statues and paintings, rare books and coins, vintage wines and the like. He adds the remark that these goods "constitute only a very small part of the goods which are exchanged in the open market every day." If it be considered that this class of goods also includes all real estate, plus the myriad goods involving patents, copyrights and trade secrets, the extent of these "exceptions" will be found to be by no means inconsiderable.[79]

2]   In the second place, all goods which are produced by skilled rather than unskilled labor constitute exceptions. The product of a day's
299 work performed by a sculptor, an expert cabinet maker, a maker of violins, a mechanical engineer, etc. does not embody more labor than the product resulting from the work done by a common laborer or a factory hand. And yet the former product has an exchange value greater than that of the latter, and often it will be many times as great. Naturally, the adherents of the labor theory of value could not overlook this exception. Strangely enough, they pretend that this is no true exception, but only a little variant, which really still falls within the rule. Marx, for instance, hits upon the device of calling skilled labor a multiple of ordinary labor. He says (*on p. 19*), "More complicated labor counts as simple labor raised to a higher power, or rather, simple labor multiplied. Thus a smaller quantity of complicated labor is equal to a greater quantity of simple labor. Experience shows that this reduction process goes on constantly. A commodity may be the product of the most complicated kind of labor, but its value places it on a par with the product of simple labor, and the commodity therefore represents merely a certain quantity of simple labor."

There, forsooth, is a bit of legerdemain in the theorizing line that is astounding in its naiveté! We can concede that it is quite possible to rate a sculptor's working day as equivalent to a ditchdigger's five in some respects—for instance as to emolument. But certainly no one will care to maintain that the sculptor's 12 working hours actually *are* 60 hours

79. Cf. Knies, *Der Credit*, Part II, p. 61.

of ordinary labor. Now in matters of theory, such as the inquiry into the principle of value, it is not a question of the fictions that men may choose to deal with, but a question of that which really is. As a matter of theory the product that the sculptor brings into being in a day is the product of *one* day's work and that is final. And if the product of one day's work is worth as much as another good which is the product of *five* day's work, then the case presents an exception to the ostensible rule that the exchange value of goods is determined by the amount of human labor they represent. And it remains an exception, no matter what fictions man may create to deal with it. Suppose a railroad sets up a tariff schedule which, generally speaking, scales the charges in accordance with the distance that passengers and freight are transported. But suppose, further, that the schedule provides that distances over a certain stretch where conditions make operation especially costly, shall be computed as two miles for each mile of the road elsewhere. In such case can anyone maintain that the distance traveled is *really* the sole principle employed by the railroad in fixing its tariffs? Of course not. A *fiction* is employed, making distance the ostensible principle. In effect, however, the principle is modified by taking into consideration the *nature of the terrain* which comprises the distance. The situation is the same with respect to the theoretical consistency of the labor principle, and no amount of prestidigitation can save it.[80]

I trust it requires no further details to establish that a considerable proportion of commercial products falls into this class of exceptions. In fact almost all goods, strictly speaking, fall into this category. For almost every commodity will require, somewhere in the course of its 300 production, specialized labor of some kind—that of an inventor, a manager, a foreman and the like. And that—in terms of the labor theory of value—raises the value of that commodity somewhat above the level that it would have attained on the basis of the quantity of labor alone.

3] There is a third class of exceptions to add to the foregoing. But if the theorist is content to account for this limited influence of labor on exchange value, he is spared the necessity of seeking a motivation sufficiently basic to make labor the key to that earlier and more inclusive proposition. It is an embarrassing necessity because no such motivation exists. I refer to such things as handwork done by women, embroidery, needlework, knitting and such. The products of such labor then also have an abnormally low exchange value. It is not unusual, for instance, that the product of three days' work by a plain seamstress will have an exchange ratio that is not equal even to that of the product of two days' labor by a factory girl.

All the exceptions that I have mentioned so far tend to exempt

80. I have repeatedly referred to my essay "Zum Abschluss des Marxschen Systems," where I have treated this point, too, in greater detail. See my p. 80 ff.

[For modern English translation see *Shorter Classics of Böhm-Bawerk*, Essay IV, with the title, "Unresolved Contradiction in the Marxian Economic System." — Libertarian Press] certain groups of goods entirely from the operation of the labor value law. That is to say, they restrict the domain in which that law obtains. Really, they leave subject to that law only those goods which encounter no obstacles of any kind to reproduction in any desired volume, and at the same time require only unspecialized labor in their production. But even this restricted domain is not subject to the sway of the labor law of value without exception. Rather is it the case that even here exceptions bring about a further easing of the strictness with which the law may be applied.

4]   A fourth exception to the labor principle is offered by one phenomenon that is universally known and admitted. Even those goods the exchange value of which, by and large, is in harmony with the quantity of their labor costs, still do not exhibit that harmony at all times. Fluctuations in supply and demand often cause the exchange value to rise above or fall below an amount which would correspond to the quantity of labor these goods embody. That quantity represents a center of gravity toward which the exchange value is drawn, rather than a fixed point at which it rests. To my way of thinking the socialist adherents of the labor principle are far too ready to shrug off this exception nonchalantly. Yes, they do confirm its existence, but they treat it as an ephemeral little irregularity, the existence of which by no means impairs the great "law" of exchange value. But it cannot be denied that all these irregularities constitute just that many examples of exchange values which are the result of factors other than the quantity of labor costs. At the least, this should have started an investigation into the question as to whether there might not be some other principle of exchange value. Might there not be a more general principle which would account simultaneously not only for the "regular" manifestations of exchange value, but also for those which, from the point of view of the labor theory, appear as irregular? But you may look in vain for an investigation of that sort by the theorists of the school we are discussing here.

301   5]   Finally, there is a fifth deviation from the law. Aside from the aforementioned momentary fluctuations, the exchange value of some goods fails to correspond to the quantity of labor they embody, in a way which is *enduring* and to a degree which is not inconsiderable. Of two goods, the production of which costs the same amount of labor in terms of the average prevailing in a given society, that one will command a higher exchange value which requires the greater advance outlay of "preliminary" labor. As we know, Ricardo discussed in detail this departure from the labor principle in two sections of the first chapter of his *Principles*. Rodbertus and Marx, in the course of deriving their theories,[81]

---

81. Marx does not make express mention of it until his third and posthumous volume. The result is—and it could not have been expected to be otherwise—that he now finds himself in conflict with the laws in the first volume, which had been formulated in disregard of the exception.

ignore it without expressly denying it—a thing they could not legitimately do. An oak tree that is 100 years old has a higher price than can correspond to the half minute it takes to plant the acorn. That is a fact too well known to be successfully denied.

Let us summarize. The alleged "law" provides that the exchange value of goods is determined by the quantity of labor embodied in them. It is a law which a considerable proportion of goods *does not obey at all,* and the rest *not always,* and *never exactly.* Such is the empirical material with which he must deal who would formulate a theory of value.

What conclusions can the impartial theorist draw from such material? Surely not that the origin and determinant of all value is to be found solely in labor. A conclusion like that would be no whit better than to conclude, let us say, as follows: Electricity, experience tells me, often results from rubbing, and also often, to be sure, in other ways. Therefore there is a law, "All electricity is the result of friction."

On the other hand one can fairly conclude that expenditure of labor is a circumstance which has a far-reaching influence on the exchange value of many goods. It should be carefully noted, however, that this applies to labor, not as an ultimate cause, but as a specific intermediate factor. Any ultimate cause of value would have to be possessed in common by all value phenoma. However, in accounting only for this more limited influence of labor on exchange value, the theorist would be relieved of the embarrassing necessity of discovering as basic a motivation as was sought—necessarily in vain, of course—in the attempt to prove labor to be the key to that earlier and more inclusive proposition. It might be quite interesting and quite important to pursue further the question of the influence of labor on the exchange value of goods, and to formulate the results in the shape of laws. Only it would be imperative never to lose sight of the fact that those would then only be specific laws of value, which do not affect the general nature of value.[82] I might make use here of an analogy. The laws which formulate the influence of labor on the exchange value of goods stand in the same relation to the general law of value, as that in which the law "East wind brings rain" stands to a general theory of rain. East winds are a widespread intermediate cause of rain, just as expenditure of labor is a widespread intermediate cause of the value of goods. But the essential nature of rain is no more attributable to the east wind than that of value is to labor expended.

---

82. For that reason I think Natoli in his *Principio del valore,* recently published, goes much too far. He is keenly aware that labor exercises neither a primary nor a universal influence on the value of goods. He is, in fact, well cognizant of the fact that such value depends, without exception, on the *grado di utilità* (marginal utility). And he also knows, finally, that in Ricardo's labor theory of value, cause and effect are interchanged (*op. cit.,* p. 191). Yet in spite of all this, Natoli alleges that ultimately an *equazione utilitaria* (equation of utility) between value and labor can always be established. And by way of that equation he detours to the point where he declares the coinciding of value and labor to be the fundamental law of value. Indeed, he calls it the basic "cardinal law of all economy" (*op. cit.,* pp. 191, 244, 277 and 391).

15. How Marx Worsened Ricardo's Error

302   Ricardo himself overstepped the legitimate bounds only by very little. As I have already shown, he knows very well that his labor law of value is only a specific one. He knows, for instance, that the value of "rare goods" has an entirely different basis. His only error is that he greatly overestimates the extent to which his law is valid and practically ascribes to it almost universal applicability. A related phase of the same error consists in his tendency in the later stages to forget entirely the lightly regarded exceptions to his law which he had very correctly mentioned himself toward the beginning of his work. In consequence he comes to speak—quite incorrectly—of his law in phrases that imply that his law really is a universal law of value.

It was only his successors who, exercising less foresightedness than he, committed the almost incomprehensible error of positing labor, with complete and conscious assurance, as the universal principle of value. I say "almost incomprehensible error" because it is really difficult to understand how scientifically trained men after mature deliberation can maintain a doctrine for which they can simply not find a shred of logical support. There is none in the nature of the problem, for that shows absolutely no necessary connection between value and labor. There is none in experience, for that, quite on the contrary, shows that value for the most part does *not* harmonize with the expenditure of labor. Nor, finally, is there any even in authority, for the authorities on whom they rely never maintained the proposition in that pretentious all-inclusiveness with which their successors were fond of endowing it.

And the socialist adherents of the exploitation theory seek to maintain such a proposition, built on sand as it is! Nor do they employ it just incidentally, and to shore up some inconsequential angle of the structure of their theory. Indeed, they make of it a keystone to support the very façade of their most vital and practical claims. They uphold the law that the value of all goods consists in the labor time they represent. Then the next moment they attack any creation of wealth that is in conflict with this "law," such as the differences in exchange value which accrue to the capitalist as a surplus value. They call it "contrary to the law," "unnatural," "unjust," and recommend that it be abolished. That is to say, first they ignore the exception, in order to be able to proclaim their law of value as having universal validity. And after their furtive theft of that quality of universal validity, they revive their memories of the exceptions, to brand them as violations of the law. This method of argumentation is truly just as bad as that which would be followed by one who, observing that there are many foolish men, ignores the fact that there are also some wise men, in order to derive the "universally valid law," that "all men are foolish," and then demands the extirpation of the "unlawfully" existent wise men!

16. Two Contradictory Posthumous Volumes of Marxian System (by Engels; Vol. II in 1885, and Vol. III in 1894)

THE foregoing is substantially the verdict that I rendered many years ago, on the subject of the labor theory of value in general, and of Marx's arguments in its favor in particular. That was in the first edition 303 of this book. In the meantime the posthumously published third volume of Marx's *Kapital* appeared. Its publication had been awaited with a certain eager curiosity among economists of all persuasions. They were eager to learn how Marx would solve a certain difficulty which was the inevitable consequence of the doctrine he had laid down in the first volume. It was a difficulty which he had not only failed to solve in the first volume, but had hitherto left completely unmentioned.

In discussing Rodbertus I have already called attention to the absolute incompatibility of two of his assumptions. The first of these is that goods are exchanged on the basis of the relative quantities of labor with which they are indued. The other, and incidentally one which is indubitably corroborated empirically, is that earnings on capital are subject to an averaging process.[83] Naturally Marx in *his* presentation was beset by the same difficulty, and in fact he was more drastically vulnerable still, because just that part of the doctrine which contains the bone of contention is formulated by him with such special emphasis that it virtually invites objection.

For Marx distinguishes, within the capital which serves the capitalist as his means of acquiring a surplus, two component parts. The first is the part which is the source of labor's compensation, and which Marx calls the "variable capital"; the second is the part that constitutes the outlay for concrete materials of production such as raw materials, instruments, machines and such, and which Marx calls the "constant capital." Since only the labor of living persons can really create new additional values, only that part of capital which has been converted into labor power can change and increase in value during the process of production. That is why Marx calls it the "variable" capital. That part alone reproduces its own value and something in excess of it, the surplus value. The value of the consumed means of production, on the other hand, is merely preserved intact, since it reappears in the value of the product, altered in form, unaltered in magnitude. That is why Marx calls it the "constant" capital. It is not capable of "putting on surplus value." From this it necessarily follows (nor does Marx neglect to point out the syllogism with all possible emphasis) that the amount of surplus which can be produced with a capital can be in direct proportion to *the variable part* of the capital, but not to *the total capital*.[84] And it follows further,

83. See foregoing p. 277 f.
84. "At a given rate of surplus value and with a given value of labor power the amounts of the surplus value are in direct proportion to the amounts of the advanced variable capitals." "The amounts of value and surplus value produced from different capitals, are, in the case of a given value and of equal rates of exploitation of labor power, in direct proportion to the magnitudes of the variable components of these capitals, that is to say, of so much of their component parts as have been converted into live labor power" (Marx, Vol. I, p. 311 f.).

that equal capitals must produce unequal quantities of surplus value, if they differ as to their composition, with respect to relative amounts of constant and variable capital. This is what Marx calls their "organic composition." Let us accept, for a bit longer, Marx's terms and call the ratio of surplus value to that portion of the variable capital which is paid for wages the "rate of surplus value." And for its ratio to the total capital employed by the capitalist—what the latter in practice ordinarily uses as the base on which to compute the surplus value he has gained— let us use the term "profit rate" or "rate of return." Marx would now say, if the degree of exploitation is equal or the rate of surplus value is equal, then capitals of varying organic composition must yield unequal "rates of return." Capitals which are of such composition that the variable portion predominates, must bear a higher "rate of return" than those in the composition of which the constant capital predominates. But experience says that because of the operation of the law of the leveling of returns, capitals will in the long run bear equal "rates of return" without regard to their composition. Accordingly there is a manifest conflict between that which is, and that which, according to the Marxian doctrine, ought to be.

304

Marx himself was not unaware of the existence of this conflict. In his first volume he had already made laconic mention of it as "merely apparent," and referred his readers for his solution to the parts of his system which were to come later.[85] The long suspense in which the world had waited interminably to learn how Marx would try to extricate himself from this awkward dilemma was finally relieved through the appearance of his third volume. It contains a detailed discussion of the problem, but of course no solution. He merely corroborates the irreconcilable contradiction (nor could anything else have been expected) in what proved to be an abandonment of the doctrine in his first volume—veiled, unacknowledged, glossed over, to be sure—but still an abandonment.

For now Marx develops the following doctrine. He admits explicitly that in reality, and because of competition, the rate of return on capitals, quite irrespective of their organic composition, is leveled off, and necessarily must be leveled off to a uniform average rate.[86] In addition he admits explicitly that a uniform return rate, in the case of varying organic composition of capitals, is possible only if the individual commodities are interexchanged in a proportion other than that which reflects their value as determined by the labor they contain. Indeed, the exchange will be such that commodities produced with capital that is predominantly

---

85. Vol. I, p. 312 and p. 542.

86. "Aside from unimportant, fortuitous and mutually compensating variations, there can be no doubt that in reality a difference in average profit rates as between different branches of industry does not exist, nor could it exist without destroying the whole system of capitalistic production" (Vol. III, p. 132). "As a result of the varying organic composition of the capitals invested in various branches of production . . . the profit rates prevailing in different branches of production are originally widely different. These differing profit rates are levelled off by competition to a general profit rate, which is the average of all these different profit rates" (Vol. III, p. 136).

constant will be exchanged at more than their value, and those produced with predominantly variable capital at less than their value. Here he adds the term "capital of higher composition" for capital with a higher percentage of constant capital; conversely "lower composition" designates capital with a lower percentage of constant capital and a higher percentage of variable capital.[87] And finally Marx admits explicitly that the determination of prices in practical life really takes place in this way. On page 136 of the third volume he defines the "price of production" of a commodity as containing three things. In addition to repayment of wages paid plus means of production consumed (the "cost price") it also contains the average return for the capital employed in production. This price of production "is actually the same thing that Adam Smith calls 'natural price,' Ricardo calls 'price of production,' the physiocrats '*prix nécessaire*,' because in the long run it is the condition on which the supply, the reproduction of commodities in each particular sphere of production depends" (*Vol. III, p. 178*). In real life then, goods are no longer exchanged according to their values, but according to their prices of production. Or as Marx is fond of saying euphemistically (*for instance, Vol. III, p. 176*) "values are transformed into prices of production."

No one can fail to realize that these concessions and affirmations in the third volume are a striking contradiction of the fundamental principles laid down in the first volume. In the latter the reader was presented with a logical thesis to the effect that out of the essential nature of exchange arises the necessity that two commodities that have been accorded equivalence by virtue of the exchange must contain a common element in equal magnitude, and that this common element of equal magnitude is labor. In the third volume the reader is informed that when commodities are rated as equivalents in an exchange, they actually and regularly contain, and necessarily must contain, unequal amounts of labor. In the first volume (*p. 142*) we had read, "It is true that commodities may be sold at prices that are at variance with their values, but this variation constitutes a violation of the law of the exchange of commodities." And now we read that the law of the exchange of commodities provides that they are sold at their prices of production, and that the latter, as a matter of principle, cannot coincide with their values! I do not imagine there ever was a system of which the end repudiated the beginning so conclusively, so scathingly!

305

87. Marx develops this principle by giving an example in schematic form which embraces five classes of commodity and five productive industries with capital of varying organic composition. He supplies a comment on the results revealed by his schematic arrangement in the following words: "Together the commodities are sold at $2 + 7 + 17 = 26$ above their value, and at $8 + 18 = 26$ below their value. Thus the price deviations cancel out reciprocally. This takes place through an equalizing distribution of the surplus or by addition of the average 22% profit to the cost prices of the respective commodities I to v. Some of the commodities are sold above their value in the same proportion as the rest are sold below their value. And only their sale at such prices makes it possible for the profit rate to be a uniform 22% for commodities I to v, irrespective of the differing organic composition of capitals I to v." The same thought is then discussed in detail on the succeeding pp. 135-144.

Of course Marx will not admit there is any contradiction. Even in this third volume he still claims that the law of value, as it is stated in the first volume, governs the actual conditions of the exchange of goods. And he expends many an effort, resorts to many a subterfuge, in his attempt to prove that in some degree, in some way or other, it still continues so to govern. I have discussed all these subterfuges elsewhere and in detail,[88] and exposed their futility. At this point I should like to comment expressly on just one of them. This is partly because it might really, at first blush, appear to have something alluring about it, and partly because Marx is not the only one to employ it. For I find its counterpart in the writings of one of the most capable among the theorists of the socialist school in the present generation. In 1889, which means before the publication of Marx's third volume, an attempt was made by Konrad Schmidt to carry to completion the part of Marx's system that was then still lacking. It was to be an independent creation, but presumably in the Marxian spirit.[89] And so he was led to a construction of the problem which likewise modified its provisions to the effect that individual commodities cannot, as the letter of the law—the Marxian law of value—demands, be exchanged in the ratio of the quantities of labor they represent. And so of course he found himself face to face with the question how far he could maintain the validity of the Marxian law of value if indeed he could maintain it at all, after such an admission. And Schmidt, as early as that, attempted to rescue the validity of the law by means of the same dialectician's argument that crops up again in Marx's own third volume.

The course which that argument takes is as follows. Individual commodities admittedly are exchanged in part above, and in part below their values. But these deviations compensate each other or cancel out, so that, for all the exchanged commodities taken together, the total of the prices paid is equal to the total of the values. Hence the law of value, applied to the totality of all branches of production, does after all find enforcement "as the governing trend."[90]

88. In my "Zum Abschluss des Marx-schen Systems," pp. 25-62. Since that time Hilferding has published an apologia by way of refutation, which appeared in Vol. I (1904) of the *Marx-Studien*, but nothing in it has caused me to change my opinion in any respect. More specifically, I wish to insist at this point on bringing up the matter of some observations by Heimann in his "Methodologisches zu den Problemen des Wertes," excerpt reprinted from the *Archiv für Sozialwissenschaft*, Vol. XXXVII, p. 19. I cannot forego remarking that the schedules I presented (*op. cit.*, p. 53) are entirely correct and appropriate. Hilferding's "corrected versions" of them are as arbitrary as they are irrelevant.

89. *Die Durchschnittsprofitrate auf Grund des Marxschen Wertgesetzes*, Stuttgart, 1889.

90. "In the same proportion in which one part of the commodities is exchanged above its value, another part is exchanged below its value" (Vol. III, p. 135). "The total price of commodities I to v" (i.e., in the schematic example used by Marx) "would therefore equal their total value . . . And thus, taking the totality of all branches of production into account, in society itself the sum of the prices of production of the commodities produced equals the sum of their values" (Vol. III, p. 138). The divergence of the prices of production from values balances out "in that the excessive amount that is diverted to surplus value in the case of one commodity is offset by a corresponding deficiency in another, and in that the deviations from value which are lodged in the prices of production offset each other" (Vol. III, p. 140). Similarly, K. Schmidt (*op. cit.*, p. 51) says: "The necessary divergence of the actual price from the value in the case of particular commodities vanishes . . . as soon as one takes into account the sum of all the individual commodities, that is to say, the annual national production."

The dialectical web of this pseudo argument however, can be very 306 easily torn asunder, and that, too, I have already demonstrated on another occasion.[91]

For what is the purpose of the law of value, anyhow? Certainly it can only be to explain the ratio of exchange as we observe it in real life. We want to know, for instance, why a coat is the equivalent of 20 yards of linen cloth, why 10 pounds of tea is considered to have the same value as half a ton of iron, and so on. And that is the way Marx himself conceived the task of explaining the law of value. Obviously one can speak of an exchange *ratio* only in the sense of the relation of two individual and dissimilar goods *to each other*. But as soon as we consider all goods *taken together* and add up the prices of them, we necessarily and deliberately ignore whatever internal relations may exist within that totality. The relative differences in price as between members within the group are compensated out of existence in the total. The amount by which tea is worth more than iron is the amount by which iron is worth less than tea, and vice versa. In any case, we get no answer to our question as to the exchange ratio of goods in an economic system, when we are told the total price that all goods combined will command. We might just as well ask by how many minutes or seconds did the winner of a foot race better his competitors' time for the distance, and then be told, "All the men in the race, taken together, took 25 minutes and 13 seconds"!

Now the situation is this. In answering the question of the problem of value, the Marxists begin with their law of value, that commodities are exchanged in the ratio of the labor time they embody. Then they make a disavowal—disguised or undisguised—of their first answer, so far as it concerns the exchange of individual commodities. But of course the question has no significance at all, except insofar as it does concern these. And then the Marxists claim complete validity for their answer only so far as it concerns the entire sum of the "national production." And that of course is a field in which the question has no point at all. They are thus forced to admit that the facts belie the "law of value" as an answer to the real question of the problem of value. And the only application which does not belie the law is then no longer an answer to the problem to which we really require a solution, but could at best be an answer only to some other question.

But it is not even an answer to another question. It is no answer at all, it is rank tautology. For every economist knows that if we pierce through the veil of money transactions, we perceive that commodities are really exchanged for other commodities. Every commodity that is the subject of exchange is at one and the same time a commodity and the price of what is received in exchange. Accordingly the total of the commodities is identical with the total of the prices paid for them. Or it can

---

91. The first was in a discussion of the aforementioned article by Schmidt which I published in the *Tübinger Zeitschrift*, 1890, p. 590 ff.

be put this way. The price of the total national product taken together is nothing more nor less than the total national product itself! Under these circumstances it is, to be sure, quite correct to say that the total price which is paid for the whole national product combined, is equal
307 to the total exchange value that is "crystallized" in that national product. But this tautological dictum does not represent any genuine addition to our knowledge. Neither is it of any particular use as a test of the correctness of the alleged law which provides that goods are exchanged in the proportion of the labor they embody. By use of that method it is possible to supply just as good a proof—or rather just as bad a proof—of any "law" you wish to name. Let us imagine a law providing that goods are exchanged in the proportion of their *specific gravity!* For even though it be true that as an "individual commodity" a pound of gold can be exchanged, not for one pound of iron, but for 50,000 pounds of it, nevertheless the *total* price that is paid for a pound of gold plus 50,000 pounds of iron *combined* is not more and not less than 50,000 pounds of iron and one pound of gold. Accordingly the total weight of the total price, 50,001 pounds, is exactly equal to the total weight embodied in the total commodities, namely likewise 50,001 pounds. Consequently *weight* is the true standard by which the exchange relationship of goods is governed!

V
Marxian Doctrine as Interpreted by His Successors

UNLESS I am mistaken, the appearance of Marx's third volume signified the beginning of the end of the labor theory of value. That was the rock on which Marxian dialecticism foundered so manifestly, that blind faith inevitably began to weaken, even in the ranks of the most devout believers. Literary signs are already noticeable. For the time being these consist in attempts to rescue the doctrine, now no longer tenable in the exact words in which Marx set it down, by subjecting it to new interpretations.

1. Werner Sombart's Reinterpretation

In very recent times several serious theorists have proclaimed such interpretations. Werner Sombart openly admitted that the Marxian law of value is not tenable if it is put forward with a claim that it is in accordance with empiric reality. His idea is to interpret the Marxian doctrine as only an attempt to provide us with a "device for assisting our thinking," that device being Marx's concept of value. Value, as Marx defines it, does not appear in the exchange relation as it concerns the objects of capitalist production. Nor does it play any part as a factor in the distribution of the annual "national product." Consumers' goods, because of their qualitatively heterogeneous character are otherwise not commensurable. But by means of this auxiliary concept our minds are enabled to conceive of them as quantitative entities and they are thus rendered commensurable for our thinking. The Marxian concept of value becomes defensible when it functions in this capacity.[92]

---

92. "Zur Kritik des ökonomischen Systems von Karl Marx," from the *Archiv für soziale Gesetzgebung,* Vol. VII, No. 4, p. 573 ff.

In my opinion this proposition bears all the earmarks of a compromise that is quite unacceptable to both sides, and I have already expressed that opinion elsewhere.[93] It cannot satisfy the Marxians because it is in direct contradiction to the most unequivocal pronouncements of Marx himself, and because it contains a complete surrender of the very essence of the Marxian doctrine. For it is self-evident that a theory which by its own admission is not in accordance with reality cannot have any significance for the explanation and evaluation of real conditions. And as a matter of fact voices have already been raised in disavowal in the camp of the Marxists.[94]

On the other hand, neither can the impartial theorist be satisfied with this compromise from the point of view of purely scientific requirements. For even auxiliary concepts, while they may be assumptions made in neutral disregard of reality, must not be a contradiction of it. So I consider Sombart's attempt at a new interpretation to be a pronouncement which will hardly win many friends and impel them to take up their pens and champion its cause.

2. Konrad Schmidt's Reinterpretation

Konrad Schmidt recently announced a pending fresh attempt at a reinterpretation of Marx which may be expected to provide more material for discussion than Sombart's. He commented on my previously mentioned *Zum Abschluss des Marxschen Systems* and conducted his discussion with commendable objectivity and impartiality. He comes to the conclusion that Marx's law of value, in the light of the facts recorded in the third volume, does actually lose the meaning "which, according to its presentation in the first volume, it seemed to have," and against which my criticism was leveled. But, says Schmidt, by that very fact it gains "a new and deeper significance, which only needs to be worked out more clearly in its contrast to the original version of the law of value." By a "revised thinking out" of the law of value "along lines that Marx concededly has not clearly laid down" it will be possible "at least in principle" to reconcile the contradictions that I pointed out. And Schmidt does give a hint of the basic lines along which his revised thinking will proceed.

He says price and labor time are both measurable quantities. A twofold relationship between them is thinkable. "Either the magnitude of the price is in direct proportion to the labor time contained in the commodity, or there are variations from this direct relation which follow certain rules that can be formulated, at least in a general way." Since the latter alternative is as readily conceivable as the former, it would not be permissible to do more than consider as a hypothesis the law of value which

93. "Zum Abschluss des Marxschen Systems," p. 103 ff.
[See "Unresolved Contradiction in the Marxian Economic System," Essay IV in *Shorter Classics of Böhm-Bawerk."* — Libertarian Press]

94. For instance, Engels in his most recent work appearing in the *Neue Zeit,* Nos. 1 and 2 of the 14th annual vol. (1895-1896) entitled, "Ergänzung und Nachtrag zum dritten Buch des Kapitals."

is based on the former of the two alternatives and it is "the task of further concrete investigation, either to confirm that hypothesis or further to modify it." Marx's first two volumes "pursue the original simple hypothesis to its remote conclusions" and thus are able to compose "a detailed picture of the capitalist economy, under a system of exploitation, as it would appear if price and labor time coincided exactly." But even though this picture "reflects the fundamental features of the capitalist reality," it contradicts that reality in certain respects. Therefore the hypothesis must be modified in order "to reconcile the partial contradiction between it and reality." And that is what takes place in the third volume. "The simple rule according to which the two factors coincide, which was absolutely necessary for a preliminary orientation, must now be modified. 309 It must now be said that in reality prices deviate from the assumed norm in accordance with a rule which can be formulated in general terms." By this circuitous route, and only by this circuitous route, is it possible to arrive at recognition and detailed understanding of the actual relationship between prices and labor time. And that means an understanding of the real method of exploitation.[95]

I cannot prophesy any brighter future for this attempt at reinterpretation than I did for the original by Marx. Konrad Schmidt is a keen dialectician, and it may well be that when he proceeds to the detailed delineation of the doctrine he has sketched out, he will attempt to present it agreeably, with many a clever turn of phrase and many an alluring argument. But with all his artistry of presentation and argumentation, he will not be able to avoid foundering on two objective rocks which, judging by the sketch he has submitted of his program, are certain to lie athwart his course. That program already reveals two methodological sins, one of commission, one of omission. The first is a self-contradictory question-begging assumption, the second is the inherent untenability of his point of departure.

I spoke of a self-contradictory begging of the question (*petitio principii*). Let us occupy the point of view that Schmidt invites us to take. Let us for the present regard as a mere hypothesis the "law of value" according to which the exchange ratio of commodities is determined solely by the labor embodied in them. It is a hypothesis of which the correctness is not yet established, but is only to be put to the test by a more searching examination of the facts. What is the outcome of that test?

It is frankly conceded by its protagonists that the test does not completely and fully confirm the hypothesis. Quite on the contrary, it must be admitted that the quantity of the embodied labor does not constitute the sole determinant of the prices which the owner of commodities receives for them. Now, it must be remembered that the really distinctive and characteristic feature of Marx's law of value is its claim that labor is the *exclusive* determining factor. That it is a contributing influence is admitted under any theory of value. It now appears that the "less than

95. Supplement to the issue of *Vorwärts* of April 10, 1897.

full and complete confirmation" in this case, really signifies a *refutation* of the hypothesis with regard to its one essential feature.

My next query is, "What right has Schmidt to postulate that this hypothesis, which is unconfirmed as to its principal point, nevertheless 'reflects the fundamental features of capitalist reality'; and more specifically, that it does so in depicting the receiving of interest by the capitalists as based, in principle, on a 'genuine exploitation' of the workers?" If Schmidt advanced any other considerations which could prove the exploitative character of interest, we should of course have to make an independent examination of those considerations. But Schmidt does not establish any such additional independent reasons in his program, nor can he supply any, as we shall see in a moment. His only argument to prove the exploitative character of interest lies in the hypothetical law of value. However, the hypothesis bases its conclusion as to the exploitative char-

310   acter of interest on the premise—and exclusively on the premise—that in the labor that is incorporated in the commodity is to be found the sole cause of exchange value, and of the magnitude of that value. Schmidt must demonstrate that not an atom of exchange value can arise from any other cause than labor, in order to establish that any share of the value which a nonworker receives out of the product, is received only at the expense of the worker, and therefore is the fruit of exploitation. But as soon as it must be admitted that the exchange value of commodities is not exactly equal to the quantity of labor they embody, then it is clear that in addition to labor some other causative factor influences the creation of exchange value. And as soon as that happens, there is no longer any certainty that the capitalist's share arises from exploitation of the workers. For it could quite conceivably, and even quite probably, arise from that other cause of exchange value which competes with labor, and concerning the nature of which nothing is as yet established. In other words, the justification for using the hypothetical "law of value" as a reason for regarding originary interest as an exploitative gain stands or falls with a *full and complete* verification of the hypothesis. To discredit it even in part is to dig the ground right out from under the feet of the thesis, because the latter took its stand upon just that unconfirmed part of the hypothesis, namely the assumption that labor is the *exclusive* determinant of exchange value. Thus Schmidt presents an assumption, suspended in mid-air, to the effect that the exploitation hypothesis "reflects the fundamental features of capitalist reality." But he treats that suspended hypothesis as an ostensibly verified proposition which follows logically from the corroborated portion of the law of value, and in so doing he is guilty of an obvious *petitio principii,* assuming as true exactly what needed to be proven to be true.

And that blunder is made even more vicious by the presence of a contradiction. The mere presumption without proof of the exploitative character of interest would still not get Schmidt to his goal. In the course of the logical argument which is supposed to lead to an explanation of the phenomenon of interest as it actually exists, he is forced into that contradiction. Again it pertains to that ill-starred proposition, that the magnitude of the value is determined exclusively by the amount of labor it represents. Schmidt is forced to treat it in two ways, first as having validity in actual practice, then as not having validity in actual practice. That is because he is required to explain not only the cause of interest, but its amount as well. In doing so he takes the same position as the Marx of the third volume. He explains the determination of the interest rate as follows. The total surplus predatorily acquired by the capitalists is distributed uniformly and in accordance with the "law of the equalization" of profits, over all capitals employed, in proportion to their amounts and to the length of time for which they are invested. In order to make this portion of his explanation hold good, Schmidt has to concede expressly that the tentative hypothesis of the law of value is not in accord with actual practice, that is to say, that the exchange of commodities is *not* exactly in proportion to the labor incorporated in them—in short, 311 that the hypothesis does not have validity.

But that is not yet quite enough to explain the interest rate. There still has to be an assumption and an explanation on the subject of how large that divisible quantity is, which is to be uniformly distributed, in other words that total of the capitalists' predaciously acquired surplus value. For this portion of his explanation Schmidt joins forces with the Marx of all three volumes. He assumes that the capitalists are able, in disposing of the commodities that they have their workers produce, to realize a price for them which is in complete accord with the hypothesis of the law of value—a price which corresponds in magnitude exactly to the number of labor hours which are embodied in the commodities. And so at two stages of a single explanatory line of reasoning he treats the law of value, first as empirically valid, then as empirically invalid. Even that possibility might be entertained if the two stages in his explanatory line of reasoning corresponded to two distinct stages in the empirical course of events. That is to say, if the creation of the surplus value were *one* separate and independent process, and the distribution of the surplus value, after its creation, were another independent and subsequent process. That would correspond to the business experience of a corporation. There the gaining of surplus proceeds and the amount of them are determined by the business transactions of the year. But the distribution of them does not take place until later, and by action completely independent of the business activity that brought about the surplus, namely by the declaration of a dividend in accordance with a resolution of the board of directors. But that is not the situation with respect to the "surplus" of the capitalists. The very contention of the Marx-Schmidt doctrine is that the creation and the distribution of the surplus are not divisible into distinct actions, but that they result from one and the same action, namely, the creation of the exchange value of commodities. The surplus value is created in the manner and to the extent that Marx claims, because the exchange value of commodities which is realized by the entrepreneur capitalists is determined entirely and solely by the number of labor hours embodied in them. And the surplus value is distributed in the manner that Marx declares because *the same* exchange value of commodities which is realized by the entrepreneur capitalists is *not* determined entirely and solely by the number of labor hours embodied in them! And so it is literally true that with respect to one and the same fact, namely the determination of the exchange value of commodities, Schmidt maintains that the law of value is a complete empirical reality, and that it is *not* a valid hypothesis!

In the Marxian camp there is a fondness for pronouncements that are analogous to the laws and the hypotheses in the natural sciences. And comfort is derived from the fact that the empirical effectiveness of those laws is subject to certain modifications by reason of disturbing factors, without causing those laws for that reason to be considered any less valid. If the law of gravity, for instance, governed in strict conformity with its terms, falling bodies would behave distinctly differently from the way they actually do when their actions are affected by disturbing factors such as air resistance and the like. Nevertheless the law of gravity is not questioned as a genuine, valid and scientific law. The same is true, they say, of the "law of value." The law is correct, only in practice its application is distorted because of the existence of the institution of private capital which demands a uniform rate of return. Just as air resistance prevents falling bodies from moving at the exact speed assigned to them under the law of gravity, so the influence of the institution of private capital, with its claim to uniform interest rates, prevents the exchange value of commodities from conforming completely to the quantities of labor incorporated in them.

It is a lame analogy. The Marxian syllogism exhibits a deformity that does not and cannot find its counterpart in the impeccable syllogism of the physicist. The latter is quite clear on the principle that in a vacuum gravity is the only determinant of the velocity of falling bodies. He is equally clear as to the fact that in atmospheric space the velocity of falling bodies is essentially a result of the interaction of a number of causes. He is therefore careful to avoid making a statement with respect to atmospheric space that is valid only where gravity may be assumed to be the only force at work. Not so the Marxists. Even after they have introduced the existence of the institution of private capital into their hypothesis (as analogous to air resistance) they still maintain, as we have seen, that exchange value is determined solely by embodied quantities of labor. It is not until they explain the distribution of the total value over the individual parts of capital that they begin to remember the existence of a competing cause. That is just as if the physicist were to say that the total velocity of a falling body is the same in atmosphere as it is in a vacuum, only the velocity is distributed differently over the successive stages traversed in atmosphere, from the way it is distributed in a vacuum!

Moreover, the physicist has a very good reason for his assumption that at least in a vacuum falling bodies would conform exactly to his law of gravitation. But the Marxist does not occupy the same position with respect to his analogous assumption. To do so he would have to be justified in assuming that in an economy without the institution of private capital the exchange value of commodities would follow exactly the law of value which he claims to be in force. But for such an assumption the Marxist has neither a good nor a bad reason, he simply has no reason at all. And that brings me to the second cardinal sin of Schmidt's program, namely the literal untenability of his point of departure.

It is my opinion that the Marxists make it somewhat too easy for themselves in positing the "hypothesis" of the value of labor. The hypothesis certainly contains nothing which is basically and *a priori* unthinkable or impossible. But even that is not enough to justify setting up a hypothesis as the basis of a theory that is to be taken seriously. It is not *a priori* unthinkable, either, that exchange value might be determined by specific gravity! Now you cannot defend the contention that a hypothesis is entitled to be considered valid until its literal, palpable refutation has been achieved. I might, for instance, set up the hypothesis that the universe 313 is filled with an infinitude of large and small sprites which push and pull bodies about, and by means of these pushings and pullings bring about those phenomena which the physicists, following another hypothesis, term gravitational attraction. Any theorist will grant me that an unimpeachable refutation of that fantastic hypothesis, extravagant though it be, is impossible with the knowledge available to us. It will never be possible to prove that the pushing and pulling sprites do not exist. The best that could be done would be to show that their existence is extremely improbable. And yet I should deservedly be the object of ridicule, were I to claim that my hypothesis were entitled to consideration in preference to any other until such time as it had been absolutely refuted. It has been held since time immemorial in all scientific research that only those hypotheses can lay claim to serious scientific consideration which offer some positive reason for considering them to be good hypotheses, or at least to be relatively the best.

But in the present stage of economic knowledge there is just no support at all for the hypothesis that the value of commodities is based on their embodied labor alone. We have already seen that it is certainly not an axiom, carrying direct conviction and capable of dispensing entirely with proof. The only attempt to furnish logical proof of it is Marx's, and that was a failure. And apparently Schmidt has abandoned it as a failure. For it is obviously asking too much of us to believe that we necessarily must conceive of every exchange as an exchange of equal amounts of labor. How can we, when Marx himself in his third volume proves to us that under certain circumstances it is an economic necessity that *unequal* amounts of labor be considered equivalents? Nor do we have that strict coincidence of hypothesis and empiric reality which, under some circumstances, can replace proof and indeed must replace it in all cases in which we are dealing with ultimate facts incapable of any further analysis. We know the very reverse to be true, for, as has been sufficiently emphasized, experience shows numerous flagrant exceptions, and throughout the whole investigation no exact coincidence of "hypothesis" and reality. A final possibility, which also would require internal proof, is an analysis of the forces in operation when exchanges take place. The object would be to prove thereby, or to make understandable, a tendency inherent in values toward agreement with the quantities of labor—a tendency which is blocked only by external obstacles. Nothing along this line was ever attempted by the Marxists since any such attempt would have been foredoomed to failure. I feel, on the contrary, that everything experience reveals to us and teaches us concerning the motivating forces that actuate exchanges, compels us to assume that value and amounts of labor never could be in harmony. That is no less true of a real world marked by the existence of private capital than it would be of a noncapitalist society. In any form of society, in any distribution of wealth, man is swayed by considerations of usefulness and cost. Those considerations indubitably include that of the amount of labor expended, but just as indubitably do not consist of that exclusively.

314 And especially would the length of time required for goods to deliver their usefulness play a part. And for that part the unrealistic hypothesis of the labor value of goods has no room.

3. Edward Bernstein's Reinterpretation

IN MOST recent times a remarkable publication has issued from the camp of the socialists. It withdraws a short but important distance behind even the line that Konrad Schmidt defended, and no longer makes any claim at all that the law of value lends proof and support for the socialists' exploitation theory. It is true that the author, Edward Bernstein[96] does devote to the law of value a sort of lukewarm apology, that contains a line of reasoning about midway between Sombart's and Schmidt's. The unrealistic character of the law of value is freely admitted, insofar as it is supposed to apply to the conditions under which single commodities are exchanged. Labor value is declared to be a "purely intellectual creation," "a purely intellectual fact built up on an abstraction"; he calls it "absolutely nothing but a key, a symbol, like the animated atom." With his "imputation" that single commodities are sold at their value, Marx had wanted only to use a "hypothetical individual case" in order to make it possible to "visualize" the process that, in his opinion, total production did in fact go through. The fact that he has in mind is "surplus labor." However Bernstein has no intention of proving "surplus labor" on the basis of the law of value. He probably

96. *Die Voraussetzungen des Sozialismus und die Aufgaben der Sozialdemokratie,* Stuttgart, 1899.

has the feeling that the law of value is itself far too unsound to be used as a foundation for anything else. At any rate he says, "Whether Marx's theory of value is correct or not, is a matter of complete indifference, so far as the proof of surplus labor is concerned. The theory is in this respect not a corroborative thesis, but a means of analysis and visualization."[97]

And it is significant that to this concession Bernstein adds the following further admissions. The value of labor, even as a key, "fails to serve its purpose after a certain point has been reached and so has brought disaster upon almost every student of Marx." In any event "the doctrine of value is no more a criterion by which to judge the justice or injustice of the distribution of the product of labor, than the theory of the atom is a criterion by which to judge the beauty or ugliness of a statue." "The marginal utility of the Gossen-Jevons-Böhm school" which, just like the Marxian labor value, does have "some relation to reality" as a basis but is built on abstractions, bears still further resemblance to it in that "for certain purposes" and "within certain limitations" it can lay "claim to validity." In view of the fact that Marx, too, had emphasized the significance of use value, it is impossible "to dismiss the Gossen-Böhm theory with a few supercilious phrases."[98]

Now what will be Bernstein's replacement for the supporting proof which the older Marxian school had sought in the theory of value, and which Bernstein has renounced? There must be such a replacement if he is to continue, as he does, to support the exploitation theory. He takes refuge in an extraordinarily simple premise, but one that is, to be sure, also extraordinarily questionable as to its conclusiveness. He simply points out the fact that "the production and distribution of commodities is achieved by the active participation of only a part of the entire population. Another part consists of persons who either receive an income for services that have no direct bearing on production, or who receive income without doing any labor. The total labor that is contained in production therefore supports a considerably greater number of human beings than those who actively participate in it. And over and above that, statistics on income show that the share appropriated by the ranks of those not active in production is a far larger fraction of the total product than would correspond to their numerical relation to the productive workers. The surplus labor contributed by the latter is an empirical fact, demonstrable through actual experience, which needs no deductive proof."[99]

Of course Bernstein thinks of "surplus labor" in pronouncedly Marxian vein as exploited work. Therefore he states, in effect, the following. It is a simple fact that something less than the entire national product is paid out in wages to the productive workers, and that there are other forms of income. That simple fact, Bernstein would have us understand, constitutes *empirical* proof of the exploitation of the workers, so that

315

97. *Op. cit.*, pp. 38, 41, 42, 44.
98. *Op. cit.*, pp. 45, 41, 42.
99. *Op. cit.*, p. 42.

there is no need for any further enlightenment by deductive reasoning on the correctness of that conclusion. But I say the conclusion is on the contrary, so obviously premature, shows so patently that he takes for granted what he intends to prove, that there really is no need to make a proper refutation. Using the same method of argumentation it would be possible to outdo even the physiocrats and prove that all humanity lives by an exploitation of the agricultural population. For it is a fact, after all, that the products of the soil which the workers on the farms produce provide sustenance for a great many other people!

But the problem is really not that simple. Experience shows most clearly that production arises from the cooperation of human labor and material means of production. The latter are in part natural (land) and in part man-made in origin (capital goods). The natural product is then distributed, by some formula or other, among those who contribute the cooperating forces. Now a person might entertain the very debatable opinion that of all those who actually participate in that distribution only one has any right to do so, so that participation of any others is, from the outset, an exploitation of the one. But the holder of that opinion would certainly be under the duty of casting a clear light on the relations between the contributing forces and of presenting grounds from which the whys and wherefores can be deduced. He would have to explain why, despite the multiplicity of cooperators, one of them means everything—everything in general, or at least everything in respect to distribution specifically, and why therefore the one is entitled to claim everything for himself, and why the others have no claim at all. And Marx did conceive the problem in those terms. Goods have significance in economic life in accordance with their value, and therefore Marx was entirely logical. In order to prove that the worker had the sole right to the entire value of his product, he attempted to show that value is specifically the creation of labor alone. His law of value was to him a means of proof by which the landowner's and the capitalist's claim to participation were to be deduced out of existence.

I do not suppose Bernstein himself expects that he can get along without any deducing at all. Evidently his proof, purely empirical though he alleges it to be, does nevertheless contain an unspoken deductive factor, namely the proposition out of Rodbertus that from the economist's point of view all goods are purely the product of labor. Once the Marxian law of value has been expressly excluded from the premise which is to serve as the basis of a process of proof, Bernstein must avail himself of Rodbertus's proposition at least, in order to set up his chain, otherwise his syllogism would lack formal completeness. But this deductive premise to which Bernstein is forced to retreat, is not capable of lending support to the exploitation theory any more effectively than is the Marxian law of value. The Rodbertian proposition, as we know, is absolutely erroneous, insofar as it fails to recognize and to admit the significance for man's economy and production of the rare gifts of nature.[100]

316

100. See foregoing p. 257 f.

And what is more important for our question of interest is the fact that, even to the extent that it is correct, it does not furnish any support for that concept and those conclusions which the exploitation theorists would have it support. For, be it remembered, the exploitation theory does not restrict itself to claiming for the workers all that they create, but in addition claims it at an earlier date than that at which they create it; and this artificial prematurity has neither any natural title, nor any title naturally derived, the disregard of which could on principle be branded as "exploitation." The adherents of the exploitation theory do not provide themselves or their readers with any very clear idea of this interpolated factor, unnatural as it is, if indeed it should not be said that it flies in the face of nature. It represents an element intruded into their set of postulates which are alleged to be derived from self-evident natural principles; and while its nature is not clear, its existence is not to be denied. I made my point in this respect in discussing Rodbertus, and illustrated with an example, in miniature, as it were.[101] Now, in refutation of Bernstein I shall make the point again but on a large scale. For it seems, now that the episode of the remarkable Marxian law of value is at last approaching final disposition, that the battle over the exploitation theory is about to resume and to achieve ultimate decision in the same positions in which Rodbertus marshalled his theorems.

Bernstein summarizes the thought content of the point at issue in a concept of disconcerting simplicity by pointing out that other people beside the productive workers live off the natural production. I intend to oppose to that a few facts no less simple and elementary.*

It is a fact that the production methods customarily practiced today involve long range preparatory measures calling for "indirect labor" on materials, tools, machines, auxiliary materials, means of transportation and so on. And it is also a fact that these methods are far more productive than those which do not include such long-range preparations. It is likewise a fact that if we consider as one whole process all the labor that has been expended, directly and indirectly, on a finished consumers' good, we must be aware that we cannot get possession of the end product, ready for our use and enjoyment, before the expiration of a long period of time covering several or even many years, all filled with labor. And it is a fact that the socialists lay claim to this whole product, or to its exchange value, exclusively for the workers engaged in producing it, as the "full product of their labor"; that they are however by no means disposed to tolerate postponing the distribution of this entire value among the workers until such time as the product they have cre-

317

---

101. See foregoing p. 263 ff.

* PUBLISHER'S NOTE: The refutation of Bernstein's reinterpretation of Marx's ideas on the exploitation of labor is clear although brief, but for the full force of Böhm-Bawerk's argument to be appreciated it is necessary to read his *Positive Theory of Capital*, Volume II of *CAPITAL AND INTEREST*. There is no more closely reasoned description of the use of Capital for modern production.

ated is completed and ready for distribution; that they demand, on the contrary, that each worker, immediately upon performance of his quota of the labor, shall receive the full value equivalent of that which will not eventuate from the cooperative labors of all of them until several years have passed.

And at this point a second series of facts joins forces with the first. It is a fact, that if any distribution at all is to be made to the workers before the completion of their work, it must be made from goods which are ready for use and service, and are on hand before the workers' labor is concluded. That can be possible only when the goods to be distributed are derived from some other source. It is a further fact that only under such conditions is it possible to direct labor to objectives representing temporally remote enjoyment of the product. That is another way of saying that only under such conditions is it possible to adopt roundabout methods of greater productivity. Failing that, it becomes necessary to put up with the smaller returns from labor to which we are restricted when we employ production methods characterized by less efficient preparation and less roundabout processes. Such supplies of goods are at present in the hands of the capitalists, being handed on and increased from generation to generation. Let us ignore for the time being the question as to whether the acquisition of those supplies may have been partly legitimate and partly illegitimate. The fact remains however that the creation and preservation of this supply of goods must be credited to individuals other than the ones who are to be maintained and paid during the course of the production process already begun.

And so it is not even to be credited entirely to the workers active today, to *their* industry and *their* skill alone, that a certain more abundant product will one day come into existence, after the passing of so and so many years. Part of the origination and part of the credit is due to some group of people who did advance work, who provided for the creation and preservation of the stored up supplies of goods. And are we then being told that the services of these workers of today confer on them an unquestionable claim, not merely to be the recipients of that larger more abundant product to the full extent of its value, but over and above that, to receive it in full before the product itself has achieved existence?

That is what the exploitation theory would have us believe, but even the warmest friend of labor could never be convinced of it if he looked
318   all the facts straight in the face. But of course the exploitation theory does not do that. Until now that theory, in whatever terms it may have been formulated, has evaded the salient point at issue, that of the time difference. This is a twofold evasion, for it concerns not only the interval between the payment of wages and the completion of the product, but also the significance of the time element for the technological production process and for the evaluation of goods. Either it leaves this subject untouched, or it touches upon it in a misleading and mistaken fashion.

And Marx has his share of sins to answer for in this particular, too. On one occasion he says that for the creation of the value of goods it is "a matter of complete indifference" that part of the labor necessary for the producing of a finished product had to be expended in an earlier period, that "it is in the pluperfect tense."[102] In another place he even reverses the argument, and by a bit of maddening casuistry contrives to show that the custom of distributing wages on periodic "pay days" is not an anticipation but a delay in the payment of wages, which is to the workers' disadvantage. He maintains that since the workers are not in the habit of receiving their wages until the *end* of the day, or week, or month during which they have already been working for the entrepreneur, it is not he who advances their wages, but on the contrary the workers who advance their labor![103]

Of course that statement would be entirely correct if it were made by someone who takes the position that the worker's claim to compensation has no further concern with the product that results from his labor. Such a position would also mean maintaining that the entrepreneur does not buy the future product that will result from the labor, but merely the present physical performance of labor by the worker. It would also mean contending that, once the wage contract has been performed, neither the worker nor his claim to wages is in the least affected by the degree of usefulness, if any, to which the product may attain, that question being one which concerns the entrepreneur alone. One who takes that position could of course say with full justification that whenever wages are paid upon completion of the performance of labor, it is not the entrepreneur who advances the wage, but the worker who advances the labor. But Marx and the socialists consider the claim to wages a direct claim to the product itself which will result from the labor, and maybe that claim is not without justification. They therefore base their criticism and their decisions concerning the payment of wages on the very relation that exists between those payments and the end product of the labor. But if that is so, then they must not overlook and deny that the payments, even though they may follow the performance of the individual installments of labor by a negligible period of time, do precede by a considerable interval the completion of a good that is ready for use or service. That entails recognizing further than when the entrepreneur pays wages which are actually a claim to the product itself, he is really satisfying the claim before it is due. And finally it means recognizing that since there is a difference in value between present goods and future goods, the anticipation in satisfying the claim must receive some compensation, which it does through the adjustment of the wages **319** paid.

I have always expressed myself reservedly and rather negatively whenever in the foregoing pages it devolved upon me to discuss the rest of

---

102. Vol. I, p. 175.   103. Vol. II, p. 197 ff.

the participants in production. It befitted the nature of my present task to do so. The correctness or incorrectness of the exploitation theory does not depend on whether or not those parts of the national product which are not expended as wages are dispensed on an accurately graded scale which is in accordance with the true deserts of the participating parties. It depends solely and only on whether it can be proved that what the workers have earned constitutes an unqualified claim to an artificially premature payment to them of the total product. If that cannot be proved, then the exploitation theory is wrong. Then part of the product remains, and other claimants may then urge their legal or just pretensions to it. In the absence of such claims let an enlightened system of law dispose of it in accordance with such considerations of expediency as give due regard to the permanent advancement of the common good. Such might be quite possible, and indeed there seems to be a strong tendency in that direction in the development of our system of jurisprudence as evidenced by modern social security, graduated income taxes, increasing government ownership and controls and so on. Yes, it is quite possible, I say, that the share of the workers, based on naturally justified claims, will be increased temporarily by our laws through artificial measures based on considerations of expediency in the best sense of the word. And the increase would come out of that part of the national product still available after wages. And so, directly or indirectly, there would be a limitation of the income that is derived solely by virtue of possession. But the consideration and decision of these matters involve reasons which are completely disparate from those to which the exploitation theory appeals, and which it considers to have determining force. The significance of the exploitation theory, in the last analysis, can be summed up as follows. It first advances a specious claim to imagined rights, and aims thereby to cut off discussion; then when it comes to a settlement concerning that part of the national product not covered by a valid and just claim of the workers, the exploitation theory refuses to allow the genuinely pertinent considerations and reasons to be heard.

VI
Conclusion

I HAVE devoted an exceptionally and disproportionately large amount of space to the discussion of the exploitation theory. I have done so advisedly. Certainly none of the other doctrines has approached it in the influence it exercised on the thoughts and the emotions of whole generations. And just our era has seen it at its apogee. And unless I am mistaken, its descent has already begun.* But it is to be expected that there will still be attempts at stubborn defense or at revivification by metamorphosis. And so I thought I should be serving the good cause if I avoided restricting myself to a purely retrospective critique of the developmental stages of the doctrine, now definitely terminated. I thought it would be well to look forward, and even now cast some critical illumination on the intellectual theatre of operations to which, according to definitely discernible signs, its adherents are intending to transfer the renewed controversy.

So far as that old socialist theory of exploitation is concerned, which has been presented here in the person of its two most distinguished protagonists, Rodbertus and Marx, I cannot render a verdict any less severe than the one I handed down in the first edition of this book. It is not only fallacious but, considered from the point of view of theoretical soundness, it occupies one of the lowest places among all theories of interest. Grievous as may be the errors in logic made by the representatives of other theories, I hardly think that anywhere else are the worst errors concentrated in such abundance—frivolous, premature assumptions, specious dialecticism, inner contradictions and blindness to the facts of reality. The socialists are excellent critics, they are exceptionally weak theorists. The world would have been convinced of that long since, if the positions of the two parties had happened to be reversed, and if a Marx or a Lassalle had mustered for an attack against the socialist

320

---

* PUBLISHER'S NOTE: Böhm-Bawerk was too optimistic when he expressed this view.

theories the same brilliant rhetoric and the same accurately aimed, mordant irony, which they directed against the "bourgeois economists."

The wide extent to which faith was—and is—placed in the exploitation theory, despite its essential weakness is attributable, in my opinion, to the influence of two circumstances. The first of these is the fact that it drew up the line of battle on a field where the heart, as well as the head is wont to speak. What people wish to believe, they believe very readily. The situation of the working classes is indeed wretched, for the most part, and every philanthropist must desire to see it improve. Many capital earnings are indeed fished up from turbid waters, and every philanthropist must hope those streams will run dry. When the implications of a theory point toward raising the claims of the poor and lowering those of the rich, many a man who finds himself faced with that theory will be biased in its favor from the outset. And so he will in large measure neglect to apply the critical acuity which he ordinarily would devote to an examination of its scientific justification. Naturally it goes without saying that the great masses will become devotees of such doctrines. Critical deliberation is of course no concern of theirs, nor can it be; they simply follow the bent of their wishes. They believe in the exploitation theory because of its conformity to their preferences, and despite its fallaciousness. And they would still believe in it, if its scientific foundations were even less stable than they actually are.

A second circumstance that redounded to the benefit of the exploitation theory and to its wide dissemination was the weakness of its opponents. As long as the scientific controversy was conducted on the basis of such equally vulnerable theories as those of productivity, abstinence or remuneration, and in the manner of a Bastiat or a McCulloch, of a Roscher or a Strasburger, the battle could not have an outcome unfavorable to the socialists. Their enemies could not attack their true
321   weaknesses from such ill-chosen positions; their opponents' weak attacks could be repulsed without any great difficulty, and the enemy victoriously pursued into his own camp. And the socialists managed to do so with a felicity that equalled their skill. That fact, and that fact almost alone, accounted for the support that socialism furnished to the cause of the theory. If some socialist writers have achieved lasting significance in the history of economic theory, they owe it to the energy and adroitness with which they succeed in destroying many an old and deep-rooted fallacious doctrine. To be sure, the socialists were not able themselves to replace error with truth—less able, even, than many of the opponents whom they so deeply despised.*

* PUBLISHER'S NOTE: Readers should be informed on the idea that *all* theories explaining interest, including popular *capitalist* theories, are equally discredited in Böhm-Bawerk's *History and Critique of Interest Theories,* Volume I in his *CAPITAL AND INTEREST.* To get a good perspective of the whole complex of ideas it is necessary to read Volume II, *Positive Theory of Capital;* and Volume III, *Further Essays on Capital and Interest.*

Eugen von Böhm-Bawerk
and the
Discriminating Reader

Evaluation of CAPITAL AND INTEREST *

By Ludwig von Mises†

The publication of a new English-language translation of Böhm-Bawerk's monumental work on *Capital and Interest** raises an important question. There is no doubt that Böhm-Bawerk's book is the most eminent contribution to modern economic theory. For every economist it is a must to study it most carefully and to scrutinize its content with the utmost care. A man not perfectly familiar with all the ideas advanced in these three volumes has no claim whatever to the appellation of an economist. But what about the general reader, the man who does not plan to specialize in economics because his strenuous involvement in his business or in his profession does not leave him the leisure to plunge into detailed economic analysis? What does this book mean to him?

To answer this question we have to take into account the role that economic problems play in present-day politics. All the political antagonisms and conflicts of our age turn on economic issues.

It has not always been so. In the sixteenth and seventeenth centuries the controversies that split the peoples of Western civilization into

---

*In three volumes: Vol. I, *History and Critique of Interest Theories,* 512pp.; Vol. II, *Positive Theory of Capital,* 480pp.; Vol. III, *Further Essays on Capital and Interest,* 256pp.; Libertarian Press, South Holland, Illinois 60473, U.S.A.

†The Austrian School of economics, in the final quarter of the nineteenth century, showed the cost or labor theory of value to be untenable and advanced instead the free market or subjective or marginal utility theory. Consumers determine prices, according to their evaluation of an article as compared with other goods, and the consequent decision to buy or to use a substitute. This is individual liberty in its economic aspect, and it is the cornerstone of a free society.

Ludwig von Mises, Visiting Professor of Economics at New York University, is by general consent the leading exponent of the Austrian School—an established master of his subject, ranking among the greatest names in the discipline. [*Capital and Interest* was published in 1959 at which time Dr. Mises wrote the foregoing evaluation; it is equally timely today (1975). Dr. Mises was born September 29, 1881 and died at age 92 on October 10, 1973.]

feuding parties were religious. Protestantism stood against Catholicism, and within the Protestant camp various interpretations of the Gospels begot discord. In the eighteenth century and in a great part of the nineteenth century constitutional conflicts prevailed in politics. The principles of royal absolutism and oligarchic government were resisted by liberalism (in the classical European meaning of the term) that advocated representative government. In those days a man who wanted to take an active part in the great issues of his age had to study seriously the matter of these controversies. The sermons and the books of the theologians of the age of the Reformation were not reserved to esoteric circles of specialists. They were eagerly absorbed by the whole public. Later the writings of the foremost advocates of freedom were read by all those who were not fully engrossed in the petty affairs of their daily routine. Only boors neglected to inform themselves about the great problems that agitated the minds of their contemporaries.

In our age the conflict between economic freedom as represented in the market economy and totalitarian government omnipotence as realized by socialism is the paramount matter. All political controversies refer to these economic problems. Only the study of economics can tell a man what all these conflicts mean. Nothing can be known about such matters as inflation, economic crises, unemployment, unionism, protectionism, taxation, economic controls, and all similar issues, that does not involve and presuppose economic analysis. All the arguments advanced in favor of or against the market economy and its opposites, interventionism or socialism (communism), are of an economic character. A man who talks about these problems without having acquainted himself with the fundamental ideas of economic theory is simply a babbler who parrot-like repeats what he has picked up incidentally from other fellows who are not better informed than he himself. A citizen who casts his ballot without having to the best of his abilities studied as much economics as he can fails in his civic duties. He neglects using in the appropriate way the power that his citizenship has conferred upon him in giving him the right to vote.

Now there is no better method to introduce a man to economic problems than that provided by the books of the great economists. And certainly Böhm-Bawerk is one of the greatest of them. His voluminous treatise is the royal road to an understanding of the fundamental political issues of our age.

The general reader should start with the second volume in which Böhm analyzes the essence of saving and capital accumulation and the role capital goods play in the process of production. Especially important is the third book of this second volume; it deals with the determination of *value and prices.* * Only then should the reader turn to the first volume that gives a critical history of all the doctrines advanced on the source of interest and profit by earlier authors. *In this historical review the most important part is the chapter that analyzes the so-called exploitation doctrines, first of all the doctrine that Karl Marx developed in his* Das Kapital, *the Koran of all Marxians. The refutation of Marx's labor theory of value is perhaps the most interesting, at any rate the politically most momentous chapter of Böhm's contribution.*

The third volume consists of fourteen brilliant essays in which Böhm-Bawerk deals with various objections raised against the validity of his theory.

The new translation was made by Professor Hans Sennholz, the chairman of the department of economics at Grove City College, and by Mr.George D. Huncke. Mr. Frederick Nymeyer is to be credited with the initiative to make the whole work of Böhm-Bawerk accessible to the English-reading public. The hitherto only available translation is obsolete as it was made from the first edition of the treatise which consisted only of two volumes. The new translation gives the full text of the revised and considerably enlarged third edition which Böhm-Bawerk completed a few weeks before his premature death in 1914.

A book of the size and profundity of *Capital and Interest* is not easy reading. But the effort bestowed upon it pays very well. It will stimulate the reader to look upon political problems not from the point of view of the superficial slogans resorted to in electoral campaigns but with full aware-ness of their meaning and their consequences for the survival of our civilization.

Although Böhm-Bawerk's great opus is "mere theory" and abstains from any practical application, it is the most powerful intellectual weapon in the great struggle of the Western way of life against the destructionism of Soviet barbarism.

Ludwig von Mises

[*Reprinted from the August, 1959 issue of* The Freeman, *published by Foundation for Economic Education, Inc., Irvington-on-Hudson, New York 10533.*]

* [See Extract, *Value and Price,* revised second edition published in 1973 by Libertarian Press, South Holland, Illinois 60473; 272 pages.]

Publisher's Postscript

Problem When Reading "Extracts"

Doubts about the soundness of publishing *Extracts* from technical and voluminous works can very reasonably be entertained.

In the introduction which Einstein and Infeld wrote to a popular book which they coauthored, they affirm that their popularization (in that book) of Einstein's new ideas should be understandable to a person of average intelligence; but they drily add an important qualification, namely, that the ideas in the book must be read in the order as presented, beginning at the very beginning of their book; otherwise, apparently, they expected that browsing or beginning in the middle would not contribute to the book being understandable. In short, to understand a pioneering and difficult book, it is requisite that the reader begin at the beginning and not in middle of the book.

When the reader reads this "book," he begins on page 241 of a large and revolutionary book of more than twelve-hundred pages.

However, few people have the time, interest and perseverance to read *all* that is presented in the three-volume book which is the source of this *Extract.* Hopefully, this "Publisher's Postscript" will help a reader for various reasons, of which one is that although this book shows why the exploitation answer about the origin of interest is wrong, it does not show what is the correct positive answer.

Böhm-Bawerk's most famous and longest book has the title, *CAPITAL AND INTEREST.* The focus of attention should be the word *interest.* Interest here means all *unearned* income, that is, interest on money, rent on land, and profit in business. Is "interest" in that broad sense legitimate? Is a society just which allows *unearned* income, in addition to *earned* income (wages, salaries, fees)?

The world is split into two camps, Capitalism versus Socialism-Communism. These two systems are not accidental enemies; they are by basic difference of views natural enemies. Whoever is a sincere capitalist, must reject socialism-communism; whoever is a sincere socialist-communist, must be hostile to capitalism.

The largest single item in the bill of complaints of socialism-communism against capitalism is that capitalism is exploitive, that is, that those people who are capitalists (the folk who collect interest, rent or profits) have, by their ownership of capital goods, obtained an income to which they are not *justly* entitled because this income is at the expense of other people (so-called employees) who are (allegedly) proportionately exploited (robbed). The distinction between earned income and unearned income is therefore of critical importance.

It should be helpful to a reader, when he begins to read this *Extract,* to have an understanding of the thought structure of *CAPITAL AND INTEREST,* which (in modern editions) runs into three volumes.

Volume I,
History and Critique of Interest Theories

This volume (512 pages) explains, criticizes and evaluates a dozen or so interest theories. For each of the several interest theories Böhm-Bawerk explains the theory first (that is, gives the *explanation* of unearned income as put forward by socialists-communists, or capitalists, or other economists). After explaining each theory, Böhm-Bawerk sets himself the task of showing the theory to be a *false* explanation of unearned income. He is as devastating in his critique of capitalist theories justifying interest, as he is of socialist theories condemning interest. The twelfth chapter in Volume I considers the Exploitation Theory of socialism-communism.

The chapter captions in Volume I, *History and Critique of Interest Theories,* are as follows:

Volume II,
Positive Theory of Capital

This volume (480 pages) presents Böhm-Bawerk's *new* and novel explanation of the *correct* interpretation and justification of unearned income. It is, in our view, scholarly, thorough and cogent. (It is in this connection that Böhm-Bawerk must explain the exact nature of "capital," relative to the phenomena of interest [all unearned income]; hence the significance of "Capital" in the title, *CAPITAL AND INTEREST.*)

Böhm-Bawerk breaks new ground in Volume II; the contents are not critical but constructive, or to use Böhm-Bawerk's term, "Positive." The ideas of Smith, Ricardo and other economists are rejected; the concepts with which they worked are erroneous, rather than helpful. The famous Classical economic structure of Adam Smith and David Ricardo as a system collapses; brilliant and abiding individual insights of Smith and Ricardo remain, but those insights fail to explain the universal and necessary phenomena of "unearned income."

In Volume II, one brilliant and helpful segment has the caption, "Value and Price," but typical readers will have difficulty adequately understanding its revolutionary significance unless they apply the Einstein-Infeld advice (previously quoted) to "Value and Price" in its whole and proper sequence and context. [This segment is available as a separate Extract of which a revised second edition was published by Libertarian Press in 1973 with the title, *Value and Price,* 272 pages.]

Volume III,
Further Essays on Capital and Interest

This volume (256 pages) is an addendum to Volume II. Böhm-Bawerk's ideas were widely misunderstood and vigorously attacked. Volume III presents Böhm-Bawerk's rejoinders to his critics.

*　　*　　*

The substance of the content of *CAPITAL AND INTEREST* is that all forms of interest have a cosmological origin and not an ethical (moral or immoral) origin. The technical term is *originary* interest.

Basically originary interest stems from the nature of how the world was put together, and from the mortality of people. Men act according to their "values," and those "values" are systematically affected by the prospects of change in their lives, and their ultimate death.

Consequently people assign a *greater value* to a *presently* enjoyable good, than to an otherwise identical but *future* good. Unearned income, therefore, rests on people's ideas of v a l u e s, which values are affected (influenced) by the *time* when the good or service will be available. *Present* value is different from *future* value merely because of "timing."

This Extract, *The Exploitation Theory of Socialism-Communism*, has an intriguing quality; it makes the phenomena of unearned incomes tolerable and natural; the socialist-communist critique of unearned income evaporates. But Böhm-Bawerk is not "picking" on socialists-communists. He shows, for example, that the Productivity Theory of capitalists presumably justifying unearned income is self-deception.

Böhm-Bawerk on Rodbertus

When presenting the Exploitation Theory of socialism-communism, Böhm-Bawerk adopts the method of considering not all socialist-communist writers, but two outstandingly representative men, Karl Johann Rodbertus and Karl Marx.

Rodbertus (1805-1875) has been described as the "real founder of modern scientific socialism in Germany." He is appraised by many economists as a better economist than Karl Marx. Professor Adolph Wagner described Rodbertus as "the most distinguished theorist of the purely economic side of scientific socialism." Rodbertus and Wagner were close friends, as was also true about Rodbertus and Ferdinand Lassalle. Rodbertus was influential with Lassalle, who was an active political socialist, but with whom Marx was much at odds.

Rodbertus was of upper-class gentry stock in northern Germany. His father was professor of law and a judiciary in Pomerania. Rodbertus was first a barrister. When twenty-seven years old he changed his activities from law to political economy. In his travels at about that time he was impressed by social tensions related to industrialization. Whereas his friend Lassalle was interested in politics, Rodbertus insisted that the socialist movement restrict itself to economics and abstain from political objectives.

Rodbertus was an early representative of the so-called Socialists of the Chair, a school of socialist thought which flourished in German academic circles, particularly in Berlin, in the latter half of the nineteenth century. Representative names are Adolph Wagner, Gustav Schmoller, Lujo Brentano, Albert Schäffle and Werner Sombart.

The Socialists of the Chair (or as they were known in Germany, *Katheder Sozialisten*) became influential in Prussian and German politics through their ideas, through their support of imperialism in Germany, and through their influence on Bismarck who accepted key ideas of this school of economic thought to (1) undermine socialist theories which were more radical, (2) improve the conditions of the working classes, and (3) strengthen the Hohenzollern dynasty. The Socialists of the Chair were also called, somewhat derisively, the "intellectual bodyguard of the Hohenzollerns." Members of the Austrian Neoclassical school of economic thought (to which Böhm-Bawerk belonged) were aggressive in their ideological conflict with the *Katheder Socialists*.

The ideas of the Socialists of the Chair were expressed by Schmoller at a gathering at Eisenach in 1872 as follows (*Social Economic Movements* by Harry W. Laidler, page 738, 1949, Thomas Y. Crowell Company):

> We preach neither the upsetting of science nor the overthrow of the existing social order, and we protest against all socialistic experiments. But we do not wish, out of respect for abstract principles, to allow the most crying abuses to become daily worse, and to permit so-called freedom of contract to end in the actual exploitation of the laborer. We demand that [the state] should concern itself, in an altogether new spirit, with his [the laborer's] instruction and training, and should see that labor is not conducted under conditions which must have for their inevitable effect the degradation of the laborer.

The Socialists of the Chair were genuinely preoccupied with an anxiety about the "actual exploitation of the laborer"; and the fear that without special legislation to protect the laborer, the "degradation of the laborer" (in a free labor market) would be "inevitable."

Rodbertus analyzes the economic and social effects of the institution of private property. Where there is private property, labor degenerates into a commodity, and land becomes capital; eliminate private ownership, and then all goods might economically be considered to be products of labor only; then values and prices would depend exclusively on the amount of labor incorporated in the production. This is a theory that the values and prices of commodities and services depend on *costs,* and that the costs should be *labor* costs only.

Rodbertus considered that the laborers in primitive societies would naturally be deprived of everything except the urgent necessaries of life; laborers would be at the subsistence level, held down by the "iron law of wages," (an erroneous law but widely accepted at the time). See the article by Ludwig von Mises, page 147. When growth and productivity, however, rose above an alleged subsistence level, Rodbertus held that the poorer classes should be granted a greater share in the social product. Free markets and *laissez-faire* would not yield that to the laborers, and therefore he favored government intervention in order to enlarge the worker's share.

Rodbertus was a bureaucrat, and not revolutionary in his approach as either his friend Lassalle, or as Marx; he was a "law and order" man, and favored an evolutionary program. In the future, he looked forward to the "total elimination of the private ownership of the means of production and of land." Politically, Rodbertus considered every revolution a detour, since it involved disturbance of law and order; as a theorist he advocated a guided system of social planning (modernly called, state interventionism), in lieu of *laissez-faire.*

Rodbertus held ideas which have become common in the twentieth century. One of the current assaults on capitalism may be called, "The assault on [private] saving." That term is title to Chapter XXIV in Henry Hazlitt's brief text, *Economics In One Lesson.* Hazlitt comments that a spendthrift (designated as Alvin, one of two brothers) is a disciple (to go no further back) of Rodbertus who declared, in the middle of the nineteenth century, that capitalists "must expend their income to the last penny in comforts and luxuries" for if they "determine to save . . . [then inventories of] goods [will] accumulate, and part of the workmen will have no work [become unemployed]." Readers will recognize from the foregoing that Rodbertus held to fallacies which are a part of present-day (1975) Keynesianism. (Hazlitt, in his chapter referred to, demolishes the idea that private savings will necessarily be accompanied by unemployment.)

When reading that part of Böhm-Bawerk's description and critique of the Exploitation Theory of socialism-communism that discredits Rodbertus's version of the theory of exploitation of the laborer (see pages 15-52 herein), the analysis is negative and not positive, to wit, although the erroneous theory of Rodbertus is shown to be just that, the correct theory is not explicated here; the reader must be prepared to read more than this Extract to get the "positive" (the correct) explanation for the phenomenon of unearned income, to wit, Volume II, *Positive Theory of Capital*. Böhm-Bawerk here does no more than adumbrate the correct answer to the question about the origin of unearned income.

What Böhm-Bawerk shows in this Extract, in connection with his description and critique of Rodbertus's ideas, is that valuations will be different when there is a time factor—*present* valuations of present goods versus present valuations of the same *future* goods—if justice is to prevail. He affirms that there is a difference in the value a person puts on a *present* good immediately consumable versus the value that a person puts on the same good consumable after the lapse of a year, or more years, that is, in the future. He shows how among five workmen a *present* good will be preferred to a delayed *future* good. That difference in valuation, between immediately consumable goods versus goods consumable only in the future, is the explanation—the *only* ultimate explanation—of unearned income.

To comprehend that, the reader should pose the problem to himself in rather implausible terms, such as, How much lower would a person value a million dollars available 200 years from now versus available to him at once? Relatively, he would despise the *future* good and avidly choose the *present* good. (But all the requisite "positive" reasoning to support that could not be presented by Böhm-Bawerk in this context.)

To make the negative reasoning cogent, Böhm-Bawerk places the problem in a purely socialistic-communistic society and imagines it takes five years to build an engine, that five men work at it, each for one year. After five years the engine is completed. If the engine commands a price of $5,500 when finished, should each man get $1,100? The answer is *No*. The first-year worker should get more, namely, $1,200; the next man should get $1,150; the third man, $1,100; the fourth man, $1,050; and the last man should get an even $1,000. (These figures assume an annual interest rate of five percent.)

Böhm-Bawerk's argument cannot, in this brief illustration, give the whole answer, but it cannot fail to alert readers that the Exploitation Theory of socialism-communism involves a fallacy. Böhm-Bawerk's introduction of the *time* factor, in this material on Rodbertus, is the first foreshadowing by Böhm-Bawerk that the difference in valuation between present and future goods is indeed the correct explanation of unearned income. The essential problem is posed on pages 34 to 40 herein.

The reader should note another interesting and, in a sense, astounding part of Böhm-Bawerk's exposition. He clearly and without qualification declares that the laborer is entitled to get *all* the value he produces—everything. This sounds like a paradox, but it is not; it gets down to this:

In capitalism as a system, the owner of capital is not entitled to *anything* that the laborer actually produces. If a reader has understood so much, he will begin to appreciate that he is reading a fragment in a book of remarkable significance.

In several ways, the description and critique of Rodbertus's ideas overshadow the immediately following description and critique of Marx's ideas, although Marx was far more famous than Rodbertus.

Böhm-Bawerk on Karl Marx

The history of Karl Marx's life and ideas are well known, and his influence is of such monumental proportions that he needs no detailed introduction at this point. The characteristics of his life are presented later in the article by Erik von Kuhnelt-Leddihn, which see. Special attention to Marx's significance for weel or woe to the modern world is also given attention. At this point let us consider what was Böhm-Bawerk's appraisal of Marx. That appraisal comes near the end of this book, and for those readers who do not read that far, Böhm-Bawerk's personal conclusion is entitled to special emphasis. What follows is from Section VI herein, pages 99 and 100.

> I HAVE devoted an exceptionally and disproportionately large amount of space to the discussion of the exploitation theory. I have done so advisedly. Certainly none of the other doctrines has approached it in the influence it exercised on the thoughts and the emotions of whole generations. . . .
>
> So far as that old socialist theory of exploitation is concerned, which has been presented here in the person of its two most distinguished protagonists, Rodbertus and Marx, I cannot render a verdict any less severe than the one I handed down in the first edition of this book. It is not only fallacious but, considered from the point of view of theoretical soundness, it occupies one of the lowest places among all theories of interest. Grievous as may be the errors in logic made by the representatives of other theories, I hardly think that anywhere else are the worst errors concentrated in such abundance—frivolous, premature assumptions, specious dialecticism, inner contradictions and blindness to the facts of reality. The socialists are excellent critics, they are exceptionally weak theorists. The world would have been convinced of that long since, if the positions of the two parties had happened to be reversed, and if a Marx or a Lassalle had mustered for an attack against the socialist theories the same brilliant rhetoric and the same accurately aimed, mordant irony, which they directed against the "bourgeois economists."
>
> The wide extent to which faith was—and is—placed in the exploitation theory, despite its essential weakness is attributable, in my opinion, to the influence of two circumstances. The first of these is the fact that it drew up the line of battle on a field where the heart, as well as the head is wont to speak. What people wish to believe, they believe very readily. The situation of the working classes is indeed wretched, for the most part, and every philanthropist must desire to see it improve. Many

capital earnings are indeed fished up from turbid waters, and every philanthropist must hope those streams will run dry. When the implications of a theory point toward raising the claims of the poor and lowering those of the rich, many a man who finds himself faced with that theory will be biased in its favor from the outset. And so he will in large measure neglect to apply the critical acuity which he ordinarily would devote to an examination of its scientific justification. Naturally it goes without saying that the great masses will become devotees of such doctrines. Critical deliberation is of course no concern of theirs, nor can it be; they simply follow the bent of their wishes. They believe in the exploitation theory because of its conformity to their preferences, and despite its fallaciousness. And they would still believe in it, if its scientific foundations were even less stable than they actually are.

A second circumstance that redounded to the benefit of the exploitation theory and to its wide dissemination was the weakness of its opponents. As long as the scientific controversy was conducted on the basis of such equally vulnerable theories as those of productivity, abstinence or remuneration, and in the manner of a Bastiat or a McCulloch, of a Roscher or a Strasburger, the battle could not have an outcome unfavorable to the socialists. Their enemies could not attack their true weaknesses from such ill-chosen positions; their opponents' weak attacks could be repulsed without any great difficulty, and the enemy victoriously pursued into his own camp. And the socialists managed to do so with a felicity that equalled their skill. That fact, and that fact almost alone, accounted for the support that socialism furnished to the cause of the theory. If some socialist writers have achieved lasting significance in the history of economic theory, they owe it to the energy and adroitness with which they succeed in destroying many an old and deep-rooted fallacious doctrine. To be sure, the socialists were not able themselves to replace error with truth—less able, even, than many of the opponents whom they so deeply despised.

So much for two famous socialist thinkers who developed the theory that all unearned income is exploitation of the employee by the employer. Let us turn now to the school of economic thought to which Böhm-Bawerk belonged.

Austrian Neoclassical Economics

Nobody who aims to be realistic affirms that every individual practicing capitalism is moral and just. Good *systems* as well as bad are subject to individual abuses, intended or unintended. The problem that must be faced is: Is the *system* of capitalism unjust, and is the *system* of socialism-communism just? The contention here by Böhm-Bawerk is that the socialist-communist critique of capitalism, as *exploitation,* is incorrect; and that it is socialism-communism as a *system* which genuinely must be unjust.

Those who defend the capitalist system have over-ready answers about capitalism being more productive, and that thrift exercised to accumulate capital is a meritorious abstainment of current consumption. Productivity resulting from supplying tools, etc., and/or abstinence from consumption should be rewarded, they say; and that is what the capitalist system precisely provides. Such arguments by capitalists in favor of capitalism are superficially as plausible as socialist-communist arguments against capitalism, based on the theme of exploitation. However, in several chapters Böhm-Bawerk destroys the customary pro-capitalist arguments based on the "productivity of capital," and the "reward for abstinence." This of course imposes on him the eventual burden of coming up with the correct explanation for the phenomena of "unearned income," which he undertakes to do in his Volume II, *The Positive Theory of Capital*. The whole volume is devoted to what Böhm-Bawerk submits to be the only correct positive explanation and justification for "unearned income."

It is natural that the several incorrect explanations concerning unearned income can be grouped depending how people fall into different categories:

1. People who already possess capital defend unearned income. This class is supplemented by those who are self-confident of their abilities and self-discipline (thrift), so that they expect to become owners of capital. (Probably these last are the most vehement of the pro-capitalist classes. The capitalist system motivates them powerfully.)

2. People who do not possess any capital, and who do not expect they will ever acquire much capital, naturally are inclined to doubt the validity—justice and morality—of unearned income.

3. It is possible to straddle the problem so as to satisfy a wider range of people; there are socialists who have proposed this tactfully. Their position is that there should be public ownership of capital for production purposes (land, factories and tools) only; but that ownership of houses and other "consumers' goods" may (and should) be privately owned. (This is essentially a socialist-communist program, modified to take into account the psychology of folk of modest means and ambition, to own strictly personal property and their own homes.)

The books of Rodbertus and Marx (particularly the latter) are dull and boring reading. Summaries of their ideas by Böhm-Bawerk are more rewarding reading than the originals. But it is not to be gainsaid that the whole subject, historically obscure until the late nineteenth century, is still not easy reading.

To place the ideas of Böhm-Bawerk in proper perspective it should be worthwhile to present an over-all picture of Austrian Neoclassical economic thought. Böhm-Bawerk in his lifetime was asked by the editors of *The Annals* of the American Academy of Political and Social Science, to describe the Austrian Neoclassical school of economic thought. The English translation by Henrietta Leonard of what Böhm-Bawerk wrote appeared in the January, 1891 issue of *The Annals,* with the title, "The Austrian Economists."*

The Austrian Neoclassical school of economic thought was r e v o l u-t i o n a r y . When reading the following, the reader should keep in mind:

1. That Böhm-Bawerk and his associates held that they had thoroughly discredited the basic ideas of Adam Smith and David Ricardo. The economics of Smith and Ricardo were a marvelous advance over earlier economics, but still fundamentally defective.

2. Smith and Ricardo were wholly wrong in their explanation of value and of price determination. They alleged that value and price were determined by *cost.* The Austrians categorically reversed that; value and price were not the "effect" of costs. Values and prices determined by consumers were the "cause" which determined what costs were tolerable, and would permit an entrepreneur to stay in business. Either the Classical economists had "the cart before the horse," or else the Austrians were in that predicament. (Marx had declared that only *one* factor in costs—namely, the *labor* factor—should determine values and prices.)

What follows, pages 116 to top of 135, will enlighten a reader of Böhm-Bawerk's *CAPITAL AND INTEREST,* including this Extract, *The Exploitation Theory of Socialism-Communism.*

A list of the sideheadings in this descriptive material of the Austrian Neoclassical economists will help the reader before he begins with the text itself, to wit:

> The Most Important Doctrines of Classical
> Economists No Longer Tenable
>
> The Austrians, Although Primarily Interested in
> Theory, Have Been Obliged to defend Their Views
> on Method
>
> Features of Austrian Theory of Value—Final Utility
>
> The Vital Point: Final Utility Rests on Substitution
> of Goods

*This translation is reprinted here (as it appeared earlier in *Shorter Classics of Böhm-Bawerk,* Libertarian Press, 1962, South Holland, Illinois 60473).

The First Complication, Arising From Exchange

Escaping the *"circulus vitiosus"* [circular reasoning]
of the Expression, Supply and Demand, as Explanation
for Price

The Second Complication, Arising From "Production"

How the Foregoing Leads to the Determination of Value
of Goods Producible at Will

Cost is not the Regulator of Value, but the Value
of the Completed Product Determines the Value of
Factors of Production Which are Used

The Correct Principle has Long been Recognized in
Specific Cases, but the General Principle has Not
been Appreciated

Vacillation is not Justified; either Costs Regulate
Value, or Value Regulates Costs

The Problem of the Valuation of Complementary Goods

The Old Bad Habit of Circular Reasoning on the Value
of Complementary Goods

The Error of Attempting to Evade the General Problem

Austrian Contributions to the Theories of Distribution,
Capital, Wages, Profits and Rent

The Hitherto-Neglected Doctrine of Economic Goods

Increasing Attention to Practical Problems

Purpose of the Austrians; Renaissance of Economic
Theory; Character of Renaissance

Two Distinct Problems: Relations of Men to Things;
Relations of Men to Each Other

Past Underestimation of Problems of Relations of Men
to Things; The Yawning Defect of Classical Economics

Discontent with the necessity of Rebuilding the Science
of Economics is not Apropos; We Must Build Better than
the Pioneers in Economics

The German Historical School has Not Contributed Much
to Solution of the Problem of Improving Economics

THE AUSTRIAN ECONOMISTS
Eugen von Böhm-Bawerk

The editors of this magazine have requested from my pen an account of the work of that group of economists which is popularly called the Austrian School. Since I am myself a member of the group, possibly I shall prove to be no impartial expositor. I will, nevertheless, comply with the request as well as I can, and I will attempt to describe what we Austrians are actually doing and seeking to do.

The Most Important Doctrines Of Classical Economists Are No Longer Tenable

The province of the Austrian economists is *theory* in the strict sense of the word. They are of the opinion that the theoretical part of political economy needs to be thoroughly transformed. The most important and most famous doctrines of the classical economists are either no longer tenable at all, or are tenable only after essential alterations and additions. In the conviction of the inadequacy of the classical political economy, the Austrian economists and the adherents of the historical school agree. But in regard to the final cause of the inadequacy, there is a fundamental difference of opinion which has led to a lively contention over methods.

The historical school believes the ultimate source of the errors of the classical economy to be the false method by which it was pursued. It was almost entirely abstract-deductive, and, in their opinion, political economy should be only, or at least chiefly, inductive. In order to accomplish the necessary reform of the science, we must change the method of investigation; we must abandon abstraction and set ourselves to collecting empirical material — devote ourselves to history and statistics.

The Austrians, Although Primarily Interested In Theory, Have Been Obliged To Defend Their Views On Method

The Austrians, on the contrary, are of the opinion that the errors of the classical economists were only, so to speak, the ordinary diseases of the childhood of the science. Political economy is even yet one of the youngest sciences, and it was still younger in the time of the classical economy, which, in spite of its name "classical," given, as the event proved, too soon, was only an incipient, embryonic science. It has never happened in any other case that the whole of a science was discovered, at the first attempt, even by the greatest genius; and so it is not surprising that the whole of political economy was not discovered, even by the classical school. Their greatest fault was that they were forerunners; our greatest advantage is that we come after. We who are richer by the fruits of a century's research than were our predecessors, need not work by different methods, but simply work better than they. The historical school are certainly right in holding that our theories should be supported by as abundant empirical material as possible; but they are wrong in giving to the work of collection an abnormal preference, and in wishing either entirely to dispense with, or at least to push into the background, the use of abstract generalization. Without such generalization there can be no science at all.

Numerous works of the Austrian economists are devoted to this strife over methods;[1] among them the *Untersuchungen über die Methode der Sozialwissenschaften*, by C. Menger, stands first in deep and exhaustive treatment of the problems involved. It should be noticed in this connection that the "exact," or, as I prefer to call it, the "isolating" method recommended by Menger, together with the "empirico-realistic" method, is by no means purely speculative or unempirical, but, on the contrary, seeks and always finds its foundation in experience. But although the strife of methods, perhaps more than anything else, has drawn attention to the Austrian economists, I prefer to regard it as an unimportant episode of their activity. The matter of importance to them was, and is, the reform of positive theory. It is only because they found themselves disturbed in their peaceful and fruitful labors by the attacks of the historical school, that they, like the farmer on the frontier who holds the plow with one hand and the sword with the other, have been constrained, almost against their will, to spend part of their time and strength in defensive polemics and in the solution of the problems of method forced upon them.

1. Menger : *Untersuchungen über die Methode der Sozialwissenschaften, 1883.* [The original German-language text was republished in *Collected Works of Carl Menger*, Vol. II, London School of Economics and Political Science, University of London, 1933. (Reprint No. 18).]

   Menger : *Die Irrtümer des Historismus in der deutschen Nationalökonomie, 1884.* [Republished in "Kleinere Schriften zur Methode und Geschichte der Volkswirtschaftslehre," *Collected Works of Carl Menger*, Vol. III, London School of Economics and Political Science, 1935 (Reprint No. 19).]

   Menger : "Grundzüge einer Klassifikation der Wirtschaftswissenschaften," in Conrad's *Jahrbuch für Nationalökonomie und Statistik*, N. F., Vol. XIX, 1889. [Republished in "Kleinere Schriften zur Methode und Geschichte der Volkswirtschaftslehre", *Collected Works of Carl Menger*, Vol. III, London

Features Of Austrian Theory Of Value —
Final Utility

What, now, are the peculiar features which the Austrian school presents in the domain of positive theory?

Their researches take their direction from the theory of value, the cornerstone being the well-known theory of final utility. This theory can be condensed into three unusually simple propositions. (1) The value of goods is measured by the importance of the want whose satisfaction is dependent upon the possession of the goods. (2) Which satisfaction is the dependent one can be determined very simply and infallibly by considering which want would be unsatisfied if the goods whose value is to be determined were not in possession. (3) And again, it is evident that the dependent satisfaction is not that satisfaction for the purpose of which the goods are actually used, but it is the least important of all the satisfactions which the total possessions of the individual can procure. Why? Because, according to very simple and unquestionably established prudential considerations of practical life, we are always careful to shift to the least sensitive point an injury to well-being which comes through loss of property. If we lose property that has been devoted to the satisfaction of a more important want, we do not sacrifice the satisfaction of this want, but simply withdraw other property which had been devoted to a less important satisfaction and put it in place of that which was lost. The loss thus falls upon the lesser utility, or — since we naturally give up the least important of all our satisfactions — upon the "final utility." Suppose a peasant has three sacks of corn: the first, *a*, for his support; the second, *b*, for seed; the third, *c*, for fattening poultry. Suppose sack *a* be destroyed by fire. Will the peasant on that account starve? Certainly not.

School of Economics and Political Science, 1935 (Reprint No. 19). English translation by Louise Sommer, "Toward A Systematic Classification of the Economic Sciences," Chapter I in *Essays in European Economic Thought*, D. Van Nostrand, New Jersey, 1960.]

Sax   : *Das Wesen und die Aufgabe der Nationalökonomie*, 1884.

Philippovich : *Über Aufgabe und Methode der politischen Ökonomie*, 1886.

Böhm-Bawerk: "Grundzüge der Theorie des wirtschaftlichen Güterwerts," in Conrad's *Jahrbuch*, N.F., Vol. XIII, 1886, pp. 480ff. [Republished by London School of Economics and Political Science, 1932 (Reprint No. 11).] Review of Brentano's "Classische Nationalökonomie in the *Göttinger Gelehrten Anzeigen*, 1-6, 1889. Review of Schmoller's "Litteraturgeschichte" in Conrad's *Jahrbuch*, N. F., Vol. XX, 1890; translation in *Annals* of the American Academy, Vol. I, No. 2, October, 1890.

Or will he leave his field unsown? Certainly not. He will simply shift the loss to the least sensitive point. He will bake his bread from sack *c*, and consequently fatten no poultry. What is, therefore, really dependent upon the burning or not burning of sack *a* is only the use of the least important unit which may be substituted for it, or, as we call it, the final utility.

As is well known, the fundamental principle of this theory of the Austrian school is shared by certain other economists. A German economist, Gossen, had enunciated it in a book of his which appeared in 1854, but at that time it attracted not the slightest attention.[2] Somewhat later the same principle was almost simultaneously discovered in three different countries, by three economists who knew nothing of one another and nothing of Gossen — by the Englishman W. S. Jevons,[3] by C. Menger, the founder of the Austrian school,[4] and by the Swiss, Walras.[5] Professor J. B. Clark, too, an American investigator, came very near the same idea.[6] But the direction in which I believe the Austrians have outstripped their rivals, is the use they have made of the fundamental idea in the subsequent construction of economic theory. The idea of final utility is to the expert the open sesame, as it were, by which he unlocks the most complicated phenomena of economic life and solves the hardest problems of the science. In this art of explication lies, as it seems to me, the peculiar strength and the characteristic significance of the Austrian school.

The Vital Point: Final Utility Rests On Substitution Of Goods

And here everything turns upon one point: we need only take the trouble to discern the universal validity of the law of final utility throughout the manifold complications in which it is involved in the highly developed and varied economy of modern nations. This will cost us at the outset some trouble, but the effort will be well rewarded. For in the process we shall come upon all the important theoretical questions in their order, and, what is the chief point, we shall approach them from the side from which they appear in their most natural form, and from which we can most easily find a solution for them. I will attempt to

2. *Entwickelung der Gesetze des menschlichen Verkehrs.*
3. *Theory of Political Economy*, 1871, 2nd edition, 1879.
4. *Grundsätze der Volkswirtschaftslehre*, 1871. [English translation: *Principles of Economics*, The Free Press, Glencoe, Illinois, 1950.]
5. *Eléments d'économie politique pure*, 1874.
6. "Philosophy of Value," in the *New Englander*, July, 1881. Professor Clark was not then familiar, as he tells me, with the works of Jevons and Menger.

make this plain for a few of the most important cases, at least so far as it is possible to do so without entering into details of theory.

The law of final utility rests, as we have seen, upon a peculiar substitution of goods, due to sound prudential considerations. Those goods which can most easily be dispensed with must always stand ready to fill the breach which may at any time be made at a more important point. In the case of our peasant with the sacks of corn, the cause and the consequence of the substitution are very easy to understand. But in highly developed economic relations, important complications take place, since the substitution of goods will extend in various directions beyond the supply of goods of the same species.

The First Complication, Arising From Exchange

The first complication is that due to exchange. If the only winter coat I possess be stolen, I shall certainly not go shivering and endanger my health, but I shall simply buy another winter coat with twenty dollars which I should otherwise have spent for something else. Of course, then, I can buy only twenty dollars' worth less of other goods, and, of course, I shall make the retrenchment in goods which I think I can most easily dispense with; *i.e.*, whose utility, as in the foregoing example, is the least; in a word, I shall dispense with the final utility. Satisfactions, therefore, which are dependent upon whether or not I lose my winter coat are the satisfactions that are most easily dispensed with, the satisfactions which, in the given condition of my property and income I could have procured with twenty dollars more; and it is upon those other satisfactions, which may be very different in nature, that, through the workings of substitution by exchange, the loss, and with it the final utility dependent on it, is shifted.[7]

Escaping The "circulus vitiosus" Of The Expression, Supply And Demand, As Explanation For Price

If we carefully follow out this complication we shall come upon one of the most important of theoretical problems: namely, upon the relation between the market price of given goods, and the subjective estimate which individuals set upon those goods according to their very various wants and inclinations on the one hand, and their property and income on the other. I will merely remark in passing that the complete solution of this problem requires very subtle

7. Böhm-Bawerk, *Grundzüge*, pp. 38 and 49 [also, *Positive Theory of Capital*, p. 151f., Libertarian Press, South Holland, Illinois, 1959]; Wieser, *Der natürliche Wert*, 1889, p. 46ff. [English translation: *Natural Value*, Kelley and Millman, Inc., New York, 1956.]

investigation, which was first undertaken by the Austrian economists, and I will proceed to show the results which they have obtained. According to their conclusions, the price or "objective value" of goods is a sort of resultant of the different subjective estimates of the goods which the buyers and sellers make in accordance with the law of final utility; and indeed, the price coincides very nearly with the estimate of the "last buyer." It is well known that Jevons and Walras arrived at a similar law of price. Their statement, however, has considerable deficiencies, which were first supplied by the Austrians. It was the latter who first found the right way of escape from the *circulus vitiosus* in which the older theory of price as dependent upon supply and demand was involved. Since it was undeniable that, on the one hand, the price which can be asked in the market is influenced by the estimate which the buyer sets upon the goods, but, on the other hand, it is just as undeniable that in many cases the buyer's estimate is influenced by the state of the market (as, for instance, the final utility of my winter coat is materially less when I can replace it in the market for *ten* dollars than when it costs me twenty dollars) ; the theorists who found a more exact psychological explanation necessary for the law of supply and demand in general,[8] have usually allowed themselves to be beguiled into reasoning in a circle. They more or less openly explained the price by the estimate of the individual, and, vice versa, the estimate of the individual by the price. Of course, such a solution is not one upon which a science that wishes to deserve the name of a science can rest. An attempt to get to the bottom of the matter was first made by the Austrian economists by means of the subtle investigation of which I have spoken above.[9]

The Second Complication, Arising From "Production"

A second interesting and difficult complication of the substitution of goods is due to *production:* namely, given a

8. As, for example, in Germany, the highest authority on the theory of price, Hermann; cf. Böhm-Bawerk, *Grundzüge*, pp. 516, 527.

9. Austrian literature on the subject of price: Menger, *Grundsätze der Volkswirtschaftslehre*, p. 142ff. [*Principles*, 1950, 164ff.] ; Böhm-Bawerk, "Grundzüge der Theorie des wirtschaftlichen Güterwerts," Part II, Conrad's *Jahrbuch*, N. F., Vol. XIII, p. 477ff., and on the point touched upon in the text, especially, p. 516; Wieser, *Der natürliche Wert*, p. 37ff. [*Natural Value*, 1956] ; Sax, *Grundlegung der theoretischen Staatswirtschaft*, 1887, p. 276ff.; Zuckerkandl, *Zur Theorie des Preises*, 1889. I will not lose this opportunity to refer to the excellent account given by Dr. James Bonar, some years ago, of the Austrian economists and their view of value in the *Quarterly Journal of Economics*, October 1888.

sufficient time, the goods whose substitution is under consideration could be replaced by production. As in the former case the goods were replaced by the use of money, so in this case they can be replaced directly by the conversion of materials of production. But, of course, there will be less of these materials of production left for other purposes, and just as surely as before the necessary diminution of production will be shifted to that class of goods which can be most easily dispensed with, which is considered least valuable.

Take Wieser's example:[10] If a nation finds weapons necessary to the defense of its honor or its existence, it will produce them from the same iron which would otherwise have been used for other necessary, but more or less dispensable utensils. What, therefore, happens to the people through the necessity of procuring weapons is that they can have only somewhat less of the most dispensable utensils which they would have made of the iron; in other words, the loss falls upon the least utility, or the final utility, which could have been derived from the materials of production necessary to the manufacture of the weapons.

How The Foregoing Leads To The Determination Of Value Of Goods Producible At Will

From this point, again, the way leads to one of the most important theoretical principles, which under a certain form has long been familiar. This principle is that the value of those goods which can be reproduced at will without hindrance shows a tendency to coincide with the cost of production. This principle comes to light as a special case of the law of final utility, occurring under given actual conditions. The "cost of production" is nothing else than the sum of all the materials of production by means of which the goods or a substitute for the same can be reproduced. Since then, as pointed out in the foregoing, the value of the goods is determined by the final utility of their substitute, it follows that so far as that substitution can be made *ad libitum*, the value of the product must coincide with the final utility and value of the materials of production, or, as is usually said, with the cost of production.

"Cost" Is Not The Regulator Of Value, But The Value Of The Completed Product Determines The Value Of Factors Of Production Which Are Used

As to the final cause of this coincidence the Austrians have a theory quite different from the older one. The older theory explained the relation between cost and value to be

10. *Der natürliche Wert*, p. 170 [*Natural Value*, 1956].

such that cost was cause, indeed the final cause, while the value of the product was the effect; it supposed the scientific problem of explaining the value of goods to be satisfactorily solved when it had appealed to cost as the "ultimate regulator of value." The Austrians, on the contrary, believe that herein only half, and by far the easier half, of the explanation is to be found. The cost is identical with the value of the materials of production necessary to the manufacture of the goods. Cost rises when and because the materials of production (fuel, machinery, rent, labor) rise; it falls when and because the value of the materials declines. Hence, it is evident that the value of materials of production must first be explained. And the interesting point is that when the explanation is carefully carried out it leads us to see that the value of the completed product is the cause. For without doubt we place a high estimate upon materials of production only when and because they are capable of furnishing valuable products. The relation of cause and effect is, therefore, exactly the reverse of what the older theory stated. The older theory explained the value of the product as the effect, and the cost — that is, the value of the materials of production — as the cause, and thought no further explanation necessary. The Austrian economists found: (1) that the value of the materials of production needs, first of all, to be explained; and (2) that after this explanation is made, and after the net of complicated relations is untangled, the value of the materials of production is seen in the end to be the effect, and the value of the product the cause.

The Correct Principle Has Long Been Recognized In Specific Cases, But The General Principle Has Not Been Appreciated

I know very well that this thesis will seem strange to many readers at the first glance. I cannot here attempt to demonstrate it or even to guard it against certain misapprehensions to which it is liable. I will call attention to only one circumstance. In the case of certain materials of production, whose true causal connection was for special reasons easy to see, the old theory recognized the principle; as, for instance, in regard to the value of the use of land, which is expressed in rent, Adam Smith observed that the price of the products of the soil is not high or low because rent is high or low; but, vice versa, rent is high or low according as the price of the product is high or low. Or again, no one supposes that copper is dear because the stock of the mining companies is high; but obviously the value of the mines and the stock is high when and because copper is dear. Now, just as well might the water of one river flow up hill while that of the river beside it flows down, as that in the case of different sorts of materials of production the causal connections should run in opposite directions. The law is one and the same for all materials of production. The difference is only that in case of certain materials the true relation of cause and effect is very easy to see, while in others, owing to manifold obscuring complications, it is very hard to see. The establishment of the law for those cases also, when deceptive appearances had led to the opposite explanation, is one of the most important contributions of the Austrian school.

Perhaps it is the most important of all. Every political economist knows what a vast part cost of production plays in the theory of political economy — in the theory of production no less than in that of value and price, and in this no less than in that of distribution, rent, wages, profit on capital, international trade, etc. It is safe to say that there is not one important phenomenon of economic life for the explanation of which we are not compelled either directly or indirectly to appeal to cost of production. And here rises the question which having once been thrown into the world is no more to be put out of it: What place does this much-appealed-to cost properly hold in the system of phenomena and their explanation? Does it play the part of a center about which as a fixed and absolute middle point all the other phenomena of value turn? Or is cost, the value of materials of production, in spite of all contradictory appearances, the variable part, determined by the value of the product?

Vacillation Is Not Justified; Either Costs Regulate Value, Or Value Regulates Costs

That is a question as fundamental for political economy as the question between the Ptolemaic and Copernican systems was for astronomy. The sun and earth turn, as every child knows, but one cannot be much of an astronomer today without knowing whether the earth turns about the sun or the sun about the earth. Between the value of the product and the value of the materials of production there exists a no less obvious and indubitable relation. But whoever wishes to understand this relation and the countless phenomena that depend upon it must know whether the value of the materials of production is derived from the value of the product or the reverse. From the first instant when this alternative comes into view in discussion everyone who wishes to be an economist must have an opinion, and a definite opinion. An eclectic vacillation, such as up to this time has been almost universal, will not do; in a scientific system we cannot have the earth turning about the sun and the sun turning about the earth alternately. Whoever, therefore, today wishes to contend that the cost of production is "the ultimate regulator of value" may continue to do so; but he will not find his task so easy as it has been heretofore. We shall justly expect him to attempt to explain to the bottom, without deficiency or contradiction, in accordance with his principle, the phenomena of value, and especially the value of materials of production. Probably, if he takes his task seriously, he will come upon difficulties. If he does not find them himself he must at least take account of those which others have met in the same path, by which they have finally been compelled to attempt the explanation of phenomena of value according to the opposite principle. At any rate, this part of economic theory will in future be treated with a considerably greater degree of care and scientific profundity than has before now been customary, unless our science wishes to deserve the reproach which has both in former and later days been so often cast upon it; that it is more a babbling over economic matters than a real, earnest science.[11]

The Problem Of The Valuation Of Complementary Goods

The question of the relation of cost to value is properly only a concrete form of a much more general question — the question of the regular relations between the values of such goods as in causal interdependence contribute to one and the same utility for our well-being. The utility furnished by a quantity of materials from which a coat can be produced is apparently identical with the utility which the completed coat will furnish. It is thus obvious that goods or groups of goods which derive their importance to our welfare through the medium of one and the same utility must also stand in some fixed, regular relation to one another in respect to their value. The question of this regular relation was first put into clear and comprehensive form by the Austrian economists; it had previously been treated only in a very unsatisfactory manner under the head of "cost of production." There is, however, a corollary to this general and important proposition which is not less important and interesting, but which has hitherto never received the modest degree of attention in economic theory which has been bestowed upon the problem of cost.

11. Austrian literature on the relation of cost and value: Menger, *Grundsätze*, p. 123ff. [*Principles*, 1950, p. 149ff.]; Wieser, *Über den Ursprung und die Hauptgesetze des wirtschaftlichen Wertes*, 1884, p. 139ff.; *Der natürliche Wert*, p. 164ff. [*Natural Value*, 1956]; Böhm-Bawerk, *Grundzüge*, p. 61ff., p. 534ff.; *Positive Theorie des Kapitals*, 1889, p. 189ff., p. 234ff. [*Positive Theory*, 1959, pp. 121-256].

Very commonly several goods combine simultaneously to the production of one common utility; for example, paper, pen, and ink serve together for writing; needle and thread for sewing; farming utensils, seed, land and labor for the production of grain. Menger has called goods that stand in such relation to one another "complementary goods." Here rises the question, as natural as it is difficult: How much of the common utility is in such cases to be attributed to each of the cooperative complementary factors? and what law determines the proportionate value and price of each?

The fate of this problem hitherto has been very remarkable. The older theory did not rank it as a general problem at all, but was nevertheless compelled to decide a series of concrete cases which depended *implicitè* upon that problem. The question of the distribution of goods especially gave occasion for such decisions. Since several factors of production — soil, capital, hired labor, and labor of the employer himself—cooperate in the production of a common product, the question as to what share of value shall be assigned to each of the factors, in compensation for its assistance, is obviously a special case of the general problem.

**The Old Bad Habit Of Circular Reasoning
On The Value Of Complementary Goods**

Now, how were these concrete cases decided? Each one was decided by itself without regard to the others, and hence, eventually, they formed a complete circle. The process was as follows: If rent was to be explained, it was decided that to the soil belonged the remainder of the product after the payment of cost of production, under which term was included the compensation of all the other factors — capital, labor, and profit of manager. Here the function of all the other factors was regarded as fixed or known and the soil was put off with a remainder varying according to the quantity of the product. If then it was necessary in another chapter to determine the profits of the entrepreneur, it was decided again that to him should be given the overplus left after all the other factors were compensated. In this case the share of the soil, the rent, was reckoned along with labor, capital, etc., as fixed, and the entrepreneur's profit was treated as the variable, rising and falling with the quantity of the product. In just the same manner the share of capital was treated in a third chapter. The capitalist, says Ricardo, receives what is left from the product after the payment of wages. And as if to satirize all these classical dogmas, last of all, Mr. F. A. Walker has completed the circle by stating that the laborer receives what is left over from all the other factors.

The Error Of Attempting To
Evade The General Problem

It is easy to see that these statements lead in a circle, and to see, also, why they so lead. The reasoners have simply neglected to state the problem in a general form. They had several unknown quantities to determine, and instead of taking the bull by the horns and straightway inquiring after the general principle, according to which a common economic result should be divided into its component factors, they tried to avoid the fundamental question — that of the general principle. They divided up the investigation, and in this partial investigation allowed themselves each time to treat as unknown that one of the unknown quantities which formed the special object of the investigation, but to treat the others, for the time being, as if known. They thus shut their eyes to the fact that a few pages earlier or later they had reversed the operation and had treated the supposed known quantity as unknown, the unknown as known.

After the Classical school came the Historical. As often happens, they took the attitude of sceptical superiority and declared altogether insoluble the problem which they were unable to solve. They thought it to be in general impossible to say, for example, what per cent of the value of a statue is due to the sculptor and what per cent to the marble.

Now if the problem be but rightly put, that is, if we wish to separate the economic and not the physical shares, the problem becomes soluble. It is actually solved in practice in all rational enterprises by every agriculturalist or manufacturer; and theory has nothing to do but rightly and carefully to hold up the mirror to practice in order in turn to find the theoretical solution. To this end the theory of final utility helps in the simplest way. It is the old song again. Only observe correctly what the final utility of each complementary factor is, or what utility the presence or absence of the complementary factor would add or substract, and the calm pursuit of such inquiry will of itself bring to light the solution of the supposed insoluble problem. The Austrians made the first earnest attempt in this direction. Menger and the author of this paper have treated the question under the heading, *Theorie der komplementären Güter* (Theory of Complementary Goods) ; Wieser has treated the same subject under the title, *Theorie der Zurechnung* (Theory of Contribution). The latter, especially, has in an admirable manner shown how the problem should be put, and that it *can* be solved; Menger has, in the happiest manner, as it seems to me, pointed out the method of solution.[12]

I have called the law of complementary goods the counterpart of the law of cost. As the former disentangles the relations of value which result from temporal and causal *juxtaposition*, from the simultaneous cooperation of several factors toward one common utility; so the law of cost explains the relations of value which result from temporal and causal *sequence*, from the causal interdependence of successive factors. "By means of the former the meshes of the complicated network represented by the mutual value relations of the cooperating factors are disentangled, so to speak, in their length and breadth; by the latter in their depth; but both processes occur within the all-embracing law of final utility, of which both laws are only special applications to special problems."[13]

Austrian Contributions To The Theories Of Distribution, Capital, Wages, Profits And Rent

Thus prepared, the Austrian economists finally proceed to the problems of distribution. These resolve themselves into a series of special applications of the general theoretical laws, the knowledge of which was obtained by a tedious, but scarcely unfruitful, work of preparation. Land, labor, and capital are complementary factors of production. Their price, or what is the same thing, rate of rent, wages, and interest, results simply from a combination of the laws which govern the value of the materials of production on the one hand with the laws of complementary goods on the other hand. The particular views of the Austrians on these subjects I will here omit. I could not, if I would, give in this paper any proper statement of their conclusions, still less a demonstration of them; I must content myself with giving a passing view of the matters with which they are busied, and, where it is possible, of the spirit in which they work. I only briefly remark, therefore, that they have set forth a new and comprehensive theory of capital[14] into

12. Menger, *Grundsätze*, p. 138ff. [*Principles*, 1950, 162ff.]; Böhm-Bawerk, *Grundzüge*, Part I, p. 56ff.; *Positive Theorie*, p. 178ff. [*Positive Theory*, 1959, pp. 161-168]; Wieser, *Der natürliche Wert*, p. 67ff. [*Natural Value*, 1956].

13. Böhm-Bawerk, *Positive Theorie*, p. 201 [*Positive Theory*, 1959, pp. 121-256, especially pp. 151-156, 161-168, 177, 248-256].

14. Böhm-Bawerk, KAPITAL UND KAPITALZINS: I *Geschichte und Kritik der Kapitalzinstheorien*, 1884; II *Positive Theorie des Kapitales*, 1889 [CAPITAL AND INTEREST, 1959, Libertarian Press, South Holland, Illinois: I *History and Critique of Interest Theories*; II *Positive Theory of Capital*; III *Further Essays on Capital and Interest*]; differing from the older teaching of Menger's *Grundsätze*, p. 143ff. [*Principles*, 1950, p. 165ff.].

which they have woven a new theory of wages,[15] besides repeatedly working out the problems of the entrepreneur's profits,[16] and of rent.[17] In the light of the theory of final utility, the last-named problem in particular finds an easy and simple solution, which confirms Ricardo's theory in its actual results and corroborates its reasoning in many details.

Of course, all the possible applications of the law of final utility have by no means been made. It is more nearly true that they are scarcely begun. I may mention in passing that certain Austrian economists have attempted a broad application of the law in the field of finance;[18] others to certain difficult and interesting questions of jurisprudence.[19]

The Hitherto-Neglected Doctrine Of Economic Goods

Finally, in connection with the foregoing efforts, much trouble has been taken to improve the implements, so to speak, with which the science has to work, to clear up the most important fundamental conceptions. And, as often happens, the Austrian economists find most to improve and correct in a department which has heretofore passed as so plain and simple that the literature of several nations — the English, for example — has scarcely a word to say about it. I refer to the doctrine of economic goods. Menger has put a logical implement into the hands of science in his conception, as simple as it is suggestive, of the subordination of goods (*Güterordnungen*),[20] a conception which will be useful in all future investigation. The writer of this paper has especially endeavored to analyze a conception which appears to be the simplest of all, but which is most

---

[15.] Böhm-Bawerk, *Positive Theorie, passim* and pp. 450-452 [*Positive Theory*, 1959, pp. 308-312].

[16.] Mataja, *Der Unternehmergewinn*, 1884; Gross, *Die Lehre vom Unternehmergewinn*, 1884.

[17.] Menger, *Grundsätze*, p. 133ff. [*Principles*, 1950, p. 157ff.]; Wieser, *Der natürliche Wert*, p. 112ff. [*Natural Value*, 1956]; Böhm-Bawerk, *Positive Theorie*, p. 380ff. [*Positive Theory*, 1959, pp. 334-337].

[18.] Robert Meyer, *Die Principien der gerechten Besteuerung*, 1884; Sax, *Grundlegung*, 1887; Wieser, *Der natürliche Wert*, p. 209ff. [*Natural Value*, 1956].

[19.] Mataja, *Das Recht des Schadenersatzes*, 1888; Seidler, "Die Geldstrafe vom volkswirtschaftlichen und sozialpolitischen Gesichtspunkt," Conrad's *Jahrbuch*, N. F. Vol. XX, 1890.

[20.] Menger, *Grundsätze*, p. 8ff. [*Principles*, 1950, p. 55ff.].

obscure and most misused: the conception of use of goods
(*Gebrauch der Güter*).[21]

Increasing Attention To Practical Problems

Questions of practical political economy, on the contrary, have only just begun to be made the subjects of
literary work by the Austrian economists.[22] This, however,
by no means implies that they have no faculty for the
practical needs of economic life, and still less, that they
do not wish to connect their abstract theory with practice.
The contrary is true. But we must build the house before
we can set it in order, and so long as we have our hands
full with simply raising the framework of our theory, there
is little obligation to devote to numerous questions of practical detail that amount of time-absorbing care which their
literary elaboration would require. We have our opinions
upon them, we teach them from our chairs, but our literary
activities have thus far been bestowed almost exclusively
upon theoretical problems, for these are not only the fundamental ones, but are those whose long-continued neglect
by the other side, the Historical School, must be repaired.

Purpose Of The Austrians; Renaissance Of
Economic Theory; Character Of That Renaissance

What, now, is the short meaning of this long story?
What is the significance to the science as a whole of the
advent of a set of men who teach this and that in regard
to goods, value, cost, capital, and a dozen other subjects?
Has it any significance at all? In answering this question
I feel the embarrassment of belonging to the group of men
whose activity is under discussion. I must, therefore, con-
fine myself to the statement of what the Austrian economists as a body are trying to effect; others may judge
whether or not they are successful.

What they are striving for is a sort of *renaissance* of
economic theory. The old classical theory, admirable as
it was for its time, had the character of a collection of
fragmentary acquisitions which had been brought into
orderly relations neither with one another nor with the
fundamental principles of human science. Our knowledge
is only patchwork at best, and must always remain so. But
of the classical theory this characterization was particularly

---

21. Böhm-Bawerk, *Rechte und Verhältnisse vom Standpunkt der
volkswirtschaftlichen Güterlehre*, 1881, p. 57ff. [English translation:
Whether Legal Rights and Relationships Are Economic Goods,
p. 70ff. in this volume] ; *Positive Theorie*, p. 361ff. [*Positive Theory*,
1959, p. 325ff.].

22. By Sax, for example, *Die Verkehrsmittel in Volks- und Staatswirtschaft*, 1878-79; Philippovich, *Die Bank von England*, 1885; *Der
badische Staatshaushalt*, 1889.

and emphatically true. With the insight of genius it had discovered a mass of regularities in the whirlpool of economic phenomena, and with no less genius, though hindered by the difficulties that beset beginnings, it commenced the interpretation of these regularities. It usually succeeded, also, in following the thread of explanation to a greater or less distance from the surface toward the depths. But beyond a certain depth it always, without exception, lost the clue. To be sure, the classical economists well knew to what point all their explanations must be traced — to the care of mankind for its own well-being, which, undisturbed by the incursion of altruistic motives, is the ultimate motive-force of all economic action. But owing to a certain circumstance the middle term of the explanation, by means of which the actual conduct of men, in the establishment of prices of goods, of wages, rent, etc., ought to have been joined to the fundamental motive of regard for utility — this middle term was always wrong. That circumstance was the following: A Crusoe has to do only with goods; in modern economic life we have to do with goods and with human beings from whom we obtain the goods we use — by means of exchange, cooperation, and the like. The economy of a Crusoe is explained when we succeed in showing what relation exists between our well-being and material commodities, and what attitude the care for our well-being requires us to take toward such material commodities. To explain the modern economic order there is, apparently, need of two processes: (1) just as in Crusoe's economy, we must understand the relation of our interests to external goods; (2) we must seek to understand the laws, according to which we pursue our interests when they are entangled with the interests of others.

Two Distinct Problems: Relations Of Men To Things; Relations Of Men To Each Other

No one has ever been deluded into thinking that this second process is not difficult and involved — not even the classical economists. But, on the other hand, they fatally underrated the difficulties of the first process. They believed that as regards the relation of men to external goods, there was nothing at all to be explained, or, speaking more exactly, determined. Men need goods to supply their wants; men desire them and assign to them in respect of their utility a value in use. That is all the classical economists knew or taught in regard to the relation of men to goods. While value in exchange was discussed and explained in extensive chapters, from the time of Adam Smith to that of Mr. Macvane, value in use was commonly dismissed in two lines, and often with the added statement that value in use had nothing to do with value in exchange.

Past Underestimation Of Problems Of Relations Of Men To Things; The Yawning Defect Of Classical Economics

It is a fact, however, that the relation of men to goods is by no means so simple and uniform. The modern theory of final utility in its application to cost of production, complementary goods, etc., shows that the relation between our well-being and goods is capable of countless degrees, and all these degrees exert a force in our efforts to obtain goods by exchange with others. Here yawns the great and fatal chasm in the classical theory; it attempts to show how we pursue our interests in relation to goods in opposition to other men without thoroughly understanding the interest itself. Naturally the attempts at explanation are incoherent. The two processes of explanation must fit together like the two cogwheels of a machine. But as the classical economists had no idea what the shape and cogging of the first wheel should be, of course they could not give to the second wheel a proper constitution. Thus, beyond a certain depth, all their explanations dégenerate into a few general commonplaces, and these are fallacious in their generalization.

This is the point at which the renaissance of theory must begin, and, thanks to the efforts of Jevons and his followers, as well as to the Austrian school, it has already begun. In that most general and elementary part of economic theory through which every complicated economic explanation must eventually lead, we must give up *dilettanti* phrases for real scientific inquiry. We must not weary of studying the microcosm if we wish rightly to understand the macrocosm of a developed economic order. This is the turning-point which is reached at one time or another in all sciences. We universally begin by taking account of the great and striking phenomena, passing unobservant over the world of little every-day phenomena. But there always comes a time when we discover with astonishment that the complications and riddles of the macrocosm occur in still more remarkable manner in the smallest, apparently simplest elements — when we apprehend that we must seek the key to an understanding of the phenomena of great things in the study of the world of small things. The physicists began with the motions and laws of the great heavenly bodies; today they are studying nothing more busily than the theory of the molecule and the atom, and from no part of natural science do we expect more important developments for the eventual understanding of the whole than from the minutiæ of chemistry. In the organic world the most highly developed and mightiest organisms once roused the greatest interest. Today that interest is given to the simplest microorganisms. We study the structure of cells and of amœbæ, and look everywhere for bacilli. I am convinced that it will not be otherwise in economic theory. The significance of the theory of final utility does not lie in the fact that it is a more correct theory of value than a dozen other older theories, but in fact that it marks the approach of that characteristic crisis in the science of economic phenomena. It shows for once that in an apparently simple thing, the relation of man to external goods, there is room for endless complications; that underneath these complications lie fixed laws, the discovery of which demands all the acumen of the investigator; but that in the discovery of those laws is accomplished the greater part of the investigation of the conduct of men in economic intercourse with one another. The candle lighted within sheds its light outside the house.

Discontent With The Necessity Of Rebuilding The Science Of Economics Is Not Apropos; We Must Build Better Than The Pioneers In Economics

It may, of course, be to many who call themselves political economists a very inconvenient and unpleasant surprise to find that to the field which they have heretofore ploughed with intellectual toil, another new field is added — a field by no means small, whose tillage is particularly laborious. How convenient it has been heretofore to conclude an explanation of phenomena of price with reference to the shibboleth of "supply and demand" or "cost"! And now, on a sudden, these supposed pillars tremble, and we are forced to build the foundations far deeper, at the cost of great and tedious labor.

Whether inconvenient or not, there is no other course left us than to do the work which past generations have neglected. The classical economists are excusable for having neglected it. In their time, when everything was yet new and undiscovered, investigation *per saltum,* scientific exploitation, so to speak, might bring rich results. But now it is otherwise. In the first place, we of later times, since we have not the merit of being pioneers of the science, should not lay claim to the privilege of pioneers: the requirements have become higher. If we do not wish to remain behind the other sciences, we too must bring into our science a strict order and discipline, which we are still far from having. Let us not be beguiled into vain self-satisfaction. Mistakes and omissions are, of course, to be expected at any time, in every science; but our "systems" still swarm with the commonplace, superficial faults, whose frequent occurrence is a sure sign of the primitive state of a science. That our expositions end in smoke before essentials are reached; that they evaporate in empty phrases as soon as they begin to be difficult; that the most important problems are not even stated; that we reason in the most undisguised circle; that not only within the same system, but even within the same chapter, contradictory theories of one and the same matter are upheld; that by a disorderly and ambiguous terminology we are led into the most palpable mistakes and misunderstandings — all these failings are of so frequent occurrence in our science that they almost seem to be characteristic of its style. I can easily understand how the representatives of other sciences, which have become amenable to strict discipline, look down with a sort of pity upon many a famous work of political economy, and deny to the latter the character of a true science.

The German Historical School Has Not Contributed Much To Solution Of The Problem Of Improving Economics

This state of affairs must and shall be changed. The Historical School, which for the last forty years has given the keynote to all Germany, has unfortunately done nothing at all to this end. On the contrary, in its blind terror of "abstract" reasoning and through the cheap scepticism with which at almost every important point in the system it declares the given problems "insoluble," and the struggles to discover scientific laws hopeless, it has done its utmost to discourage and obstruct the scanty efforts that have been directed toward the desired end. I do not ignore the fact that in another direction, in the provision of vast empirical stores, they have conferred great benefit; but future time will impartially show how much they have helped in this direction and harmed in the other with their one-sided zeal.

But what both the classical and the historical schools have neglected, the Austrian school is today trying to accomplish. Nor are they alone in the struggle. In England, since the days of Jevons, kindred efforts, to which the great thinker gave the impulse, have been carried forward by his worthy associates and followers; and incited partly by Jevons, partly by the Austrian school, a surprisingly great number of investigators, of all nations, have in recent times turned to the new ideas. The great Dutch literature is devoted almost entirely to them; in France, Denmark and Sweden they have gained an entrance. In Italian and American literature they· are almost daily propagated; and even in Germany, the stronghold of the Historical School, against whose resistance the ground must be fought for almost inch by inch, the new tendency has taken a strong and influential position.

Can it be that the tendency which possesses so great a power of attraction is nothing but error? Does it not in reality spring from a need of our science, and supply a need which has long been repressed by one-sided methods, but which must eventually make itself felt — the need of real scientific depth?

Eugen von Böhm-Bawerk

How Böhm-Bawerk Delimited
The Field of Ethics

Ethics and economics are contiguously related sciences; see what Böhm-Bawerk wrote which is quoted on pages 131 to 133 in the foregoing. It is fundamental to come to the realization that the science of economics (in a broad sense, the relationships of men to things) is *antecedent* to ethics (the relationships of men to men), for the decisive reason that it is the competing claims of men for scarce goods and services from which flow the jealousy, envy, violence, adultery, theft and fraud which bedevil society, and constitute the subject matter of ethics.

In his exposition, Böhm-Bawerk wrote:

> To explain the modern economic order there is apparently need of two processes: (1) just as in an isolated Crusoe's economy, we must understand the relation of our interest to external goods [i.e., economics]; (2) we must seek to understand the laws, according to which we pursue our interests when they are entangled with the interest of others [i.e., ethics].

Adam Smith at the University of Glasgow was originally Professor of Moral Philosophy; from that *ethical* field he moved over into problems of the relationship of men to things, that is, into *economics*. Smith always assumed an economic society which would be operating with an underlying ethical structure—no violence, no theft, no fraud, no envy, and involving the stability of the family. Other great economists thought in equivalent terms—none of them assumed a violent or coercive society, nor alienation of goods by one man from another by theft or fraud.

However, by a re-formulation of the subject matter by Rodbertus, Marx, *et al, unearned* income has become a source of virulent envy, coercion, punitive taxation, and/or violence—by socialist-communist governments, etc.

Böhm-Bawerk did not endeavor either to annul or relax ethical laws or to enlarge their scope. But he did shrink the field of ethics by showing that unearned income was in principle not a manifestation of right or wrong. The phenomena of unearned income rests on the mortality of man and is part of the calculation of everybody, namely, a valuation of the future which is at a discount from the present; therefore it requires $105 (plus or minus, depending on the originary interest rate, in this case five percent) one year into the future, to have a subjective value per unit *equal* to $100 at present.

The *customary* way of thinking is to "add" the interest, but the real way that men think is to *discount the future* compared to the present, that is, to use the formulation of $\frac{100}{105} = .95238$; note that it *is* an equation. This equation reveals a startling fact, to wit, that really *each* of the *future* $105 is "discounted"; *each* of the $105 is *individually* less than the *individual* present dollars. At what discount (under our assumption of five percent interest) are the one-year-from-now dollars valued? If the .95238 is subtracted from 1.00000, the remainder is .04762, which is the "discount" of each dollar in the future under the present (usually expressed at 4.762% interest). The present $100 has 100 single dollars in it worth one dollar each; the year-in-the-future dollars are valued at .95238 cents each. Now multiplying the 105 future dollars by .95238 each confirms the equation (100 x $1 = 105 x .95238).

In order to understand Böhm-Bawerk merely primitively, it is necessary always to think of the *discount* at which *future* goods are valued (per unit) compared with *present* goods. The r e v o l u t i o n in Austrian Neoclassical economics will not be understood by anyone who refuses to understand the foregoing.

We talk of the sun "rising and setting" but the expression is out-of-date and confusing; identically, we "add" the interest rate, but it too is out-of-date and confusing. It is necessary that our thinking in both cases be more realistic than our formulations.

The collection of unearned income is therefore not "sin," in the opinion of people who thoroughly understand themselves and their situation. However, the definition of "sin" in the socialist-communist system nonsensically enlarges the more-restricted definition of "sin" under capitalism.

Any proposition in ethics declaring there is evil in principle from receiving unearned income is a paralogism—a "fallacy in reasoning of which the reasoner is unconscious."

Ethics has been relatively sterile for a thousand years, or at least for centuries. Unearned income from ownership of goods (i.e., goods which were not obtained by violence, theft or fraud) was mistakenly alleged to be an *ethical* problem, whereas it should have been appraised as an *economic* problem only—that is, based on the value to men of goods available at different dates, namely, the present versus various dates in the future. If the differing time intervals into the future were short, the unearned income would be proportionately small; if the time intervals into the future were long, the unearned income would be proportionately larger. Unearned income is a function of time, and not a function of exploitation.

If a person wishes to ascertain the various reasons *why* a person prefers a *present* good to a *future* good, see Böhm-Bawerk's *Positive Theory of Capital,* pages 259-289.

The problem of valuing a *present* good versus a similar *future* good is a valuation a man makes for *himself* regularly. If he employs such a method of variable valuation based on the time the good is available when he is evaluating for himself, there should be no valid objection that he employs the same method of variable valuation according to the time of availability, when somebody else is involved.

Preposterous figures can be used to illustrate Böhm-Bawerk's idea. Let us assume a million dollars can come to Mr. A either twenty years from now versus right now. Will Mr. A prefer the million dollars twenty years from now? Almost certainly he will say to himself, "I may be dead before the twenty years have elapsed; then I would never get it. I choose to get the million dollars *immediately.*" Obviously, today's valuation exceeds the one for tomorrow; and still more so, for the valuation a year hence; and more and more, the longer the good's availability is postponed into the future.

About three thousand years ago Moses defined social sin as *violence* (Sixth Commandment in the Decalogue), *adultery* (Seventh Commandment), *theft* (Eighth Commandment), *fraud* (Ninth Commandment), and *envy.* (Tenth Commandment). It is a very modest, nonpietistic list. But valuing a future good at a discount from a present good (that is, at a discount which appears to yield an unearned income) was not put in the list of sins prohibited in the promulgation of the Decalogue. To evaluate unearned income as sin is to be a counterfeiter in the field of morals. Rodbertus, Marx, other socialists-communists, and some religious leaders in the world today have confused themselves into the absurdity that valuing a *present* good more than an identical future good is evil, is sin and bears the wrath of God (if they believe in One); such an enlargement of the definition of sin is an ethical swindle.

Böhm-Bawerk should be viewed as a significant contributor to ethical "de-confusilation" in the latest one-thousand years. He has reduced the area to be denominated as sin, astoundingly. Contrarily, Rodbertus and Marx endeavored to enlarge the area of sin. As Milton's grand infernal peers, these perfervid moralists have

". . . found no end, in wandering mazes lost."

Individuals interested in ethics should read Henry Hazlitt's, *The Foundations of Morality*, (Nash Publishing, Los Angeles, California), probably the most valuable secular book on ethics yet written. Hazlitt with perspicuous clarity of judgment indicates that the new ideas he advances cogently in the field of ethics derive partly from the improved economic knowledge, resulting from the Austrian Neoclassical economic r e v o - l u t i o n , (based primarily on the original thinking on unearned income by Böhm-Bawerk); Hazlitt has presented a correct view not only because of the general soundness of his judgment but also because of his supplementary knowledge of Austrian Neoclassical economics.

Augustine, Aquinas, Descartes, Coke, Blackstone, Kant, Hume, Hegel, Comte, and Marx as "lawgivers" do not overshadow either Adam Smith or Eugen von Böhm-Bawerk. Smith pushed forward the truth that there are remarkably beneficent results to be derived from the exercise of liberty and responsibility. Smith was followed by Eugen von Böhm-Bawerk, who removed from ethical considerations that which was merely a grotesquely misunderstood and crassly underestimated *timing* problem—a discount in valuation for future goods by men whose life was at no time certain, and whose mortality was indubitably inescapable. Smith on liberty and responsibility, and Böhm-Bawerk on unearned income are among the greatest ethical teachers. Theological schools and philosophy departments should examine the reasoning of Böhm-Bawerk on the question of the origin of unearned income and conclude that it is indeed not an ethical problem, but a cosmological (timing) problem.

The new theory of socialists-communists on the evil of unearned income is an intellectual fraud of a magnitude which makes it the worst degeneration in ethics perpetrated on the peoples of the world in the latest centuries.

Marx—His Mental Traits

One of the shorter essays of Böhm-Bawerk published in 1896 had the German title, *"Zum Abschluss des Marxschen Systems."** The English translation by Alice Macdonald in 1898 was given the title, "Karl Marx

---

*This essay first appeared in *Staatswissenschaftliche Arbeiten Festgaben fur Karl Knies zur Funfundsiebzigsten Wiederkehr*, Berlin, Haering, 1896, pp. 85-205. Translation by Alice Macdonald, "Karl Marx and the Close of His System," T. Fisher Unwin, London, 1898 (The Macmillan Company, New York 1898).

and the Close of His Sytem." The English title was not felicitous; what does "close" mean? It would have been better had the translation been, "Karl Marx and the Completion of His System." The idea that was properly to be conveyed by the title should be based on the following considerations:

1. An inconsistency in Marx's system of thought became obvious rather early, when Marx published in 1867 Volume I of his *Das Kapital.*

2. Marx assured his readers that he would elucidate eventually that there was no inconsistency or fallacy in his reasoning. Marx did not redeem his promise before his death, in 1883. Posthumously, Marx's friend, Friedrich Engels, undertook to put order into Marx's unorganized notes, and dispel the impression of a grave internal contradiction. Engels "redeemed" Marx's promise in 1894 after twenty-seven years.

3. When Engels eventually published what was submitted as Marx's solution, Böhm-Bawerk undertook to show that Marx did *not* dispose of (close, complete or resolve) the contradiction.

The title, "Karl Marx and the [Completion] of His System," still does not describe the desiderata of Böhm-Bawerk's critique. In 1962 in a book, in English, of essays by Böhm-Bawerk with the title, *Shorter Classics of Böhm-Bawerk,* this publisher gave the material the title, "Unresolved Contradiction In The Marxian Economic System," which does enlighten a reader what the subject matter is. This essay of Böhm-Bawerk had the merit (briefly and clearly) of (1) describing the Marxian system, (2) revealing the inconsistency, and (3) showing that nothing posthumously published by Engels for Marx "resolved" the problem. Ninety-three pages of text in "Unresolved Contradiction In The Marxian Economic System" (see *Shorter Classics,* pages 208-301) will give a reader more enlightening information than the text in the many pages of the ponderous and boring *Das Kapital.* Note what Böhm-Bawerk writes (quoted from *Shorter Classics of Böhm-Bawerk,* pages 276-278):

> And the socialist adherents of the exploitation theory seek to maintain such a proposition, built on sand as it is! Nor do they employ it just incidentally, and to shore up some inconsequential angle of the structure of their theory. Indeed, they make of it a keystone to support the very facade of their most vital and practical claims. They uphold the law that the value of all goods consists in the labor time they represent. Then the next moment they attack any creation of wealth that is in conflict with this "law," such as the dif-

ferences in exchange value which accrue to the capitalist as a surplus value. They call it "contrary to the law," "unnatural," "unjust," and recommend that it be abolished. That is to say, first they ignore the exception, in order to be able to proclaim their law of value as having universal validity. And after their furtive theft of that quality of universal validity, they revive their memories of the exceptions, to brand them as violations of the law. This method of argumentation is truly just as bad as that which would be followed by one who, observing that they are many foolish men, ignores the fact that there are also some wise men, in order to derive the "universally valid law," that "all men are foolish," and then demands the extirpation of the "unlawfully" existent wise men. *

[Böhm-Bawerk continues:]

When Marx's Theories And The Facts Are In Harmony He Reasons Well, But Otherwise Disingenuously

By his maneuver of abstraction Marx certainly gained a great tactical advantage for his own version of the case. He, "by hypothesis," shut out from his system the disturbing real world, and did not therefore, so long as he could maintain this exclusion, come into conflict with it; and he does maintain it through the greater part of the first volume, through the whole of the second volume, and through the first quarter of the third volume. In this middle part of the Marxian system the logical development and connection present a really imposing closeness and intrinsic consistency. Marx is free to use good logic here because, by means of hypothesis, he has in advance made the facts to square with his ideas, and can therefore be true to the latter without knocking up against the former. And when Marx is free to use sound logic he does so in a truly masterly way. However wrong the starting point may be, these middle parts of the system, by their extraordinary logical consistency, permanently establish the reputation of the author as an intellectual force of the first rank. And it is a circumstance that has served not a little to increase the practical influence of the Marxian system that during this long middle part of his work, which, as far as intrinsic consistency is concerned, is really essentially faultless, the readers who have got happily over the difficulties at the beginning get time to accustom themselves to the Marxian

* *Ibid.*, p. 302.

world of thought and to gain confidence in his connection of ideas, which here flow so smoothly one out of the other, and form themselves into such a well-arranged whole. It is on these readers, whose confidence has been thus won, that he makes those hard demands which he is at last obliged to bring forward in his third volume. For, long though Marx delayed to open his eyes to the facts of real life, he had to do it some time or other. He had at last to confess to his readers that in actual life commodities do not exchange, regularly and of necessity, in proportion to the labor time incorporated in them, but in part exchange above and in part below this proportion, according as the capital invested demands a smaller or a larger amount of the average profit; in short that, besides labor time, investment of capital forms a coordinate determinant of the exchange relation of commodities. From this point he was confronted with two difficult tasks. In the first place he had to justify himself to his readers for having in the earlier parts of his work and for so long taught that labor was the sole determinant of exchange relations; and secondly—what was perhaps the more difficult task—he had also to give his readers a theoretical explanation of the facts which were hostile to his theory, an explanation which certainly could not fit into his labor theory of value without leaving a residuum, but which must not, on the other hand, contradict it.

One can understand that good straightforward logic could no longer be used in these demonstrations. We now witness the counterpart to the confused beginning of the system. There Marx had to do violence to facts in order to deduce a theorem which could not be straightforwardly deduced from them, and he had to do still greater violence to logic and commit the most incredible fallacies into the bargain. Now the situation repeats itself. Now again the propositions which through two volumes have been in undisturbed possession of the field come into collision with the facts with which they are naturally as little in agreement as they were before. Nevertheless the harmony of the system has to be maintained, and it can only be maintained at the cost of the logic. The Marxian system, therefore, presents us now with a spectacle at first sight strange, but, under the circumstances described, quite natural, namely, that by far the greater part of the system is a masterpiece of close and forcible logic worthy of the intellect of its author, but that in two places—and those, alas! just the most decisive places—incredibly weak and careless reasoning is inserted. The first place is just at the beginning when the theory first separates itself from the facts, and the second is after the first quarter of the third volume when facts are again brought within the horizon of the reader. I here refer more especially to ·the tenth chapter of the third volume (pp. 151-79).

Böhm-Bawerk in the foregoing pays high tribute to the capabilities of Marx's mind, but there is little to be said for Marx's intellectual integrity.

The last paragraph in Böhm-Bawerk's evaluation of the significance of Marx's thought reads (from *Shorter Classics of Böhm-Bawerk,* page 301) as follows:

Marx's System, Like Hegel's, Is A House Of Cards

Marx, however, will maintain a permanent place in the history of the social sciences for the same reasons and with the same mixture of positive and negative merits as his prototype Hegel. Both of them were philosophical geniuses. Both of them, each in his own domain, had an enormous influence upon the thought and feeling of whole generations, one might almost say even upon the spirit of the age. The specific theoretical work of each was a most ingeniously conceived structure, built up by a legerdemain of combination, of numerous stories of thought, held together by a marvellous mental grasp, but—a house of cards.

The reader will benefit from reading a closely reasoned, brief appraisal by Ludwig von Mises of Marx's intellectual work on pages 147 to 151 in this book, with the title, "The Marxian Theory of Wage Rates."

Further, there is a more personal evaluation of Karl Marx in the article, "Portrait of An Evil Man," by Erik von Kuehnelt-Leddihn, pages 152 to 159.

Marx—As He Can Be Evaluated By Practical Consequences

Böhm-Bawerk's appraisals of the Exploitation Theory of socialism-communism and of Marx's intellectual performance (namely, as very skillful when Marx is realistic and very dangerous when he is unrealistic) is an intellectual *tour de force* which nevertheless allows Marx to come off better than history itself reveals him to have been. Consider the historical consequences of Marxian socialism-communism under Lenin, Trotsky, Stalin, *et al,* in Russia; under Hitler in Germany; under Mussolini in Italy; and Mao in China. Nowhere has socialism-communism operated with beneficence on natives or foreigners. An apparently deliberate lack of intellectual integrity in Marx has everywhere yielded a more or less bloody and accursed harvest. Neither peace nor prosperity has flourished under the ideas of socialism-communism, which denies the right of private property and denigrates a society based on voluntary contract.

As Walter Lippmann wrote in his book, *The Good Society,* a socialist-communist system will inescapably make a government *tyranncial, bellicose,* and *poor;* but a capitalist system will invariably produce a society that is *free, peaceful* and *prosperous.* What follows is from pages xi and xii of Lippmann's Introduction to *The Good Society* (Little, Brown and Company, in association with The Atlantic Monthly Press, Boston, Massachusetts, 1941); emphasis supplied:

> The plan of the work divides itself into two parts. The first, comprising Book I and Book II, is an analytical examination of the theory and the practice of the movement [namely, socialism-communism] which has, since about 1870, been attempting to organize a *directed* social order.

> I have sought to examine this design of the future not only in its fascist and its communist embodiment, but also in the gradual collectivism of democratic states, trying to determine whether a society can be planned and directed for the enjoyment of abundance in a state of peace. The question was not whether this would be desirable, but whether it was possible. I began by thinking that while it might be difficult to find planners and managers who were wise and disinterested enough, the ideal might eventually be realized by a well-trained ruling class. But I have come finally to see that such a social order is not even theoretically conceivable; that the vision when analyzed carefully turns out to be not merely difficult of administration but devoid of any meaning whatever; that it is as complete a delusion as perpetual motion. I realized at last that a *directed* [socialist-communist] society must be *bellicose* and *poor.* If it is not both bellicose and poor, it cannot be directed. I realized then that a *prosperous* and *peaceable* society must be *free.* If it is not free, it cannot be prosperous and peaceable.

Marx—His Retrogressive Epistemology

A person can be wrong (1) because he has a motive (such as envy) which distorts his reasoning; (2) because he employs a generally unsound method; or (3) (despite a generally sound method) because he has made a simple-minded mistake when he applies his method to a particular problem.

Marx appears to have been motivated significantly by a pervasive envy or social discontent. (He posed as the champion of the weaker and poorer members of society; in fact, however, the actual consequences of Marx's ideas and activities were and are sure to injure the so-called working man, the employee whom Marx averred was being exploited.) Marx appears definitely to have been tainted with error number 1.

Böhm-Bawerk concluded that the internal evidence in Marx's argumentation indicated that Marx was not guilty of an unconscious fallacy; number 3 in the foregoing list does not account for Marx's elephantine error on unearned income; Marx's error was not a blunder, but sophisticated, disingenuous, indefensible reasoning.

But Marx in addition had a generally wrong method (error number 2) in his approach to economics and the social sciences generally. He was in medieval terms a Realist (not a Nominalist). His epistemology was comprehensively inappropriate.

Epistemology is for many of us an abstruse subject. Every master in his field comes to the point where he stands back from his work and says to himself: *How* am I approaching my problem, How far can my methods carry me; and then he asks, Is there a better approach or method?

Epistemology is, in a descriptive phrase, "the science of a science," (a term used in conversation by Ludwig von Mises). In the case of economics, that general problem poses for a competent economist a sobering question: Are my methods adequate to reach correct conclusions? In the case of Marx, it was legitimate for Böhm-Bawerk to take a critical view of Marx's methods, or Marx's epistemology.

In the Middle Ages a pervasive difference existed between philosophers. Some were known as Realists; they approached problems "in the large"; in terms of "classes," and the "Great Ideas," that is, in collective terms or generalities, such as the "rich" versus the "poor." In a sense, the modern term for economic Realism would be "macroeconomics." Realism, in the medieval sense, is not realistic in the sense of getting down to specific cases, such as the poverty or wealth of an *individual person.*

Nominalists, in contrast, avoid general terms, such as "the rich" and "the poor"; they get down to specific cases; they deal with Mr. A and Mr. B individually. They are suspicious and hostile to using "general terms" instead of specific terms and specific cases.

In Marx's thinking, in his "epistemology," he was a flagrant (medieval) Realist. He revelled in group concepts, and used general terms. His method was (is) wholly inadequate in the social sciences and in economics. Böhm-Bawerk and his associates were, in their epistemology, Nominalists; their epistemology was immeasurably better.

In the centuries-long struggle between the Realists and Nominalists (in the Middle Ages), the Nominalists eventually won, and ushered in the Modern Age of astounding progress in science and in prosperity. The Franciscan who gave Realism its *coup de grace* was Thomas of Ockham (Occam) who became head (controversially) of the Franciscan Order. Occam is famous for his expression, *Entia non sunt multiplicandum praeter necessitatem,* which roughly translated says, "Terms should not be multiplied unnecessarily," which unfortunately means little to most folk. But Occam's idea can become real to the average person in two ways, that is, (1) when he understands Occam's rule as a warning against using a *new* term in place of an *old* term, for example, new and ambiguous *justice* in place of the ancient specifics—no violence, adultery, theft, fraud, envy; and (2) when he understands Occam's rule as a protest against using a *collective* term as *rich* in place of a specific rich person named John Jones. Nominalism eschews thinking in generalities and using general terms.

In Occam's day, a breakthrough in epistemology occurred when he explicitly formulated and applied his method. In Marx's day, four centuries later, Marx adopted for his economics a retrogressive epistemology; he thought and talked in terms of classes and generalities; in the epistemology of economics he set out to reverse Occam's basic idea. Marx's epistemology was tragically retrogressive; all socialist-communist epistemology is retrogressive.

Böhm-Bawerk somewhere commented (when considering the subject of epistemology) that primitive thinking started with the big and the grand, like things so obvious as an "elephant." But he added that progress everywhere depended on shifting thought from big aggregrates to the very smallest constituents, from elephants to atoms. Since Böhm-Bawerk's time science has made progress by getting down to what is smaller and smaller in size, and what is ever more-and-more specific than even atoms.

A dead-end street in the social sciences has been entered when the thinking shifts to classes, index numbers, collective terms, averages, and "macroeconomics." The essence of the epistemology of Austrian Neoclassical economics, the school of thought of which Böhm-Bawerk was an early founder, is an application of the principles of Nominalism in the field of economics. The discoveries of the Austrian Neoclassical school of economics were brilliant and specific applications of Occam's famous rule. In contrast, the epistemology of Marx has been intellectually the most degenerative factor in our time.

*   *   *

Many a man will not be able independently to reason his way through the problem whether unearned income is or is not an injustice in itself; but a man may begin his examination with a disadvantageous bias, namely, that he feels he should be reluctant to defend the validity of anything that is *unearned; in other words, the case against unearned income has an adventitious* plausibility. Böhm-Bawerk's analysis of the Exploitation Theory of socialism-communism should certainly remove all psychological inferiority complexes from the minds of defenders of the capitalist system of distributing unearned income. Instead of being befuddled by Rodbertus or Marx, men should realize that those thinkers were guilty of the acme of folly. Men should boldly reject the conclusion of the recognized leaders of socialist-communist thought because the Exploitation Theory is obviously an intellectual structure that is contemptible.

                                                                    F.N.

June 23, 1975

The Marxian Theory of Wage Rates

Ludwig Von Mises

The most powerful force in the policies of our age is Karl Marx. The rulers of the many hundreds of millions of comrades in the countries behind the Iron Curtain pretend to put into effect the teachings of Marx; they consider themselves as the executors of the testament of Marx. In the non-communist countries there is more restraint in the appreciation of Marx's achievements, but he still is praised at all universities as one of the greatest intellectual leaders of mankind, as the giant who has demolished inveterate prejudices and errors and has radically reformed philosophy and the sciences of man. To the few dissenters who do not join in the chorus of Marx commendation but little attention is paid. They are boycotted as reactionaries.

The most remarkable fact about this unprecedented prestige of an author is that even his most enthusiastic admirers do not read his main writings and are not familiar with their content. A few passages and sentences from his books, always the same, are again and again quoted in political speeches and pamphlets. But the voluminous books and the scores of articles and pamphlets turned out by Marx are, as can be easily shown, not perused even by politicians and authors who proudly call themselves Marxians. Many people buy or borrow from a library reprints of Marx's writings and start reading them. But, bored to death, they mostly stop after a few pages, if they did not stop already on the first page.

If people were familiar with the doctrines of Marx, they would never talk, as it is often heard, about socialism "according to the designs and precepts of Marx." For neither did Marx devise the concept of socialism nor did he ever say about the organization and operation of a socialist commonwealth more than that it will be a blissful realm of unlimited abundance in which everybody will get all he needs. The idea of socialism—the abolition of private control of the material means of production and of free enterprise and the exclusive management of all economic affairs by the government—had been fully elaborated by French and British authors before Marx embarked upon his career as an author and propagandist. There was nothing left to be added to it and Marx did not add anything. Neither did he ever attempt to refute what economists had brought forward already in his time to show the illusiveness and absurdity of the socialist schemes. He derided occupation with the problems of a socialist economic system as vain utopianism. As he himself viewed his own contribution, it consisted in the discovery of the alleged fact, that the coming of socialism is inevitable and that socialism, precisely because it is bound to come "with the inexorability of a law of nature" and is the final goal to which mankind's history must necessarily lead, will be the fulfillment of all human wishes and desires, a state of everlasting joy and happiness.

The writings of Marx, first of all the ponderous volumes of his main treatise, *Das Kapital,* do not deal with socialism, but with the market economy, with capitalism. They depict capitalism as a system of unspeakable horrors and utmost detestableness in which the immense majority of people, the proletarians, are ruthlessly oppressed and exploited by a class of felonious capitalists. Everything in this nefarious system is hopelessly bad, and no reform, however well intentioned, can alleviate, still less remove the abominable suffering of the proletarians. Nothing else can be said in favor of capitalism than that precisely on account of its monstrosity and atrocity it will one day, when the evils it produces will have become intolerable, result in the great social revolution that will generate the socialist millennium.

The pith of Marx's economic teachings is his "law" of wages. This alleged law that is at the bottom of his entire criticism of the capitalistic system is, of course, not of Marxian make. It was devised by earlier authors, was long since known under the label of the iron law of wages and had already been thoroughly refuted before Marx employed it as the foundation of his doctrine. Marx chose to ignore all that has been said to show the viciousness of the reasoning implied in this alleged law. He made some sarcastic remarks about the German translation of the English term "iron law" as suggested by his main rival for the leadership of the German socialist party, Ferdinand Lassalle, but he built his entire economic reasoning, all his prognostication of the future course of economic affairs and his whole political program upon the illusory basis of this fallacious theorem.

This so-called iron law declares that wage rates are determined by the cost of the means of subsistence required for the bare maintenance of the labor force. The wage earner cannot get more than is physiologically needed to preserve his capacity to work and to enable him to support such a number of children as are required to replace him when he dies. If wages rise above this level, the wage earners will rear more progeny and the competition of these additional seekers for employment will reduce wage rates again to what this doctrine considers the natural level. The workers will not be able to feed such a number of their offspring as is needed to fill the ranks of the labor force, there will develop a shortage of laborers and then competition among the employers will bring wage rates back to the natural level.

From the point of view of this alleged iron law the fate of the wage earners under capitalism appears hopeless. They can never lift themselves above the level of bare subsistence. No reforms, no governmental minimum wage enactments, no activities of labor unions can prove effectual against this iron law. Under capitalism, the proletarians are doomed to remain forever on the verge of starvation. All the advantages derived from the improvement of technological methods of production are pocketed exclusively by the capitalists. This is what the Marxian category of exploitation means. By rights, Marx implies, all the products ought to benefit those who are producing them, the manual workers. The mere existence of the bourgeoisie is parasitic. While the proletarians suffer, the bourgeois feast and revel.

Now one has only to look around in order to detect that something must be entirely wrong with this description of capitalism's economic functioning. The great innovation that the transformation of the pre-capitalistic mode of production into the capitalistic system, the historical event that is called the Industrial Revolution, brought about was precisely the inauguration of a new principle of marketing. The processing industries of the good old days catered almost exclusively to the wants of the well-to-do. But what characterizes capitalism as such is that it is mass production for the satisfaction of the needs of the masses. The much greater part of all the products turned out by the factories is consumed, directly or indirectly, by the same people who are working in the factories. Big business is big because it produces the goods asked for and bought by the masses. Those shops that are turning out luxury goods for the few never grow above the size of medium or even small business. If you go into the household of the average common man of a capitalistic country, you will find all the products manufactured in the plants of big business. It is fantastic nonsense to assert that all the wage earner gets is the bare necessaries to sustain himself and to rear enough children to fill the jobs in the factories.

The essential shortcoming of the iron law of wages was that it denied to the wage earner his human character and dealt with him as if he were a non-human creature.

In all non-human living beings there is inwrought the urge to proliferate up to the limits drawn by the available supply of the means of subsistence. Nothing but the quantity of attainable nourishment checks the boundless multiplication of elephants and of rodents, of bugs and of germs. Their number keeps pace with the available aliments. But this biological law does not apply to man. Man aims also at other ends than those involving the physiological needs of his body. The iron law assumed that the wage earner, the common man, is not better than a rabbit, that he craves for no other satisfactions but feeding and proliferation and does not know of any employment for his earnings other than the procurement of those animal satisfactions. It is obvious that this is the most absurd assumption ever made. What characterizes man as man and elevates him above the level of the animals is that he aims also at specifically human ends which we may also call higher ends. Man is not like the other living beings exclusively driven by the appetites of his belly and his sex glands. Also the wage earner is a man, that is, a moral and intellectual person. If he earns more than the absolutely required minimum, he spends it upon the satisfaction of his specifically human wants, he tries to render his life and that of his dependents more civilized.

At the time Marx and Engels adopted this spurious iron law and asserted in the Communist Manifesto that the average wage is "that quantum of the means of nourishment [*Lebensmittel*] which is absolutely requisite (*notwendig*) to keep the laborer in bare existence as a laborer" judicious economists had already exposed the fallaciousness of this syllogism. But Marx did not heed this criticism. His whole economic doctrine set forth in the ponderous volumes of his main treatise, *Das Kapital,* is based upon the iron law. The falseness of this presumed law, which has not been questioned by anybody for about a hundred years, cuts the ground from under all his economic reasoning. And it demolishes entirely the main demagogy of the Marxian system, the doctrine that contends that the recipients of wages and salaries are exploited by the employers.

In the elaboration of his system of philosophy and economics Marx was to such an extent blinded by his passionate hatred of Western civilization that he did not become aware of the blatant contradictions in his own reasoning. One of the most essential dogmas of the Marxian message, perhaps its very core and substance, is the doctrine of the inevitability of the coming of socialism. Capitalism, Marx proclaims, "begets with the inexorability of a law of nature its own negation," that is socialism. It is this prophecy that accounts for the obstinate fanaticism of the various communist and socialist factions of our age.

Marx tried to prove this cardinal dogma of his creed by the famous prognostication that capitalism generates necessarily and unavoidably, a progressive impoverishment of the masses of the wage earners. The more capitalism develops, he says, the more "grows the mass of misery, oppressions, slavery, degradation and exploitation." With "the progress of industry" the worker "sinks deeper and deeper," until finally, when his sufferings have become unbearable, the exploited masses revolt and establish the everlasting bliss of socialism.

It is well known that this prognostication of Marx was no less disproved by the facts of social evolution than all other Marxian prophecies. Since Marx wrote the lines quoted in 1848 and 1867 the standard of living of the wage earners has in all capitalistic countries improved in a way unprecedented and undreamt-of.

But there is still something more to say about this piece of Marx's argumentation. It contradicts the whole Marxian theory of the determination of wage rates. As has been pointed out, this theory asserts that wage rates are under capitalism always and necessarily so low that for physiological reasons they cannot drop any further without wiping out the whole class of wage earners. How is it then possible that capitalism brings forth a progressing impoverishment of the wage earners? Marx in his prediction of the progressive impoverishment of the masses contradicted not only all the facts of historical experience; he also contradicted the essential teachings of his own theory.

The Marxian economic system, so much praised by hosts of self-styled intellectuals, is a hodge-podge of arbitrary statements conflicting with one another.

Ludwig von Mises

(Reprinted with permission from May, 1961 issue of *Christian Economics,* published by Christian Freedom Foundation, Inc., 7960 Crescent Avenue, Buena Park, California 90620.)

Portrait of an Evil Man

ERIK VON KUEHNELT-LEDDIHN

IN THE "German Democratic Republic" they tell the story about a weary old man who tries to gain entrance into the Red Paradise. A Communist Archangel holds him up at the gate and severely cross-questions him:

"Where were you born?"

"In an ancient bishopric."

"What was your citizenship?"

"Prussian."

"Who was your father?"

"A wealthy lawyer."

"What was your faith?"

"I converted to Christianity."

"Not very good. Married? Who was your wife?"

"The daughter of an aristocratic Prussian officer and the sister of a Royal Prussian Minister of the Interior who persecuted the Socialists."

"Awful. And where did you live mostly?"

"In London."

"Hm, the colonialist capital of capitalism. Who was your best friend?"

"A manufacturer from the Ruhr Valley."

"Did you like workers?"

"Not in the least. Kept them at arm's length. Despised them."

"What did you think about Jews?"

"I called them a money-crazy race and hoped that they would vanish from the Earth."

"And what about the Slavs?"

"I despised the Russians."

"You must be a fascist! You even dare to ask for admission to the Red Paradise — you must be crazy! By the way, what's your name?"

"Karl Marx."

Man, indeed, is a very strange animal. This has been proved in

Dr. Kuehnelt-Leddihn is a European scholar, linguist, world traveler, and lecturer.

Reprinted with permission from September, 1973 THE FREEMAN, published by The Foundation for Economic Education, Irvington-on Hudson, New York 10533.

many ways, but especially by the Marx-renaissance of recent decades. And yet the ideas of this odd and by no means constructive thinker are responsible all over the world for rivers of blood and oceans of tears. There can be no doubt that without the Communist challenge National Socialism, its competitor, would never have succeeded. Hitler boasted to Rauschning that he was the real executor of Marxism (though "minus its Jewish-Talmudic spirit"); thus the macabre death dance of our civilzation in the past fifty years is due to that scurrilous, evil and unhappy man who spent half his life copying endless passages from books in the British Museum Library's reading room. Yet, with the exception of numerous pamphlets and the first volume of a book, he left nothing but badly assembled, unpublishable manuscripts and a mountain of notes. It was his friend Friedrich Engels who, with the most laborious efforts, had to bring them into shape.

New Interest from the Left

This Marx-renaissance is due largely, but not solely, to the rise of the New Left which argues that the dear old man had been thoroughly misunderstood by the barbaric Russians. Also a number of men and women would be horrified to be called Socialists or Communists but still have a soft spot in their hearts for a man who "at least was filled with compassion for the poor and was an admirable father and a tender husband." Surely, Marx was a complex and contradictory person, and the renewed attention paid to him has produced a number of German books analyzing this most fatal figure of our times. Destructive ideas almost unavoidably derive from a destructive and – in this case – rather repulsive person.

Karl Marx was born in Trier, of Jewish parents, in 1818. Only a few years earlier this Catholic bishopric was forcibly incorporated into the Kingdom of Prussia and Karl Marx's father embraced the Lutheran faith of the Prussian occupants. The children and the rather reluctant mother were baptized by a Prussian army chaplain only at a later date. The deism of Enlightenment was the true faith of Heinrich Marx who, however, was a cultured man and a devoted father. Young Karl finished high school-college with flying colors at the age of seventeen and set out to study law which he shortly abandoned for philosophy, eyeing the possibility of an academic career. He first matriculated in Bonn, then in Berlin where he fell under the spell of the Hegelians. He received his Ph.D. from the University of Jena, but renounced the idea of becoming a professor. He also gave up writing his self-centered poetry and his dream of running a theatrical review. He then married into the Prussian nobility and established himself as a free-lance writer in

Paris where he soon clashed with the more humanitarian French socialists. He moved to Cologne, then returned to Paris and, finally — expelled from Belgium as an enemy of the established order — he took a permanent abode in London where, with interruptions, he remained until his death in 1883.

So much for the facts of his life. Within the last decade three books have been published in German analyzing Marx psychologically. These tomes are very different in scope but they hardly vary in their judgments. The authors belong to no "school" in particular, but all are serious students of our "hero's" works and personal history. These books are *Marx,* by Werner Blumenberg, a small, but exceedingly readable paperback (1962), *Karl Marx, Die Revolutionäre Konfession* by Ernst Kux (1967) and *Karl Marx, Eine Psychographie* by Arnold Künzli (1966). The last two have not been published in the United States and whoever is acquainted with the tremendous difficulties encountered by translations of learned books in the United States will not be surprised. The reasons for this state of affairs are not solely of a financial nature. This article is partly based on the work of these authors.

A Generation Gap

Let us return to the personality of the founder of socialism and communism. Even as a young man Marx does not appear to have been attractive. As a student he is liberally provided with money by his affluent father, and spends his annuity of 700 Thalers — a nice middle class income would then be around 300 Thalers — in a manner still unexplained. In spite of his love for Jenny von Westphalen he is an unhappy, "torn" person and writes in these terms to his father. Heinrich Marx ticks him off: "To be quite frank, I hate this modern expression — 'torn — used by weaklings if they are disgusted with life merely because they cannot get without effort beautifully furnished palaces, elegant carriages, and millions in the bank." And in another letter the old gentleman, knowing his son only too well, tells him that he suspects his heart not to have the same qualities as his mind. "If your heart is not pure and human, if it becomes alienated by an evil genius . . . my life's great hope will be dashed."

Karl Marx was impatient. In this connection it is worthwhile to have a look at his doctoral dissertation on Epicurus, the materialistic Greek philosopher who, as the founder of Epicureanism, made sensual pleasures the main purpose of life. Here Marx quoted several lines from Aeschylus in which Prometheus rants against the gods and ridicules the idea of being an obedient son to Father Zeus. The figure of Prometheus was, indeed, as Kux and Künzli demonstrate one of the guiding stars in Marx's life. The revolt against God (and the gods), the rebellion against the entire existing order, all quite natural in youth, remained his *leitmotiv* until his death. Marx, as our authors insist, never really grew up. His entire relationship to other people continued to be juvenile, if not infantile.

Marx's basic vision was that of a humanity freed from all oppression, repression and controls and thus open to an egotistic "self-realization" — primarily of an artistic order. There was, as he believed, a Raphael, a Michelangelo, a Shakespeare, a Bach in every man. This great liberation, however, could only be achieved by the rule, the dictatorship of the poorest and most tyrannized people, the working class. These were the ones, he thought, who could be indoctrinated to destroy the existing order entirely — and then to build a new one. They were ordained "by history" to carry out his murderous dreams.

The trouble was that he had no knowledge of the mind and mentality of the workers nor any affection for them. He only knew "statistically" about their situation, their living conditions; and these were humble, inevitably so, because at the beginning of *any* industrialization (be it capitalistic or socialistic) the purchasing power of the masses is still low and the costs of saving and investing (i.e. the buying of expensive machinery) are bound to be very high. In the period of early

capitalism the manufacturers, contrary to a widespread legend, lived rather puritanically and were by no means bent on luxury. But none of this endeared the workers to Marx in any way. He had only words of contempt for them, except as they might be mobilized against the "bourgeois" society which Marx so hated.

Glaring Inconsistencies

Despite his entirely "bourgeois" background this is the way his lifelong opposition against his family, above all against his parents, took shape. Interestingly enough, Marx's anti-middle-class complex was not accompanied by any marked loathing for the aristocracy to which his wife belonged. He probably preferred her father to his own. The young leader of the German Worker's Movement directed his wife to have her calling cards printed: "Jenny Marx, née baronne de Westphalen." He also sported a most feudal-looking monocle and was a real snob. His two closest friends belonged to the hated *grande bourgeoisie*: Friedrich Engels, the Presbyterian textile manufacturer; and August Philips, a Dutch banker, a Calvinist of Jewish origin who was his maternal cousin.

Apart from these two, Marx had no real friends. Budding friendships he destroyed almost automatically through his pettiness, his envy, his rancor and his urge to domineer. He was one of the greatest haters in modern history, and one of the reasons why he never really got ahead in his basic work was his endless hostile pamphleteering. If he felt slighted by anybody, if he saw in some writer a possible competitor, if an innocent author had written about a theme of interest to Marx but with conclusions differing from his, Marx immediately dropped every serious research object, sat down and wrote a vitriolic reply or an entire pamphlet. He had the most poisonous pen under the sun and used the most unfair personal arguments. Even as a scholar he never could refrain from going off on a tangent. He sometimes copied half a book which had nothing to do with his main subject; hence the mountains of undecipherable notes and casual remarks on small slips.

A Vindictive Nature

He was a brilliant talker who dominated conversations with his caustic remarks. A Prussian lieutenant named Techow, a convert to socialism, after visiting Marx said in a letter that he would be ready to sacrifice everything for him "if only his heart were remotely as good as his mind." Marx, needless to say, vilified almost everybody within his reach and despised especially the German refugees, the 48-ers, in whose company he had to live most of the time. (Significantly enough, he had hardly any contacts with genuine Englishmen who probably could not stand his manners and mannerisms.) Marx had nothing but contempt for women in general and never engaged in genuine conversations with his wife who was decidedly an intelligent and sensitive woman with a good educational background.

Part of Marx's worst ire was directed against the Jews. In this he was not in the least inhibited by his Jewish descent. His hatred for Jews had certain religious aspects but was primarily a racism of the most wicked sort.

No, Marx certainly was not a "good man". In his memoirs, Carl Schurz, the German democratic revolutionary, who later became a U. S. Senator, has given us his impressions of Marx: "The stocky, heavily built man with his broad forehead, his pitch black hair and full beard, attracted general attention . . . What Marx said was indeed substantial, logical and clear. But never did I meet a man of such offensive arrogance in his demeanor. No opinion deviating in principle from his own would be given the slightest consideration. Anybody who contradicted him was treated with barely veiled contempt. Every argument which he happened to dislike was answered either with biting mockery about such pitiful display of ignorance, or with defamatory suspicions as to the motives of the interpellant. I still well remember the sneering tone with which he spat out the word *bourgeoisie*. And as *bourgeois*, that is to say as an example of a profound intellectual and moral depravity, he denounced everybody who dared to contradict his views."

Arnold Ruge, a well-known German essayist, with whom Marx collaborated in Paris in a literary venture and who soon fell out with him, wrote to Fröbel (nephew of the famous educator of the same name) that "gnashing his teeth and with a grin Marx would slaughter all those who got in the way of this new Babeuf. He always thinks about this feast which he cannot celebrate." Heinrich Heine, who also quickly learned to dislike Karl Marx, called him a "godless self-god."

Unkempt and Undisciplined

Karl Marx was in no way an attractive man; he had no hidden charms. A Prussian detective, sent to London in order to find out what this intellectual wire-puller of Socialism was like, informed his government that Marx was leading "the true life of a gypsy. To wash, to comb his hair or to change his underwear are rare occurrences with him ... if he can, he gets drunk ... he might sleep during the day and stay up all night ... he doesn't care whether people come or leave ... if you enter his home you have to get used to the smoke of tobacco and the coal in the open fireplace with the result that it takes some time until you can see properly the objects in the rooms."

Gainful work was alien to him and when he landed a part-time job as the correspondent for the *New York Tribune* (under Charles A. Dana, an early American socialist), it was his friend Engels who had to write most of the articles during the first year. Marx could have earned money by giving language lessons, but he refused this and continued to sponge on Engels, who really made Marx. (Once Marx, as a true socialist, tried to gamble at the London Stock Exchange, but failed.) Engels was his "angel" from every imaginable point of view.

A Most Unhappy Family

The sufferings of the Marx family, and especially of poor faithful Jenny, are difficult to describe. Though they did have a housekeeper and though Friedrich Engels spent in the course of the years *at least* 4000 Pounds on Karl Marx, they lived in abject misery. The death of one child, a boy, is directly attributable to poverty and neglect. Family life must have been absolutely terrible, but Marx could not be moved — neither by entreaties, nor by tears, nor by cries of despair. For two chapters of *Das Kapital* he needed fourteen years. No wonder that only the first volume was published during his lifetime and that it was Engels' headache to assemble and to rewrite the rest, so that — as one author suggested — we should speak of Engelsism rather than of Marxism. Yet it would be a mistake to think that Marx suffered silently and proudly. By no means!

In his letters and in his conversations he never failed to complain and to lament. He had a colossal amount not only of self-hatred, but also of self-pity, but no human feelings for others, least of all for his wife whose health he had ruined completely.

Marx liked his daughters. These were — intellectually, linguistically, artistically — extremely gifted girls, but the spiritual background of the family had an adverse influence on them. Marx was a fanatical atheist, a disciple of Feuerbach who thus succinctly formulated his views: *"Der Mensch ist, was er isst* — Man is what he eats." And in an early poem Marx had declared: "And we are monkeys of an icy god." Jenny, too, had completely lost her childhood faith and her sufferings had made her practically despondent toward the end of her life. She was older than her husband and preceded him in death.

The oldest of his daughters, also named Jenny, the most beloved by the father, died of cancer at the age of thirty-nine. Karl Marx survived her only by two months. Laura, for reasons unknown, committed suicide together with her husband later in their lives. The French Socialist Party was stunned; at their grave one of the speakers was a Russian refugee, Vladimir Ilyitch Ulyanov, better known under his pen-name: Lenin. Years later, each time he looked up from his desk in the Kremlin study (now transferred to the Lenin Museum in Moscow) he saw on his desk not a crucifix, an ikon or a picture of his wife, but the statuette of a reddish ape with an evil grin. "We monkeys of an icy god!"

Eleanor, the third daughter, a quite hysterical child and later a passionate socialist and feminist, admitted that she "saw nothing worth living for." She also committed suicide. Still, in her farewell letter to her nephew Jean Longuet, she exhorted him, above all, to be worthy of his grandfather.

Who can explain the influence of this queer and sinister man on the world? Undoubtedly he was talented in many ways, but there is nothing truly valuable about his extremely negative, nay, even absurd message. However, history is not reasonable. Mankind is not either. Surely, all the prophecies of Marx in the economic and historical field have proved wrong. His philosophical insights are totally obsolete. They are not even worth refutation except, maybe, as an exercise for high school students or college undergraduates. They are, above all, proved to be wrong *empirically*. But what does it matter? Material victories or publicity triumphs are one thing, truth or goodness very different ones.

The Children of Darkness have always been more clever than the Children of Light. Socialism, moreover, has always been a "clear, but false idea." A free market economy, on the other hand, is far more complex and cannot be explained in a nutshell. In the political arena it competes poorly with the notion of collective ownership and central planning — until the latter's bankruptcy is proved in *practice*. The ideas of the hate-swollen bookworm in the library reading room can only be shown up in *life*. Here the method of trial and error, however, has its terrible pitfalls. To experience Marxism entails a captivity from which, as we know, escape is not so simple. The poor East Europeans realize all this only too well.

More than a hundred years ago the German classic poet and writer Jean Paul wrote that "In every century the Almighty sends us an evil genius in order to tempt us." In the case of Marx the temptation is still with us, but as far as the perceptive observer can see, in spite of the renewed interest in the "Red Prussian," it is now slowly, slowly subsiding.